EMPOWER
SECOND EDITION
STUDENT'S BOOK
WITH EBOOK

B1 PRE-INTERMEDIATE

Adrian Doff, Craig Thaine
Herbert Puchta,
Jeff Stranks, Peter Lewis-Jones
with Graham Burton

EMPOWER SECOND EDITION is a six-level general English course for adult and young adult learners, taking students from beginner to advanced level (CEFR A1 to C1). *Empower* combines course content from Cambridge University Press with validated assessment from the experts at Cambridge Assessment English.

Empower's unique mix of engaging classroom materials and reliable assessment enables learners to make consistent and measurable progress.

Content you love.
Assessment you
can trust.

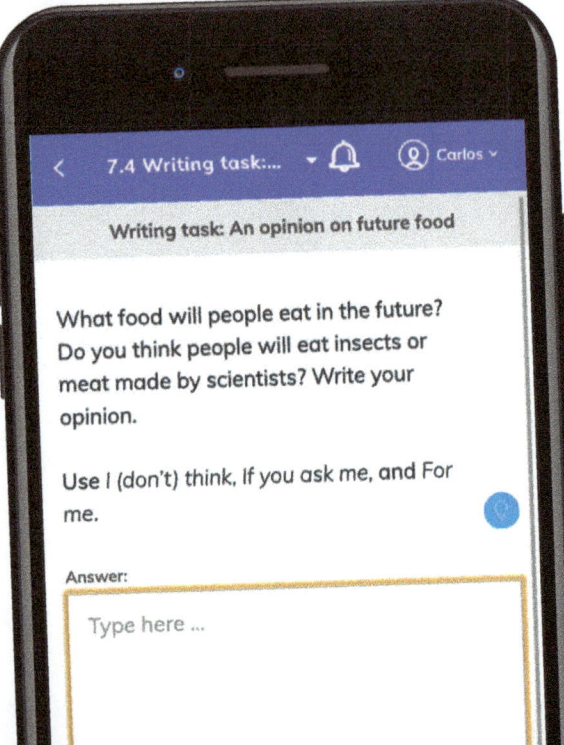

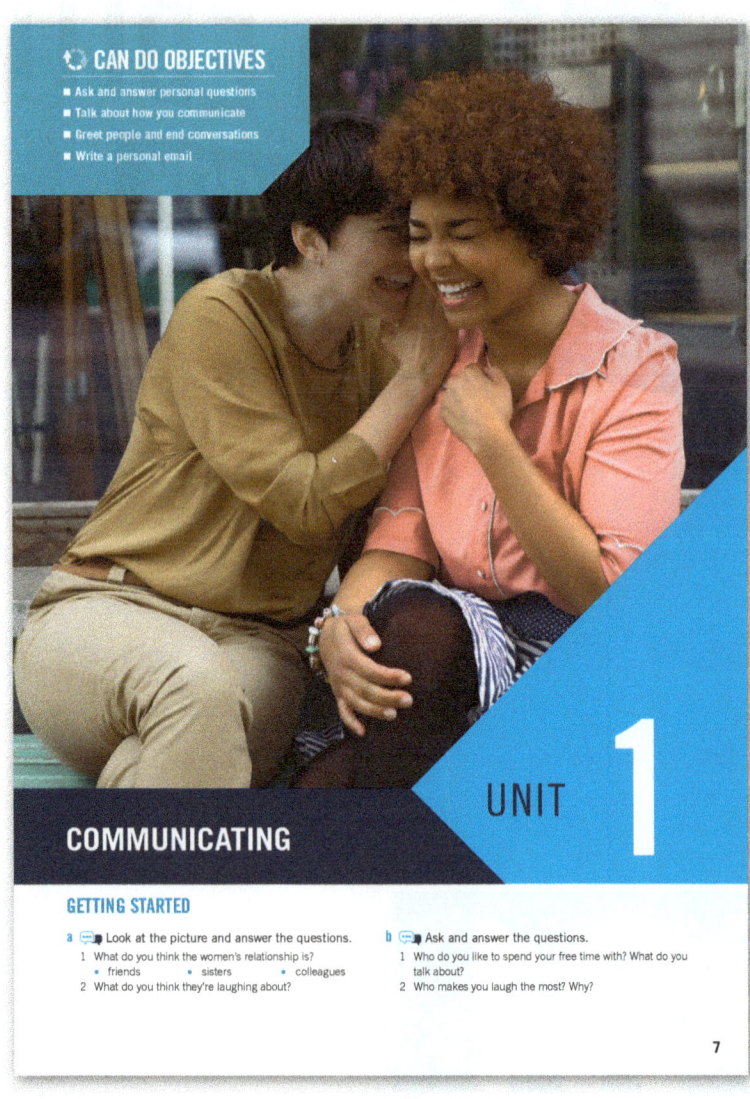

Better Learning with *Empower*

Better Learning is our simple approach where `insights` we've gained from research have helped shape `content` that drives `results`.

Learner engagement

1 Content that informs and motivates

Insights
Sustained motivation is key to successful language learning and skills development.

Content
Clear learning goals, thought-provoking images, texts and speaking activities, plus video content to arouse curiosity.

Results
Content that surprises, entertains and provokes an emotional response, helping teachers to deliver motivating and memorable lessons.

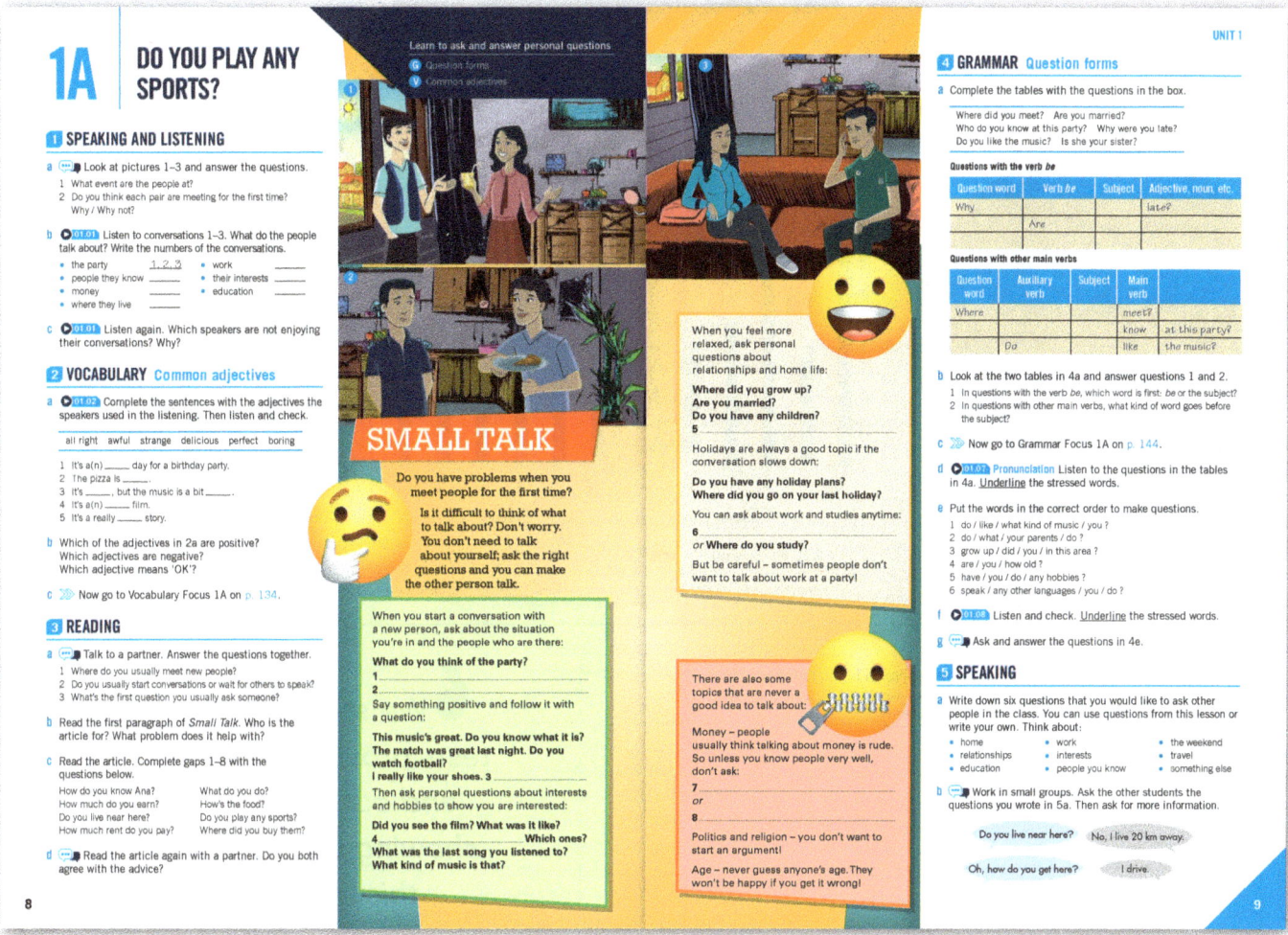

2 Personalised and relevant

Insights
Language learners benefit from frequent opportunities to personalise their responses.

Content
Personalisation tasks in every unit make the target language more meaningful to the individual learner.

Results
Personal responses make learning more memorable and inclusive, with all students participating in spontaneous spoken interaction.

"There are so many adjectives to describe such a wonderful series, but in my opinion it's very reliable, practical, and modern."

Zenaide Brianez, Director of Studies, Instituto da Língua Inglesa, Brazil

Measurable progress

1 Assessment you can trust

Insights
Tests developed and validated by Cambridge Assessment English, the world leaders in language assessment, to ensure they are accurate and meaningful.

Content
End-of-unit tests, mid- and end-of-course competency tests and personalised CEFR test report forms provide reliable information on progress with language skills.

Results
Teachers can see learners' progress at a glance, and learners can see measurable progress, which leads to greater motivation.

Results of an impact study showing % improvement of Reading levels, based on global *Empower* students' scores over one year.

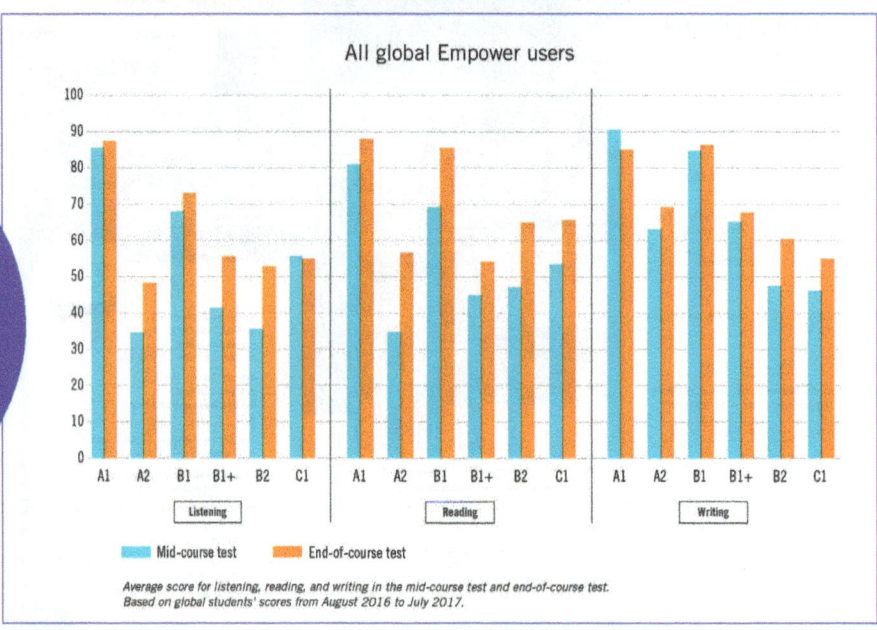

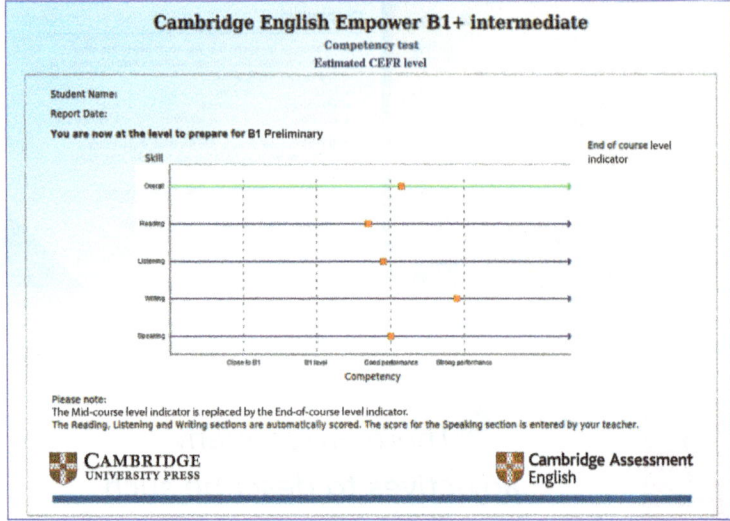

We started using the tests provided with Empower and our students started showing better results from this point until now.

Kristina Ivanova, Director of Foreign Language Training Centre, ITMO University, Saint Petersburg, Russia

2 Evidence of impact

Insights
Schools and colleges need to show that they are evaluating the effectiveness of their language programmes.

Content
Empower impact studies have been carried out in various countries, including Russia, Brazil, Turkey and the UK, to provide evidence of positive impact and progress.

Results
Colleges and universities have demonstrated a significant improvement in language level between the mid- and end-of-course tests, as well as a high level of teacher satisfaction with *Empower*.

Manageable learning

1 Mobile friendly

Insights
Learners expect online content to be mobile friendly but also flexible and easy to use on any digital device.

Content
Empower provides easy access to Digital Workbook content that works on any device and includes practice activities with audio.

Results
Digital Workbook content is easy to access anywhere, and produces meaningful and actionable data so teachers can track their students' progress and adapt their lesson accordingly.

"I had been studying English for 10 years before university, and I didn't succeed. But now with Empower I know my level of English has changed."

Nikita, *Empower* Student, ITMO University, Saint Petersburg, Russia

2 Corpus-informed

Insights
Corpora can provide valuable information about the language items learners are able to learn successfully at each CEFR level.

Content
Two powerful resources – Cambridge Corpus and English Profile – informed the development of the *Empower* course syllabus and the writing of the materials.

Results
Learners are presented with the target language they are able to incorporate and use at the right point in their learning journey. They are not overwhelmed with unrealistic learning expectations.

Rich in practice

1 Language in use

Insights
It is essential that learners are offered frequent and manageable opportunities to practise the language they have been focusing on.

Content
Throughout the *Empower* Student's Book, learners are offered a wide variety of practice activities, plenty of controlled practice and frequent opportunities for communicative spoken practice.

Results
Meaningful practice makes new language more memorable and leads to more efficient progress in language acquisition.

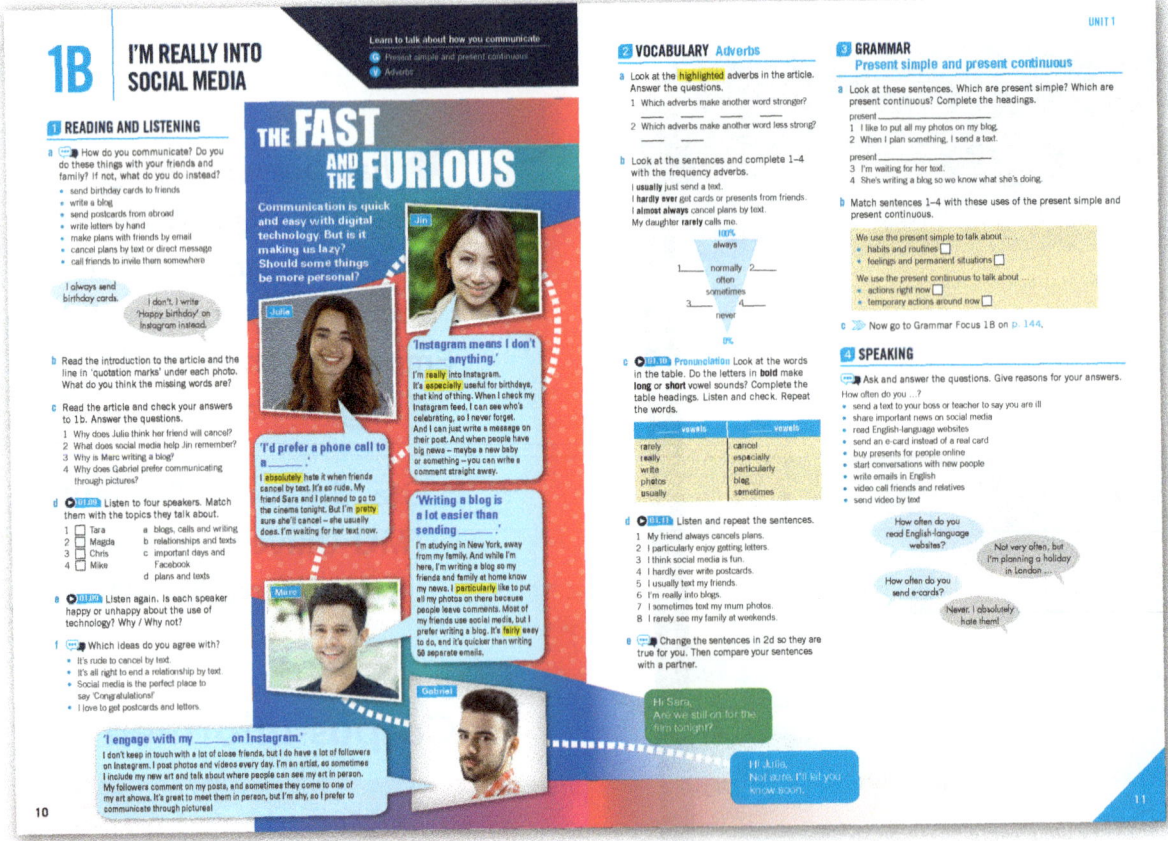

2 Beyond the classroom

"There are plenty of opportunities for personalisation."

Elena Pro, Teacher, EOI de San Fernando de Henares, Spain

Insights
Progress with language learning often requires work outside of the classroom, and different teaching models require different approaches.

Content
Empower is available with a print workbook, online practice, documentary-style videos that expose learners to real-world English, plus additional resources with extra ideas and fun activities.

Results
This choice of additional resources helps teachers to find the most effective ways to motivate their students both inside and outside the classroom.

Unit overview

Unit Opener
Getting started page – Clear learning objectives to give an immediate sense of purpose.

↓

Lessons A and B
Grammar and Vocabulary – Input and practice of core grammar and vocabulary, plus a mix of skills.

— **Digital Workbook (online, mobile):** Grammar and Vocabulary

↓

Lesson C
Everyday English – Functional language in common, everyday situations.

— **Digital Workbook (online, mobile):** Listening and Speaking

↓

Unit Progress Test

↓

Lesson D
Integrated Skills – Practice of all four skills, with a special emphasis on writing.

— **Digital Workbook (online, mobile):** Reading and Writing

↓

Review
Extra practice of grammar, vocabulary and pronunciation. Also a 'Review your progress' section for students to reflect on the unit.

↓

Mid- / End-of-course test

↓

Additional practice
Further practice is available for outside of the class with these components.
Digital Workbook (online, mobile)
Workbook (printed)

Components

Resources – Available on cambridgeone.org

- Audio
- Video
- Unit Progress Tests (Print)
- Unit Progress Tests (Online)
- Mid- and end-of-course assessment (Print)
- Mid- and end-of-course assessment (Online)
- Digital Workbook (Online)
- Photocopiable Grammar, Vocabulary and Pronunciation worksheets

CONTENTS

Lesson and objective	Grammar	Vocabulary	Pronunciation	Everyday English
Unit 1 Communicating				
Getting started Talk about spending time with friends				
1A Ask and answer personal questions	Question forms	Common adjectives	Syllables and word stress Sentence stress	
1B Talk about how you communicate	Present simple and present continuous	Adverbs	Long and short vowels	
1C Greet people and end conversations			Sentence stress	Greeting people; Ending conversations
1D Write a personal email				
Review and extension More practice		WORDPOWER *like*		
Unit 2 Travel and tourism				
Getting started Talk about holiday photos				
2A Talk about past holidays	Past simple	Tourism	*-ed* endings	
2B Describe travel problems	Past continuous	Travel collocations	Sentence stress Vowel sounds	
2C Ask for information in a public place			Connected speech	Asking for information in a public place
2D Write a travel blog				
Review and extension More practice		WORDPOWER *off*		
Unit 3 Money				
Getting started Talk about the future of cash				
3A Talk about money and shopping experiences	Present perfect or past simple	Money and shopping		
3B Talk about living with less	Present perfect with *already* and *yet*	*make / do / give* collocations	Sound and spelling: /dʒ/ and /j/	
3C Talk to people in shops			Sentence stress	Talking to people in shops; Paying at the till
3D Write an update email				
Review and extension More practice		WORDPOWER *just*		
Unit 4 Social life				
Getting started Talk about celebrations and food				
4A Talk about your plans for celebrations	Present continuous and *be going to*	Clothes and appearance	Sound and spelling: *going to*	
4B Plan a day out in a city	*will / won't / would / shall*	Adjectives: places	Sound and spelling: *want* and *won't*	
4C Make social arrangements			Sentence stress	Making social arrangements
4D Write and reply to an invitation				
Review and extension More practice		WORDPOWER *look*		
Unit 5 Work				
Getting started Talk about exciting and dangerous jobs				
5A Talk about what people do at work	*must / have to / can*	Work	Word stress	
5B Talk about the future of work	*will* and *might* for predictions	Jobs	Sound and spelling: /ʃ/	
5C Make offers and suggestions			Stressed/unstressed modals: vowel sounds	Making offers and suggestions
5D Write a job application				
Review and extension More practice		WORDPOWER *job* and *work*		
Unit 6 Problems and advice				
Getting started Talk about being afraid				
6A Give advice for common problems	Imperative; *should*	Verbs with dependent prepositions	Sound and spelling: /uː/ and /ʊ/	
6B Describe extreme experiences	Uses of *to* + infinitive	*-ed / -ing* adjectives	*-ed* endings Word stress	
6C Ask for and give advice			Main stress	Asking for and giving advice
6D Write an email giving advice				
Review and extension More practice		WORDPOWER Verb + *to*		

2

Contents

Listening	Reading	Speaking	Writing
Three conversations at a party	Article: *Small Talk*	Getting to know each other	Personal questions
Four monologues about technology and communication	Article: *The Fast and the Furious*	Ways of communicating	Sentences about communicating
Meeting an old friend		Meeting people and ending conversations; Showing interest	✓ Unit Progress Test
Conversation: keeping in touch	Three personal emails	Keeping in touch	Personal email Correcting mistakes
Audio diary: *Yes Man Changed My Life*	Diary article: *Yes Man Changed My Life*	Types of holiday; A holiday you enjoyed	
Monologue: a bad flight	Two news stories about travel problems	Retelling a news story; Travel problems	
At the train station		Asking for information in a public place; Asking for more information	✓ Unit Progress Test
Conversation: travelling to Australia	Travel blog	Making travel plans	Travel blog Linking words
Radio report: stories from a sales day	Questionnaire: *Sales Season – Can You Say No?*	Money and shopping experiences	
Radio programme: *Ways of Life*	Article: *Get Happy – Give Your Money Away!*	Living with less	Notes about living with less
Shopping for a present		Talking to people in shops; Changing your mind	✓ Unit Progress Test
Four monologues: supporting charity	Email: update on raising money for charity	Charities	Update email Paragraphing
Interview: May Ball Audio blog: Indian wedding	Article: *Life in Numbers*	Future plans; Preparations for special occasions	
Conversation: Mike and Harry in Tokyo		Tokyo highlights; Planning a day out in a city	Notes on a city you know well
Planning to meet: birthday dinner		Making plans Making time to think	✓ Unit Progress Test
Three monologues: socialising	Two emails: invitations		An invitation Writing and replying
Three monologues: cool jobs	Infographic: *The Coolest Jobs*	Job qualities and requirements	Workplace rules
Three interviews: at a career fair	Article: *Planning a Safe Future Career*	Finding a job; The future world of work	Predictions: finding a job / world of work
Leaving work early		Reassurance; Offers and suggestions	✓ Unit Progress Test
Conversation: part-time jobs	Email: job application	Summer and part-time jobs	Job application Organising an email
	Article: *How to Deal with Life's Little Problems*	Common problems and possible solutions; Advice for people who are always late	Advice for a common problem
Two interviews: *Sharks Saved My Life* (Part 2) / Skydiving accident	Article: *Sharks Saved My Life* (Part 1)	Emotional experiences; Stories about dramatic events	Notes about a dramatic event
Advising a friend		Showing sympathy; Asking for and giving advice	✓ Unit Progress Test
Three monologues: problems	Wiki: advice for learners of English	Giving advice	Message giving advice; Linking: ordering ideas and giving examples

3

Lesson and objective	Grammar	Vocabulary	Pronunciation	Everyday English
Unit 7 Changes				
Getting started Talk about different generations				
7A Talk about life-changing events	Comparatives and superlatives	*get* collocations		
7B Describe health and lifestyle changes	*used to*	Health collocations	Sound and spelling: *used to / didn't use to*	
7C Talk to the doctor		Health problems and treatments	Intonation for asking questions	Describing symptoms; Showing concern and relief; Doctors' questions
7D Write a blog about an achievement				
Review and extension More practice		WORDPOWER *change*		
Unit 8 Culture				
Getting started Talk about street art				
8A Talk about art, music and literature	The passive: present simple and past simple	Art, music, and literature	Word stress	
8B Talk about sports and leisure activities	Present perfect with *for* and *since*	Sports and leisure activities		
8C Apologise; Make and accept excuses			Intonation for continuing or finishing	Apologising; Making and accepting excuses
8D Write a book review				
Review and extension More practice		WORDPOWER *by*		
Unit 9 Achievements				
Getting started Talk about achievements				
9A Talk about future possibilities	First conditional	Degree subjects; Education collocations	Word groups	
9B Describe actions and feelings	Verb patterns	Verbs followed by *to* + infinitive / verb + *-ing*		
9C Make telephone calls			Main stress: contrastive	Calling people you don't know; Calling people you know
9D Write a personal profile				
Review and extension More practice		WORDPOWER Multi-word verbs with *put*		
Unit 10 Values				
Getting started Talk about seeing a crime				
10A Talk about moral dilemmas	Second conditional	Multi-word verbs	Sentence stress: vowel sounds	
10B Describe problems with goods and services	Quantifiers; *too / not enough*	Noun formation	Word stress; Sound and spelling: verbs and nouns	
10C Return goods and make complaints			Sentence stress	Returning goods and making complaints
10D Write an apology email				
Review and extension More practice		WORDPOWER Multi-word verbs with *on*		
Unit 11 Discovery and invention				
Getting started Talk about unusual technology				
11A Explain what technology does	Defining relative clauses	Compound nouns	Word stress: compound nouns	
11B Talk about discoveries	Articles	Adverbials: luck and chance	Word stress: adverbials	
11C Ask for and give directions in a building			Sound and spelling: /ɔː/ and /ɜː/	Asking for and giving directions in a building
11D Write a post expressing an opinion				
Review and extension More practice		WORDPOWER Preposition + noun		
Unit 12 Characters				
Getting started Talk about animals and people				
12A Tell a story	Past perfect	Animals	Sound and spelling: /ʌ/, /ɔː/ and /əʊ/	
12B Talk about family relationships	Reported speech	Personality adjectives	Sentence stress: *that*	
12C Agree and disagree in discussions			Main stress: contrastive	Agreeing and disagreeing
12D Write a short story				
Review and extension More practice		WORDPOWER *age*		
Communication Plus p. 127	**Vocabulary Focus** p. 134		**Grammar Focus** p. 144	

Contents

Listening	Reading	Speaking	Writing
Two radio monologues: *One Minute Inspiration: Steven Adams; Selena Gomez*	Quotes: life changes	Comparing yourself in the past and now; Life-changing events	Vocabulary definitions
	Article: *Health: 1970s and Today*	Changes in lifestyle and health	Sentences about changes in health
At the doctor's office		Describing symptoms; Showing concern and relief; Responding to questions	**Unit Progress Test**
Three monologues: making a change	Blog: *Living to Change*	Making positive changes	Blog: changes / achievements Linking: ordering events
	Article: *Six of the Best, Biggest, and Most Popular*	Art, music and literature	Sentences about art and music
Radio programme: *Superfans*		A famous person you admire; Sports and activities	Sentences about yourself; Notes about sports and activities
Accepting an apology		Apologising; Making and accepting excuses	**Unit Progress Test**
Three monologues: book reviews	Four book reviews	Books and reading	Book review Positive and negative comments; Linking: *although, however*
Five monologues: study habits	Article: *Unusual Degrees*	University degrees; Future possibilities	Real possibilities; Future plans
Radio interview: shyness	Article: *The Not-So-Easy Lives of Celebrities*	Shyness; Celebrity problems; Actions and feelings	
Calling people on the phone		Calling people on the phone; Dealing with problems on the phone	**Unit Progress Test**
Conversation: online courses	Two student profiles	Advantages and disadvantages of online learning	Personal profile Avoiding repetition
Radio news: illegal downloading		Dishonest behaviour; Honesty quiz	Unreal situations
Radio news: *Complaints around the World*	Article: *The Biggest Complainers in Europe*	When would you complain?	
Returning goods to a shop		Returning goods and making complaints; Sounding polite	**Unit Progress Test**
Three monologues: rudeness	Three emails: apologies	Rude behaviour	An apology email Formal and informal language
Podcast: *From Fiction to Fact*	Article: *Science Fiction through the Years*	Definitions; Describing inventions	
	Article: *Lucky Discoveries*	Unexpected events; Discoveries and inventions	Unexpected events
Lost in a building		Asking for and giving directions in a building; Checking information	**Unit Progress Test**
Radio call-in: inventions of the future	Four opinion posts: important inventions	Useful/important inventions	A post for a website Giving opinions; Expressing results and reasons
Radio news: *Willie the Parrot*	Article: *Jambo's Story*	Experiences with animals; Animal life-savers	Animals causing problems
Three monologues: sibling rivalry	Article: *Brothers and Sisters: The Facts*	Memorable things people say; Family personalities; Sibling relationships	Things people have said to you
A difference of opinion		Agreeing and disagreeing	**Unit Progress Test**
Radio report: Hurricane Harvey	Article: *Houston's Storm Bakers*	Dangerous weather	A story Linkers: past time

Phonemic symbols and irregular verbs p. 168

This page is intentionally left blank.

CAN DO OBJECTIVES

- Ask and answer personal questions
- Talk about how you communicate
- Greet people and end conversations
- Write a personal email

UNIT 1

COMMUNICATING

GETTING STARTED

a 💬 Look at the picture and answer the questions.
  1 What do you think the women's relationship is?
     • friends   • sisters   • colleagues
  2 What do you think they're laughing about?

b 💬 Ask and answer the questions.
  1 Who do you like to spend your free time with? What do you talk about?
  2 Who makes you laugh the most? Why?

1A | DO YOU PLAY ANY SPORTS?

Learn to ask and answer personal questions
- G Question forms
- V Common adjectives

1 SPEAKING AND LISTENING

a 💬 Look at pictures 1–3 and answer the questions.
1 What event are the people at?
2 Do you think each pair are meeting for the first time? Why / Why not?

b ▶ 01.01 Listen to conversations 1–3. What do the people talk about? Write the numbers of the conversations.
- the party   1, 2, 3
- people they know ____
- money   ____
- where they live ____
- work   ____
- their interests ____
- education   ____

c ▶ 01.01 Listen again. Which speakers are not enjoying their conversations? Why?

2 VOCABULARY Common adjectives

a ▶ 01.02 Complete the sentences with the adjectives the speakers used in the listening. Then listen and check.

| all right | awful | strange | delicious | perfect | boring |

1 It's a(n) _____ day for a birthday party.
2 The pizza is _____.
3 It's _____, but the music is a bit _____.
4 It's a(n) _____ film.
5 It's a really _____ story.

b Which of the adjectives in 2a are positive? Which adjectives are negative? Which adjective means 'OK'?

c ⇒ Now go to Vocabulary Focus 1A on p. 134.

3 READING

a 💬 Talk to a partner. Answer the questions together.
1 Where do you usually meet new people?
2 Do you usually start conversations or wait for others to speak?
3 What's the first question you usually ask someone?

b Read the first paragraph of *Small Talk*. Who is the article for? What problem does it help with?

c Read the article. Complete gaps 1–8 with the questions below.

How do you know Ana?   What do you do?
How much do you earn?   How's the food?
Do you live near here?   Do you play any sports?
How much rent do you pay?   Where did you buy them?

d 💬 Read the article again with a partner. Do you both agree with the advice?

SMALL TALK

Do you have problems when you meet people for the first time?

Is it difficult to think of what to talk about? Don't worry. You don't need to talk about yourself; ask the right questions and you can make the other person talk.

When you start a conversation with a new person, ask about the situation you're in and the people who are there:

What do you think of the party?
1 ....
2 ....

Say something positive and follow it with a question:

This music's great. Do you know what it is?
The match was great last night. Do you watch football?
I really like your shoes. 3 ....

Then ask personal questions about interests and hobbies to show you are interested:

Did you see the film? What was it like?
4 .... **Which ones?**
What was the last song you listened to?
What kind of music is that?

8

UNIT 1

When you feel more relaxed, ask personal questions about relationships and home life:

Where did you grow up?
Are you married?
Do you have any children?
5 ....

Holidays are always a good topic if the conversation slows down:

Do you have any holiday plans?
Where did you go on your last holiday?

You can ask about work and studies anytime:

6 ....
or Where do you study?

But be careful – sometimes people don't want to talk about work at a party!

There are also some topics that are never a good idea to talk about:

Money – people usually think talking about money is rude. So unless you know people very well, don't ask:

7 ....
or
8 ....

Politics and religion – you don't want to start an argument!

Age – never guess anyone's age. They won't be happy if you get it wrong!

4 GRAMMAR Question forms

a Complete the tables with the questions in the box.

Where did you meet?   Are you married?
Who do you know at this party?   Why were you late?
Do you like the music?   Is she your sister?

Questions with the verb *be*

Question word	Verb *be*	Subject	Adjective, noun, etc.
Why			late?
	Are		

Questions with other main verbs

Question word	Auxiliary verb	Subject	Main verb	
Where			meet?	
			know	at this party?
	Do		like	the music?

b Look at the two tables in 4a and answer questions 1 and 2.
 1 In questions with the verb *be*, which word is first: *be* or the subject?
 2 In questions with other main verbs, what kind of word goes before the subject?

c ▶ Now go to Grammar Focus 1A on p. 144.

d ▶ 01.07 **Pronunciation** Listen to the questions in the tables in 4a. Underline the stressed words.

e Put the words in the correct order to make questions.
 1 do / like / what kind of music / you ?
 2 do / what / your parents / do ?
 3 grow up / did / you / in this area ?
 4 are / you / how old ?
 5 have / you / do / any hobbies ?
 6 speak / any other languages / you / do ?

f ▶ 01.08 Listen and check. Underline the stressed words.

g 💬 Ask and answer the questions in 4e.

5 SPEAKING

a Write down six questions that you would like to ask other people in the class. You can use questions from this lesson or write your own. Think about:
 • home   • work   • the weekend
 • relationships • interests   • travel
 • education   • people you know • something else

b 💬 Work in small groups. Ask the other students the questions you wrote in 5a. Then ask for more information.

Do you live near here?   No, I live 20 km away.

Oh, how do you get here?   I drive.

9

1B I'M REALLY INTO SOCIAL MEDIA

Learn to talk about how you communicate
G Present simple and present continuous
V Adverbs

1 READING AND LISTENING

a 💬 How do you communicate? Do you do these things with your friends and family? If not, what do you do instead?
- send birthday cards to friends
- write a blog
- send postcards from abroad
- write letters by hand
- make plans with friends by email
- cancel plans by text or direct message
- call friends to invite them somewhere

I always send birthday cards.

I don't. I write 'Happy birthday' on Instagram instead.

b Read the introduction to the article and the line in 'quotation marks' under each photo. What do you think the missing words are?

c Read the article and check your answers to 1b. Answer the questions.
1 Why does Julie think her friend will cancel?
2 What does social media help Jin remember?
3 Why is Marc writing a blog?
4 Why does Gabriel prefer communicating through pictures?

d ▶ 01.09 Listen to four speakers. Match them with the topics they talk about.
1 ☐ Tara   a blogs, calls and writing
2 ☐ Magda   b relationships and texts
3 ☐ Chris   c important days and
4 ☐ Mike   Facebook
              d plans and texts

e ▶ 01.09 Listen again. Is each speaker happy or unhappy about the use of technology? Why / Why not?

f 💬 Which ideas do you agree with?
- It's rude to cancel by text.
- It's all right to end a relationship by text.
- Social media is the perfect place to say 'Congratulations!'
- I love to get postcards and letters.

THE FAST AND THE FURIOUS

Communication is quick and easy with digital technology. But is it making us lazy? Should some things be more personal?

Julie

Marc

Jin

'Instagram means I don't _____ anything.'
I'm really into Instagram. It's especially useful for birthdays, that kind of thing. When I check my Instagram feed, I can see who's celebrating, so I never forget. And I can just write a message on their post. And when people have big news – maybe a new baby or something – you can write a comment straight away.

'I'd prefer a phone call to a _____.'
I absolutely hate it when friends cancel by text. It's so rude. My friend Sara and I planned to go to the cinema tonight. But I'm pretty sure she'll cancel – she usually does. I'm waiting for her text now.

'Writing a blog is a lot easier than sending _____.'
I'm studying in New York, away from my family. And while I'm here, I'm writing a blog so my friends and family at home know my news. I particularly like to put all my photos on there because people leave comments. Most of my friends use social media, but I prefer writing a blog. It's fairly easy to do, and it's quicker than writing 50 separate emails.

Gabriel

'I engage with my _____ on Instagram.'
I don't keep in touch with a lot of close friends, but I do have a lot of followers on Instagram. I post photos and videos every day. I'm an artist, so sometimes I include my new art and talk about where people can see my art in person. My followers comment on my posts, and sometimes they come to one of my art shows. It's great to meet them in person, but I'm shy, so I prefer to communicate through pictures!

UNIT 1

2 VOCABULARY Adverbs

a Look at the highlighted adverbs in the article. Answer the questions.
1 Which adverbs make another word stronger?
___ ___ ___ ___
2 Which adverbs make another word less strong?
___ ___

b Look at the sentences and complete 1–4 with the frequency adverbs.
I **usually** just send a text.
I **hardly ever** get cards or presents from friends.
I **almost always** cancel plans by text.
My daughter **rarely** calls me.

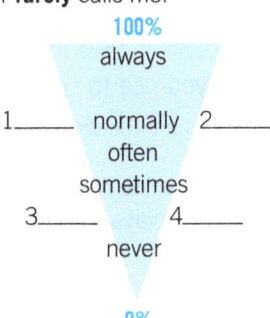

c ▶ 01.10 **Pronunciation** Look at the words in the table. Do the letters in **bold** make **long** or **short** vowel sounds? Complete the table headings. Listen and check. Repeat the words.

___ vowels	___ vowels
r**a**rely	c**a**ncel
r**ea**lly	esp**e**cially
wr**i**te	p**a**rticularly
ph**o**tos	bl**o**g
usually	s**o**metimes

d ▶ 01.11 Listen and repeat the sentences.
1 My friend always cancels plans.
2 I particularly enjoy getting letters.
3 I think social media is fun.
4 I hardly ever write postcards.
5 I usually text my friends.
6 I'm really into blogs.
7 I sometimes text my mum photos.
8 I rarely see my family at weekends.

e 💬 Change the sentences in 2d so they are true for you. Then compare your sentences with a partner.

3 GRAMMAR
Present simple and present continuous

a Look at these sentences. Which are present simple? Which are present continuous? Complete the headings.
present _____
1 I like to put all my photos on my blog.
2 When I plan something, I send a text.

present _____
3 I'm waiting for her text.
4 She's writing a blog so we know what she's doing.

b Match sentences 1–4 with these uses of the present simple and present continuous.

> We use the present simple to talk about … .
> • habits and routines ☐
> • feelings and permanent situations ☐
>
> We use the present continuous to talk about … .
> • actions right now ☐
> • temporary actions around now ☐

c ≫ Now go to Grammar Focus 1B on p. 144.

4 SPEAKING

💬 Ask and answer the questions. Give reasons for your answers.
How often do you …?
• send a text to your boss or teacher to say you are ill
• share important news on social media
• read English-language websites
• send an e-card instead of a real card
• buy presents for people online
• start conversations with new people
• write emails in English
• video call friends and relatives
• send video by text

How often do you read English-language websites?

Not very often, but I'm planning a holiday in London …

How often do you send e-cards?

Never. I absolutely hate them!

Hi Sara,
Are we still on for the film tonight?

Hi Julie,
Not sure. I'll let you know soon.

1C EVERYDAY ENGLISH
It was really nice to meet you

Learn to greet people and end conversations

- P Sentence stress
- S Showing interest

1 LISTENING

a In your country, what do you normally say and do when you …
- first meet somebody new?
- meet someone you know well?

We hug and kiss. *We shake hands and say …*

b Look at the photographs. Do you think the people in each photo know each other well? Why?

c ▶ 01.14 Watch or listen to Part 1 and check your answers to 1b.

d ▶ 01.14 Watch or listen again. Are sentences 1–5 true (*T*) or false (*F*)? Correct the false sentences.
1. ☐ The last time Rachel and Annie saw each other was six years ago.
2. ☐ Annie lives a long way from the town centre.
3. ☐ Rachel and Mark got married a year ago.
4. ☐ Annie has a boyfriend.
5. ☐ Rachel, Mark and Annie decide to go to a restaurant together.

2 USEFUL LANGUAGE Greeting people

a ▶ 01.15 Complete the sentences from Part 1 with the words in the box. Listen and check your answers.

| meet you | no see | to see you | by the way | are you | these days |

1. Long time _____!
2. How _____?
3. Great _____!
4. Where are you living _____?
5. My name's Mark, _____.
6. Nice to _____.

b Look at the phrases in 2a. Which can you use to speak to … ?
1. someone you know
2. someone you are meeting for the first time

c ▶ 01.16 Listen and note down some possible replies to the phrases in 2a. Do you know any different ways to reply to each phrase in 2a?

d Work in pairs. Take turns saying the phrases in 2a and replying.

3 CONVERSATION SKILLS Showing interest

a ▶ 01.17 Listen and complete the conversations from Part 1 with the adjectives in the box.

| fantastic | lovely | good | nice |

1. Long time no see! How are you?
   I'm great. What a _____ surprise! Great to see you.
2. We live on Compton Road.
   Oh – how _____!
3. Mark's my husband!
   Husband – wow! That's _____ news.
4. Would you both like to come?
   Yeah, that sounds _____.
   Brilliant! Let's go.

b Look at the conversations in 3a. Do the highlighted phrases give information or show interest?

c What kind of word completes each phrase 1–4? Choose the correct form from the box.

| adjective + noun | adjective |

1. What a + _____!
2. How + _____!
3. That sounds + _____.
4. That's + _____ + news.

d Work in pairs. Take turns to tell your partner about yourself. Reply using the phrases in 3c.

Tell your partner:
- where you live
- something you did at the weekend
- some news
- what job you do / what you are studying these days

12

UNIT 1

4 PRONUNCIATION Sentence stress

a ▶ 01.18 Listen to the sentences. Notice the words with stressed syllables.

I <u>think</u> it was about <u>six</u> <u>years</u> ago!
I <u>live</u> on <u>Hamp</u>ton Street.
My name's <u>Mark</u>, by the way.
<u>Mark</u>'s my <u>hus</u>band!
I'm <u>go</u>ing to the <u>ca</u>fé down the <u>street</u> now…
…to <u>meet</u> <u>Leo</u>, my <u>boy</u>friend.

b Look at the sentences in 4a. Which words have stressed syllables – grammar words or words that give information?

5 LISTENING

a 💬 Look at the picture from Part 2. Who is the fourth person at the café? Does he know Rachel and Mark?

b 🎥 ▶ 01.19 What do you think they will talk about in the café? In pairs, think of three things. Then watch or listen to Part 2. Were you right?

c 🎥 ▶ 01.19 Watch or listen again. Answer the questions.
1 Do Rachel and Mark have plans for next week?
2 What job does Rachel do?
3 Who helps Rachel at the shop?
4 What does Annie say about her job?
5 What does Mark do?
6 What is Annie doing at the weekend?
7 Why do Rachel and Mark leave?
8 What suggestion does Annie make before they leave?

6 USEFUL LANGUAGE Ending conversations

a ▶ 01.20 Listen and complete the phrases for ending a conversation.
1 We really must _____ .
2 It was really nice to _____ you.
3 It was great to _____ you again, Annie.
4 Yeah! We must _____ _____ soon.
5 _____ hello to Dan for me!

b Which phrase in 6a do you use when you say goodbye to somebody you have just met?

c Put the sentences in the correct order to make a conversation.
B ☐ Oh, that's fine. It was great to see you.
A ☐ Not far from here. Look, I'm sorry, but I really must go. I'm late for a meeting.
A ☐ 1 Dan, is that you?
A ☐ Yeah! I think I last saw you at John's wedding. How are you?
A ☐ You, too! I'll give you a call!
B ☐ I'm fine. And you? Where are you living these days?
B ☐ Hi Sarah! Long time no see!

7 SPEAKING

a ≫ Communication 1C Work in pairs. Student A: Go to 7b below. Student B: Go to p. 130.

Student A

b Read card 1. Think about what you want to say.

c Start the conversation with Student B. Use your own name.

1 You are walking down the street and you see your friend.
• say hello
• give your news:
  • you've got a new job
  • *your own idea*
• listen to your friend's news and respond
• say goodbye

d Now look at card 2. Listen to Student B and reply. Use your own name.

2 You meet a colleague for the first time.
• say who you are
• give some information:
  • your office is in building C
  • *your own idea*
• listen to what your new colleague says and respond
• say goodbye

✓ UNIT PROGRESS TEST

→ **CHECK YOUR PROGRESS**

You can now do the Unit Progress Test.

13

1D SKILLS FOR WRITING
I'm sending you some photos

Learn to write a personal email
W Correcting mistakes

1 SPEAKING AND LISTENING

a Read messages 1–3 and answer the questions.
1 What do the <mark>highlighted</mark> phrases mean?
2 Do you ever send or receive these kinds of messages? Who to/from? Why?

1. I can't seem to <mark>get in touch</mark> with you. Call me! SEND
2. Did you <mark>get</mark> my last text? SEND
3. Are you OK? We <mark>haven't heard from you</mark> for a long time. SEND

b ▶ 01.21 Listen to Nina and Chris talking about keeping in touch with friends and family. Who is better at keeping in touch: Nina or Chris?

c ▶ 01.21 Listen again and answer the questions.
1 Why doesn't Nina send many emails?
2 Why does Chris call his mother so often?
3 How often does Nina call her parents?
4 When does Nina prefer to tell her friends her news?
5 When does Chris send photos by email?

d How often do you keep in touch with friends and family? Circle the correct adverb for you.

always   often   sometimes   rarely

Think about:
1 a family member who lives in a different place
2 a friend you don't see very often.

Which of these do you do with each person? Write the first letter of their name.
- talk on the phone or make a video call
- send emails or texts
- send pictures, video or links
- hardly ever keep in touch
- meet for a chat

e Work in pairs. Talk about your answers to 1d.

> I rarely keep in touch with people. I never have time to …

> I often keep in touch with my family. I enjoy sending …

> I sometimes send photos to my sister Jane. They're usually pictures of …

> I send my friend Alex links to interesting articles.

f Which of these opinions do you agree with?
1 'It's nice to see photos of what your friends are doing.'
2 'You don't have to keep in touch with people all the time.'
3 'If your parents worry a lot, you should call them.'

2 READING

a Simon is a student from England. Look at his pictures from Salamanca, in Spain. What do you think he is doing there?

b Read the emails and check your ideas in 2a. Which email is to his … ?
☐ friend Blake   ☐ uncle and aunt
☐ younger sister Mika

c Who does Simon write to about these subjects?
- the weather
- what he does in the evenings
- the family he is staying with
- learning to speak Spanish
- the other students

d Answer the questions about Simon's emails.
1 What does he say about speaking Spanish?
2 Why do you think he says different things about this to each person?

UNIT 1

1

Hope you're both well and are enjoying the summer.
I'm in Salamanca, in Spain. This is a photo I took of the old centre. It's a beautiful old city, as you can see – and really big! It has an incredible mix of old, historical places and new, trendy areas.
As you know, I'm learning Spanish at the moment. I'm taking a two-month Spanish course here, so my Spanish is slowly improving. The classes are very good, and we also watch Spanish films.
It's pretty hot here, but it's nice and cool in the evenings.
Love to all,
Simon

2

How's it going? Are you having a good time in Berlin?
Here are some photos of my group on the Spanish course. We're all from different countries, so we usually speak English when we're together – not very good for my Spanish! Anyway, I'm having a great time here, and the time's going much too quickly. There are a lot of good cafés here, and we usually all go out at night together.
What's Berlin like? Send me some photos! See you back at college next month.
Simon

3

I'm sending you some photos of the family I'm staying with in Salamanca. They've got a daughter the same age as you (her name's Blanca). She speaks English quite well, but we usually speak Spanish together. She introduced me to some of her friends, and I speak Spanish with them, too … some of the time, not always! How's your job in the supermarket? Hope you're not working too hard and are saving a lot of money!
See you next week.
Love,
Simon xx

3 WRITING SKILLS
Correcting mistakes

a Look at the pairs of sentences A–D. Which pair has mistakes in … ?

☐ grammar ☐ punctuation
☐ spelling ☐ capital letters

A 1 Hope youre both well and are enjoying the summer
　2 Are you having a good time in Berlin,

B 1 i'm in salamanca, in spain.
　2 the classes are very good, and we also watch spanish films.

C 1 I having a great time here, and the time going much too quickly.
　2 She speak English quite good, but we are usually speaking Spanish together.

D 1 Her are some fotos of my group on the Spanish corse.
　2 We're all from diferent countrys, so we usually speak English.

b Match the rules with mistakes in five of the sentences in 3a (A1–D2).

1 ☐☐ The present continuous is formed be + verb + -ing.
2 ☐☐ When we leave out a letter, we write an apostrophe (').
3 ☐☐ We use the present simple to talk about habits.
4 ☐☐ If a word ends in -y, we change it to -ies in the plural.
5 ☐☐ Place names start with a capital letter.

c Correct all of the mistakes in the sentences in 3a. Check your answers in Simon's emails.

4 WRITING

a Write an email to a friend or family member that you don't see very often. Write about:
- how you are
- what's new for you (the place you're living or the people you're spending time with)
- what you're doing these days.

b Work in pairs. Exchange emails and read your partner's email. Circle their mistakes and write these letters at the end of the line.
- grammar **G**   • punctuation marks **P**
- spelling **Sp**   • capital letters **L**

c Work in pairs. Correct the mistakes in your emails together.

d Read other students' emails. Which email is the most interesting? Why?

15

UNIT 1
Review and extension

1 GRAMMAR

a Put the words in the correct order to make questions.
1 night / did / go / out / you / last ?
2 where / you / last / weekend / go / did ?
3 kinds of / like / you / what / do / TV programmes ?
4 do / this school / know / who / at / you ?
5 you / how / play / sport / often / do ?
6 you / do / what / at weekends / do / usually ?
7 tired / you / are / today ?

b 💬 Ask and answer the questions in 1a.

c Complete the conversation with the present simple or present continuous forms of the verbs.

JACKIE Hi, Mum.
MUM Oh, hi, Jackie. Nice of you to call. You ¹_____ (not call) very often!
JACKIE Oh, come on, Mum! I ²_____ (work) really hard at university at the moment. I never ³_____ (have) time to call! And I ⁴_____ (send) you emails all the time.
MUM I ⁵_____ (like) to talk to you and hear your voice, that's all. Your sister ⁶_____ (call) me every weekend.
JACKIE Well, we ⁷_____ (talk) now, but the world ⁸_____ (change), Mum! Some of my friends never ⁹_____ (call) home. They just ¹⁰_____ (email) or send a text.
MUM I preferred how things were in the past.

2 VOCABULARY

a Complete the sentences with the correct adjectives.
1 The film was a_ _ _ _ _ _t at the beginning, but I didn't like the ending.
2 We ate some really d_ _ _ _ _ _ _s food at the party.
3 They've got a nice house, but they live in a really u_ _y part of town.
4 It was a l_ _ _ _y day, so we decided to go to the beach.
5 I bought a g_ _ _ _ _ _s new dress to wear to my friend's wedding.
6 He listens to really s_ _ _ _ _e music – I don't know any of the bands.
7 This summer, the weather here was h_ _ _ _ _ _e – it rained all the time.
8 This is a p_ _ _ _ _t day for a walk in the park – it's so warm and sunny.

b Choose the correct answers.
1 I *absolutely / fairly* love football.
2 My parents live abroad. I *rarely / always* see them.
3 I think American films are *absolutely / quite* good, but I don't love them.
4 I *usually / particularly* go for a run once or twice a week.
5 I *really / fairly* hate rock music.
6 I love all sports, but tennis is *especially / usually* good.

c 💬 Which sentences in 2b are true for you?

3 WORDPOWER *like*

a Match sentences 1–4 with replies a–d.
1 ☐ I've got a jacket **like** yours.
2 ☐ **What was** the film **like**?
3 ☐ I enjoy visiting countries with a lot of history, **like** Greece.
4 ☐ We can go for a walk later **if you like**.

a Yes, that would be great.
b And Italy! Me, too.
c Yes, this style's popular at the moment.
d I thought it was all right, but my friend hated it.

b Match the expressions in **bold** from 3a with meanings a–d.
a ☐ what was your opinion of
b ☐ similar to
c ☐ if you want
d ☐ for example

c Complete the sentences with the words in **bold** from 3a.
1 A Is your university different from others in your country?
   B No, it's _____ most of the others.
2 A We can meet tomorrow _____.
   B OK – come to my flat for a coffee.
3 A Do you want me to bring something to the dinner party?
   B Yes. Bring something sweet, _____ some ice cream.
4 A We went to that new restaurant yesterday.
   B _____ it _____?

d We often use *like* with the verbs *look* and *sound*. Look at the examples.

- saying people or things are similar
  John **looks like** his brother – they're both tall with black hair.
  I think this new song **sounds like** all their other stuff.

- saying what you think will happen
  It **looks like** it might rain – it's very cloudy.

- giving your opinion about what you heard or read
  I spoke to Sara yesterday. It **sounds like** she had a really good holiday.

Complete the sentences with the correct forms of *look like* or *sound like*.
1 It _____ their first song. I really like it!
2 Sam invited Tom to the party, so it _____ he'll come.
3 You don't _____ your sister. She's very tall.
4 That was the last bus. It _____ we'll have to walk.

🔄 REVIEW YOUR PROGRESS

How well did you do in this unit? Write 3, 2 or 1 for each objective.
3 = very well 2 = well 1 = not so well

I CAN ...	
ask and answer personal questions	☐
talk about how I communicate	☐
greet people and end conversations	☐
write a personal email.	☐

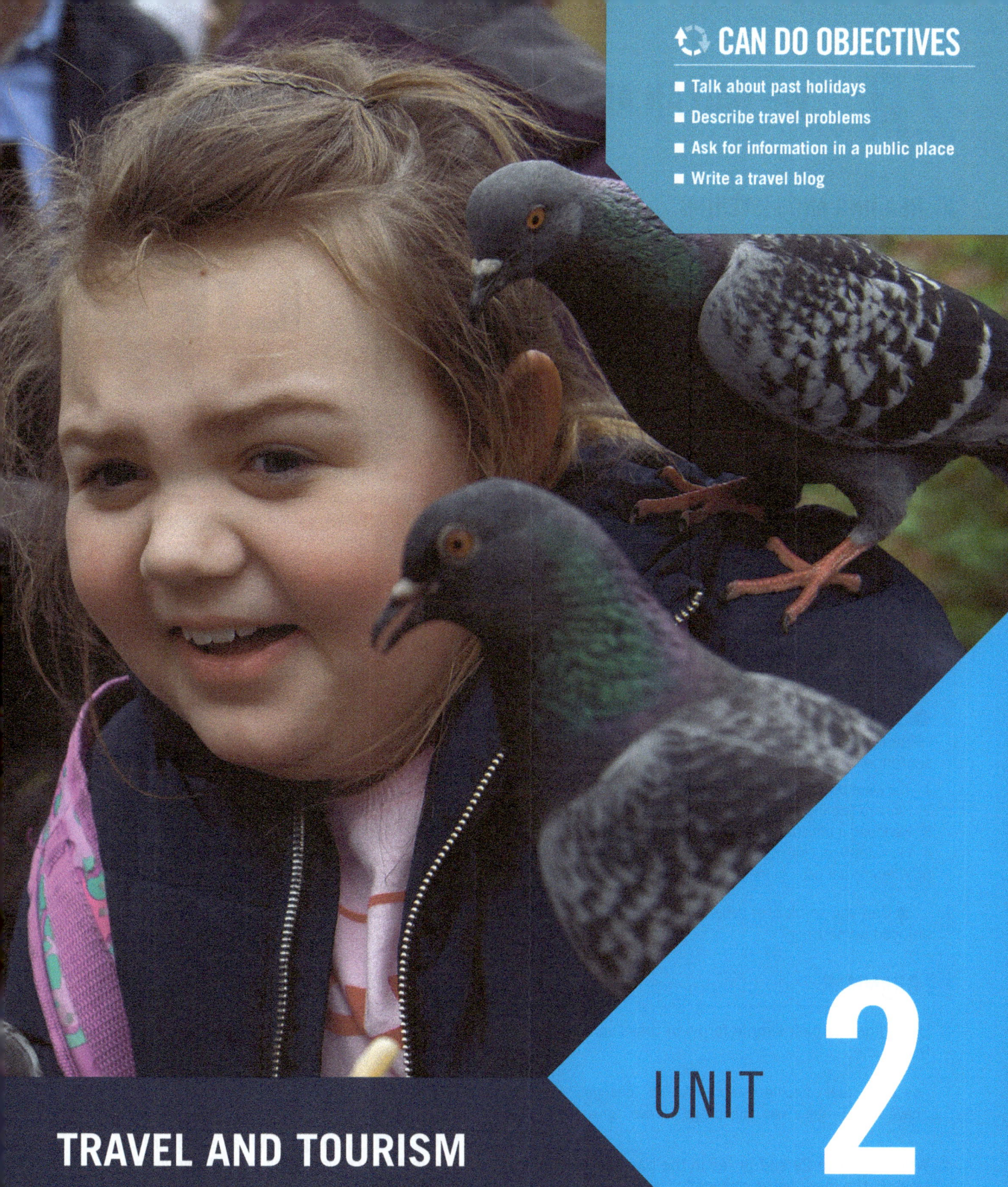

CAN DO OBJECTIVES
- Talk about past holidays
- Describe travel problems
- Ask for information in a public place
- Write a travel blog

UNIT 2
TRAVEL AND TOURISM

GETTING STARTED

a Look at the picture and answer the questions.
1 Who is the girl? What is she doing?
2 How do you think she feels? Why?
3 Do you think the photo was her idea? Why / Why not?

b Ask and answer the questions.
1 Would you like to take a photo like this on holiday? Why / Why not?
2 What is the funniest or most unusual photo you have taken on holiday? Where were you? How did you feel? Did anything go wrong?

2A | WE HAD AN ADVENTURE

Learn to talk about past holidays
- **G** Past simple
- **V** Tourism

1 READING AND LISTENING

a Ask and answer the questions.
1 Where do you like to go on holiday?
2 Do you like to try new things on holiday? What?
3 Can you think of any kind of holiday you wouldn't enjoy?

b Read *Yes Man Changed My Life* and answer the questions.
1 What is Danny Wallace's book *Yes Man* about?
2 What did Richard do after he read *Yes Man*?

c Read *Day 1* and *Day 2* and then answer the questions.
Day 1
1 Why did Richard go into the travel agent's?
2 What holiday did he book?
3 Did he book the kind of holiday he usually likes?
Day 2
1 Why did Richard go to the beach?
2 What did he buy at the beach?
3 What is he going to do on day three? How does he feel about it?

d Would you like to try water skiing? Do you think Richard will enjoy it?

e ▶ 02.01 Listen to Richard describing day 3. Are sentences 1–5 true (*T*) or false (*F*)? Correct the false sentences.
1 The class began with a lesson before they went out to sea.
2 Richard felt fine when they went out on the boat.
3 He found it difficult to stand up on the water skis.
4 He hated water skiing.
5 When he got back to the hotel, he went to bed.

f Can you think of a time when you were surprised you enjoyed something?

2 GRAMMAR Past simple: positive

a Underline the past simple forms of these verbs in the article.

| become | feel | decide | start | ask | do | change |
| have | want | get | see | sleep | go | arrive | give |

b Which verbs in 2a end in *-ed* in the past tense? How do the other verbs change?

You can find a list of irregular verbs on p. 168.

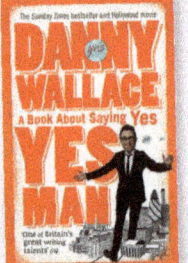

YES MAN CHANGED MY LIFE
by Richard Collins

Yes Man is the best book I've ever read. It's the true story of a year in the life of author Danny Wallace.

Before Danny Wallace became the 'Yes Man', his life was boring and he felt old. So he decided to make things more exciting. He started saying 'yes' to every question people asked him. And he did it for a whole year. From the day he started, it completely changed his life, and he had all kinds of adventures.

It's a fantastic story. When I finished the book, I wanted to change my life like Danny Wallace. So I took a holiday from work and became a 'Yes Man' for a week. This is what happened.

c Complete the sentences with the past simple forms of the verbs in brackets.
1 I _____ as a waiter for a day, for no money. (work)
2 I _____ a day fishing with five Greek fishermen. (spend)
3 I _____ at a beach party until six in the morning. (stay)
4 I _____ a dancing competition. (win)
5 I _____ the same boat trip three times. (take)
6 I _____ swimming at midnight. (go)

3 LISTENING

a ▶ 02.02 Which of the activities in 2c do you think Richard enjoyed? Tell a partner. Listen and check.

b ▶ 02.02 Listen again. What is Richard's last question? Do you think he will say *yes* or *no*? Why?

c Ask and answer the questions.
1 Do you ever say 'yes' when you don't want to? When?
2 Would you like to be a 'Yes Man' for a week? Why / Why not?

UNIT 2

DAY 1

I started on Saturday morning. At 10 am, I got my first question. I saw a poster in the window of a travel agent's. It said, 'Tired?'
(Yes – I slept badly the night before, so I was tired.) Under this, it said, 'Do you need a holiday?' (Yes, definitely.) So I went in.
The travel agent asked, me where I wanted to go. But before I could answer, she said, 'Somewhere hot?'
I don't like hot weather, but I said, 'Yes.'
'A beach holiday? Maybe in Greece?'
I don't like the beach. I prefer cities. But I said, 'Yes.'
'What kind of accommodation? A hotel? Or a … '
I hate hotels, but before she could continue, I said, 'Yes.'
Five minutes later, everything was ready. My flight was the next day.

DAY 2

I arrived at my hotel on the island of Zante at lunchtime. It was very, very hot. I just wanted to check in and unpack my suitcase, but the receptionist said, 'We have a minibus to the beach in ten minutes. Do you want to go?'
You know the answer I gave her.
It was about 40°C at the beach. Luckily, I brought suntan lotion. A man came towards me: 'Sunglasses? Do you want sunglasses?'
I had some in my bag, but I said, 'Yes.'
Five minutes later, another man came: 'Beautiful hat, sir?' I tried not to look at him.
Three hours later, I had two pairs of sunglasses, three hats, a watch and a woman's necklace.
It was difficult to carry all my new things back to the minibus. I decided: no trips tomorrow, just rest. When I got back, the receptionist asked, 'Did you like the beach?'
I didn't, but I said, 'Yes.'
'Oh, there's a water skiing course tomorrow. Do you want me to book a place for you?'
I can't swim very well, and I don't like the sea. I wanted to cry …

4 GRAMMAR
Past simple: negative and questions

a Complete the sentences with the words in the box.

   was   didn't   did   weren't

1 Some of my experiences _____ very good.
2 I _____ like the mosquitoes that bit me.
3 _____ you have a good week?
4 What _____ your favourite thing?

b Look at the sentences in 4a and answer the questions about the past simple.
1 Which sentences include the verb *be*?
2 How do we make negatives and questions …?
   • with the verb *be*   • with other verbs

c ⟫ Now go to Grammar Focus 2A on p. 146.

5 PRONUNCIATION -*ed* endings

a ▶ 02.05 Listen and tick (✓) the verbs that have an extra syllable when we add -*ed*.

change > changed ☐	play > played ☐
need > needed ☐	ask > asked ☐
decide > decided ☐	want > wanted ☐
start > started ☐	

b Complete the rule with two sounds.

> We pronounce -*ed* endings with an extra syllable /ɪd/ after ___ and ___ only.

c ▶ 02.06 Which of the verbs + -*ed* in the box have the extra /ɪd/ syllable? Listen and check.

| waited | included | arrived | looked | watched |
| shouted | smiled | stopped | ended | believed |

6 VOCABULARY Tourism

a 💬 What useful holiday items can you see on these pages? What else do people usually take?

b ⟫ Now go to Vocabulary Focus 2A on p. 134.

7 SPEAKING

a Think of a holiday you enjoyed. Think about your answers to these questions.
• When did you go?
• Where did you go?
• Was it your first time?
• How long did you go for?
• Who did you go with?
• What kind of accommodation did you stay in?
• Did you do any sightseeing?
• Who did you meet?
• Did you bring back any souvenirs?

b 💬 Tell your partner about your holiday. Listen to your partner and ask questions.

19

2B EVERYONE WAS WAITING FOR ME

Learn to describe travel problems
- G Past continuous
- V Travel collocations

1 VOCABULARY Travel collocations

a 💬 Look at the list of ways to travel. Which do you prefer? Why?
- car
- bus
- train
- plane
- coach
- on foot

b 💬 Look at the travel problems in the pictures. Which situation do you dislike the most?

c ›› Now go to Vocabulary Focus 2B on p. 135.

2 LISTENING

a 💬 Look at the picture and the headline. What do you think happened?

WOMAN ANGRY AFTER FLIGHT IN TOILET

b ▶02.11 Listen to the woman describing her experience. Were your ideas in 2a correct?

c ▶02.11 Listen again. What does the woman say about … ?
- her journey to the airport
- boarding the plane
- what the flight attendant said
- what happened when she was in the toilet
- how she feels now about what happened

d 💬 Do you believe the woman's story? Why? / Why not?

20

3 GRAMMAR Past continuous

a ▶ 02.12 Listen and complete the sentences with past continuous verbs.
1 It _____ when I left the house.
2 When I boarded the plane, all the other passengers _____ for me.
3 I _____ my book when one of the flight attendants spoke to me.
4 I _____ on the toilet when the turbulence started.

b Underline the past simple verbs in sentences 1–4 in 3a.

c Look at the sentences in 3a again and answer the questions.
1 Which action started first in every sentence: past simple or past continuous?
2 Think about when and why the past continuous action stopped in each sentence. Write the sentence numbers (1–4).
The past continuous action ... .
stopped because of the past simple action ___ ___
stopped some time after the past simple action ___ ___

d ≫ Now go to Grammar Focus 2B on p. 146.

e ▶ 02.14 Pronunciation Listen to the sentences. Notice which syllables are stressed.
1 It was <u>rain</u>ing.
2 It <u>wasn't rain</u>ing.
3 Was it <u>rain</u>ing?
4 We were <u>driv</u>ing <u>fast</u>.
5 We <u>weren't driv</u>ing <u>fast</u>.
6 Were we <u>driv</u>ing <u>fast</u>?

f ▶ 02.14 Listen to the sentences in 3e again. Do the vowel sounds in *was* and *were* sound the same in all the sentences?

g ▶ 02.15 Listen to five more sentences. Do you hear *was*, *wasn't*, *were* or *weren't* in each?

h Complete the sentences with the past continuous or past simple forms of the verbs in brackets.
1 The train _____ (leave) the station when I _____ (realise) I was on the wrong train.
2 When I _____ (travel) around Australia, I _____ (lose) my passport.
3 I _____ (run) for the bus when my bag _____ (open) and all my things _____ (fall) out.
4 I _____ (drive) to a family wedding when my GPS _____ (stop) working.
5 Someone _____ (steal) my bag when I _____ (stand) in the queue for a ticket.

i 💬 Have you had any experiences that were similar to the ones in 3h?

> I lost my passport when we were moving house.

> What did you do?

4 READING AND SPEAKING

a 💬 Read the headlines and look at the pictures. What do you think happened to the travellers?

DID YOU MEAN CAPRI?

SWEDISH TOURISTS MISS THEIR DESTINATION BY 600 KM

COACH PASSENGERS ASKED TO GET OUT AND PUSH

b ≫ Communication 2B Student A: Go to p. 127. Student B: Go to p. 128.

c 💬 Tell your partner your story. Use the questions to help you.
• Where were they going?
• How were they travelling?
• What was the problem?
• Who helped solve the problem? How?
• What happened in the end?

> Two Swedish tourists were on holiday in Italy. They ...

d 💬 Which journey do you think was worse for the travellers?

e Think of a time you experienced travel problems. Think about your answers to these questions.
• Where were you going?
• How were you travelling?
• What went wrong?
• What happened in the end?

f 💬 Work in small groups. Tell the group about your journey.

> When I was travelling to Florida, we waited for ten hours in the airport. Then they sent us to a hotel.

> Was it free?

g 💬 Who in your group has had the worst experience on ... ?
• a plane • a train • a bus

UNIT 2

21

2C EVERYDAY ENGLISH
What time's the next train?

Learn to ask for information in a public place

P Connected speech
S Asking for more information

1 LISTENING

a What kind of information do people ask for in these places? Think of two kinds of information for each place.
- train stations
- tourist offices
- airports

b 💬 Look at the picture. Where is Annie? What information do you think she is asking for?

c ▶ 02.16 Watch or listen to Part 1 and check your ideas in 1b.

d ▶ 02.16 Watch or listen to Part 1 again. Answer the questions.
1 When does the next train to Birmingham leave? _____
2 How often do the trains leave? _____
3 Which platform does the Birmingham train leave from? _____
4 Which day will Annie come back? _____
5 How much is Annie's ticket? _____
6 What does Annie want to get from the newsagent's? _____

2 USEFUL LANGUAGE Asking for information in a public place

a ▶ 02.17 Match 1–6 with a–f to make questions from Annie's conversation. Then listen and check.

1 ☐ What time's   a is a ticket?
2 ☐ How often   b pay by card?
3 ☐ Could you tell me where c the ticket office is?
4 ☐ How much   d the next train?
5 ☐ Can I   e do the trains leave?
6 ☐ Where can I   f buy a magazine?

b ▶ 02.18 Listen and complete the questions the assistant asks.
1 Yes, how _____ _____ help you?
2 Is there _____ _____ I can help you with?

c Complete the dialogue with words from the box.

| what time where can I can I how much could you tell me |

A Hi, [1]_____ where the museum is, please?
B Yes, it's not far. It's by the river. Look on the map – here.
A I see. And [2]_____ does it open?
B From 8 am till 4 pm.
A [3]_____ is a ticket?
B For adults, it's £14.
A [4]_____ buy a ticket?
B I can sell you a ticket here, or you can buy one at the museum.
A Oh, I'll buy one here. [5]_____ pay by card?
B Of course – that's no problem.

d ▶ 02.19 Listen and check. Practise the dialogue.

3 PRONUNCIATION Connected speech

a ▶ 02.20 Listen to the questions and look at the letters in **bold**.
- Where ca**n I** buy a magazine?
- How mu**ch is** a ticket?

1 Underline the correct word to complete the rule.

There *is* / *isn't* a pause between words when a consonant sound comes before a vowel sound.

2 What sound exactly do the letters in **bold** in each question make?

b Underline the letters and spaces where there isn't a pause.
1 Is anyone sitting here?   4 Do you want a drink?
2 Could I sit next to you?   5 Where do you get off?
3 What are you reading?   6 Can I have your email address?

c ▶ 02.21 Listen and check.

d 💬 In pairs, ask the questions in 3b and answer with your own ideas.

UNIT 2

4 CONVERSATION SKILLS
Asking for more information

a Look at the underlined phrases. Do the phrases show that the speaker wants to … ?
1 end the conversation
2 ask something else

ANNIE	<u>Sorry, just one more thing.</u>
ASSISTANT	Yes, of course.
ANNIE	Could you tell me where the ticket office is?
ASSISTANT	Is there anything else I can help you with?
ANNIE	<u>Actually, there is one more thing</u>. Where can I buy a magazine?

b 02.22 Listen to the phrases and repeat.

c Work in pairs. Student A: you are a tourist officer. Student B: you are a tourist in town. Use the dialogue below, and ask two more questions.

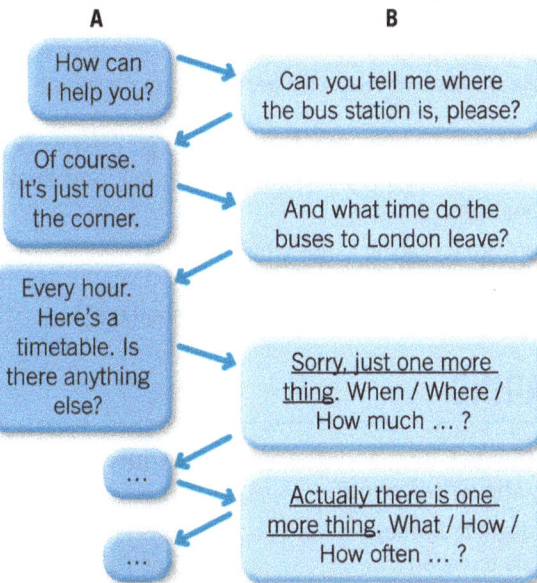

A / B

- How can I help you?
- Can you tell me where the bus station is, please?
- Of course. It's just round the corner.
- And what time do the buses to London leave?
- Every hour. Here's a timetable. Is there anything else?
- Sorry, just one more thing. When / Where / How much … ?
- …
- Actually there is one more thing. What / How / How often … ?
- …

d Swap roles. Do the dialogue again.

5 LISTENING

a Look at the picture from Part 2. Why do you think Annie runs back to the assistant?

b 02.23 Watch or listen to Part 2 and check your ideas. What mistake did Annie make? What is her last question?

c Have you ever made a silly mistake like Annie? What happened?

6 SPEAKING

a ≫ **Communication 2C** Student A: Go to 6b below. Student B: Go to p.128.

Student A

b Look at Card 1. Think about what you want to ask.

> **1**
> You need to book a train ticket.
> - 🕐 – first train to Manchester / in the morning?
> - how often / trains to Manchester?
> - £ two adult tickets?
> - pay by card?
> - where / leave luggage?
> - where / the waiting room?

c Listen to Student B and reply. Find out the information you need.

d Now look at Card 2. Start the conversation with Student B. Say 'How can I help you?'

> **2**
> You are a tourist guide in Warwick.
> - castle is in the centre of town
> - opening hours 10 am–6 pm
> - prices: adult £30.60, child £25.80
> - buy tickets at the castle or online
> - tours every hour
> - visitors can bring food, but many places to buy food

✓ UNIT PROGRESS TEST
→ CHECK YOUR PROGRESS
You can now do the Unit Progress Test.

23

2D SKILLS FOR WRITING
This city is different, but very friendly

Learn to write a travel blog

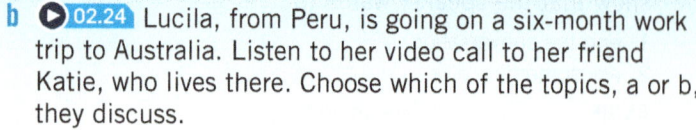
Linking: *and / but / so / because / when*

1 SPEAKING AND LISTENING

a 💬 Look at the photos of Sydney, Australia. Discuss the questions.
1 What can you see in the photos?
2 What do the photos tell you about Sydney?
3 What other things do you know about Sydney and Australia?
4 Have you been there? Would you like to go? Why / Why not?

b ▶ 02.24 Lucila, from Peru, is going on a six-month work trip to Australia. Listen to her video call to her friend Katie, who lives there. Choose which of the topics, a or b, they discuss.
1 Lucila's arrival: a passport control
                      b transport
2 Sydney: a the sea
                      b the parks

c ▶ 02.24 Listen again and underline the correct answers.
1 Katie will meet Lucila *at five / after six* o'clock.
2 They will meet at the *airport / train station*.
3 When Katie arrived in Sydney, she was *too tired to enjoy / excited by* the view.
4 Katie's home town is *similar to / different from* Sydney.
5 Katie lives in a part of Sydney that *is next to a harbour / has a lot of things to do*.
6 Lucila will stay with Katie for *her whole trip / a short time*.

d 💬 Imagine you are making plans to go on a work trip to another country for six months. Ask and answer the questions.
1 Where are you going to go? Why?
2 What do you hope to see and do?
3 What jobs do you plan to do while you are there?

2 READING

a Read Lucila's blog about arriving in Sydney. Tick (✓) the topics she writes about.
☐ her flight to Sydney
☐ public transport
☐ Katie's job
☐ a famous building in Sydney
☐ fresh food
☐ Katie's accommodation
☐ Katie's neighbourhood
☐ wildlife

b Read the text again. What does Lucila say about the topics you ticked in 2a?

24

My TRIP to OZ!

TUESDAY, NOVEMBER 7
SYDNEY – FIRST EVENING

I've arrived, and it's amazing! It was a long flight, but I slept most of the way, so I'm not tired. Katie was right – the view from the plane was spectacular! Sydney just looks so different from anywhere else I have been.

When I got off the plane, the first thing I noticed was how organised everything is. There are signs everywhere that tell you where to go and what to do. There are a lot of rules about bringing food into Australia. You can't bring in fresh fruit or anything like that because it could have diseases that are dangerous for plants in Australia.

It was really easy to find the train and get to the city centre. Katie was waiting for me at Central Station – it was wonderful to see her again. We took a train to Newtown, where she lives. The transport system here seems really efficient.

Katie lives in a lovely old-style house with two other housemates, Louise and Michaela. They were very friendly and welcoming. And they don't mind if I stay until I find my own place to live.

We all had a lovely dinner together, but after that I felt very tired. In fact, I'm finding it difficult to keep my eyes open and write this, so I'll finish now – more tomorrow.

WEDNESDAY, NOVEMBER 8
SYDNEY – MY FIRST FULL DAY!

Katie didn't have to go to work today, so we spent the day together. In the morning, we went for a walk around her neighbourhood, Newtown. It's really cool – a lot of the shops and houses there are more than a hundred years old. There are so many interesting cafés and places to eat. Some of them are quite expensive, but most of them are really cheap. Newtown is also famous for its street art.

In the afternoon, Katie took me to a part of central Sydney called The Rocks. It's a really attractive part of Sydney because it's right on the harbour.

From there, we walked around to the Opera House, which is next to Sydney Harbour Bridge. On a sunny day like today, the Opera House is beautiful and it's like no other building I know.

Then we went to the Royal Botanic Garden and sat down for a while because I was feeling tired. The plants and the trees here are unusual – different from those in Peru. And the birds! Here in Australia they're very colourful, but they're so noisy!

It's very warm here already, so tomorrow we think we'll go to Bondi Beach for a swim. Can't wait!

3 WRITING SKILLS Linking words

a Read the sentences and answer the questions about the linking words in **bold**.

1 I slept most of the way, **so** I'm not tired.
2 **When** I got off the plane, the first thing I noticed was how organised everything is.
3 They were very friendly **and** welcoming.
4 Some of them are quite expensive, **but** most of them are really cheap.
5 You can't bring in fresh fruit or anything like that **because** it could have diseases.

Which linking word do we use to … ?

a say two things happen at the same time
b add a similar idea
c add a different idea
d give the reason for something
e give the result of something

b Find and underline more examples of linking words in Lucila's blog.

c Put *but*, *when*, *so*, or *because* where you see ⌃ in the sentences.

1 We were very tired, ⌃ we went straight to bed.
2 ⌃ we got to the hotel, I unpacked.
3 It was the middle of the night, ⌃ the streets were completely empty.
4 The restaurant looked small and cheap, ⌃ the food was amazing.
5 We gave the waiter $20 ⌃ the service was excellent.
6 We ran into a shopping centre ⌃ the storm began.
7 We went to the National Museum ⌃ we wanted to understand more about the country's history.
8 We tried to check in, ⌃ we were very early and the desk was closed.

4 WRITING

a You're going to write a blog. Choose one of the topics.
- a holiday experience
- your first day doing something new (for example, starting a new class or job)
- a new place you visited recently

b Make notes. Think about:
- where you were
- how you felt
- what you saw and did
- who you talked to.

c Write your blog. Use some linking words from Ex 3a.

d Work in pairs. Read your partner's blog. Do they use linking words? Is it similar to your blog?

UNIT 2
Review and extension

1 GRAMMAR

a Complete the sentences with the past simple forms of the verbs in the box.

> ask   not take   learn   meet   need   not spend   wear

1. We _____ a lot of money because everything was very cheap.
2. She _____ the bus driver for directions.
3. I _____ to change my ticket before I got on the train.
4. I _____ the bus home because I didn't have any money.
5. He _____ his new shirt to the party.
6. _____ you _____ any interesting people on holiday?
7. I _____ how to surf when I lived in Cornwall.

b Choose the correct verb forms.

I had a terrible journey. I ¹*walked / was walking* to the train station and it started raining. And then the train was twenty minutes late. When it ²*came / was coming*, I ³*found / was finding* a seat by the window. Some girls ⁴*played / were playing* music on their phones, but it was great music, so that was OK. I ⁵*read / was reading* my book when the train ⁶*arrived / was arriving* at the next station. Two people got on, and a man ⁷*sat / was sitting* down next to me. He started talking loudly on his phone. He ⁸*told / was telling* someone about his new car, his job – everything! He was still talking when the train ⁹*got / was getting* into the station.

2 VOCABULARY

a Match clues 1–5 to the words.

> suntan lotion   map   backpack   foreign currency
> guidebook   sunglasses   passport   suitcase

1. You wear or use these two things when it's sunny.
2. This is money from another country.
3. These two things give you ideas of where to go.
4. You usually need this to travel internationally.
5. You pack clothes in these two things when you go away.

b Complete the sentences with the verbs in the box.

> change   check out   do   get
> go away   set off   travel around

1. We hope to _____ the world next year.
2. You need to _____ a visa if you want to visit China.
3. You will have time to _____ some sightseeing later.
4. You need to _____ trains in Frankfurt for Berlin.
5. We want to _____ for the weekend later this month.
6. We _____ for Scotland at seven tomorrow.
7. We need to _____ of our hotel before 10 am.

3 WORDPOWER *off*

a Match the general meanings of *off* (a–c) with the groups of sentences (1–3).

1. ☐ OK, **I'm off**. My train leaves in ten minutes.
   The traffic lights turned green and they **drove off**.
   The plane **took off** half an hour early.
2. ☐ The airline has 20% **off** tickets to New York.
   He **fell off** the chair and hurt his back.
   Can you **cut off** a piece of that cheese for me?
   Why don't you **take off** your coat? It's not cold here.
3. ☐ I tried to call him, but his phone **was off**.
   I was tired, so I **turned off** the TV and went to bed.

b Match sentences 1–8 with replies a–h.

1. ☐ There's 10% off if you buy today.
2. ☐ Is that your phone? What happened to it?
3. ☐ Why is it so cold in here?
4. ☐ When are you off?
5. ☐ Can I try some of that sausage?
6. ☐ Can you turn off the radio, please?
7. ☐ We took off an hour late.
8. ☐ So, do you know who hit your car?

a. It fell off the table.
b. Of course. I'll cut off a piece for you.
c. Great! I'll take two, please.
d. In five minutes.
e. What time did you land?
f. No, they drove off before I saw them.
g. No. I'm listening to it.
h. The heating's off.

c 💬 Work in pairs. Cover a–h in 3b and try to remember the replies.

🔄 REVIEW YOUR PROGRESS

How well did you do in this unit? Write 3, 2 or 1 for each objective.
3 = very well   2 = well   1 = not so well

I CAN ...	
talk about past holidays	☐
describe travel problems	☐
ask for information in a public place	☐
write a travel blog.	☐

CAN DO OBJECTIVES
- Talk about money and shopping experiences
- Talk about living with less
- Talk to people in shops
- Write an update email

UNIT 3
MONEY

GETTING STARTED

a 💬 Look at the picture and answer the questions.
1. What is happening in the picture?
2. How do you think the woman feels?
3. What do you think she will do next?

b 💬 Ask and answer the questions.
1. How often do you use cash these days? Do you use cash more or less than you did five years ago? Why?
2. Do you think people will stop using cash in the future? Why / Why not?

3A I'VE NEVER SEEN CROWDS LIKE THIS

Learn to talk about money and shopping experiences

G Present perfect or past simple
V Money and shopping

1 VOCABULARY Money and shopping

a 💬 In your country, what three things do people spend the most money on? Why?

> In my country, families spend a lot of money on food because they like eating well.

> Everyone thinks it's important to have a nice car – people spend a lot of money on that.

b Complete the questions with the nouns in the box. Notice the verbs in **bold** that they go with.

| discount | bargain | money | sale | loan |

1 How likely are you to **borrow** _____ from family or friends to buy something expensive? Why?
2 How easy is it for young people in your country to **get** a _____ from a bank to buy something expensive?
3 Is it fair that some shops **offer** customers a small _____ (10–20%) to encourage them to shop there? Why / Why not?
4 Do you **save up for** a big _____ so you can buy a lot of things at a cheap price? Why / Why not?
5 How does it make you feel when you **find** a really good _____ in the sales?

c 💬 Work in pairs. Ask and answer the questions.

d ≫ Now go to Vocabulary Focus 3A on p. 136.

2 READING AND SPEAKING

a 💬 Work in pairs. Ask and answer the questions.
1 When do shops have sales in your country? When is the biggest sales season?
2 What kinds of products do people buy in the sales?

b Read the text about sales around the world and answer the questions.
1 Is it similar in your country?
2 What information surprises you?

SALES MADNESS AROUND THE WORLD!

Every year in late November, shoppers in the USA rush to shops and jump online for the Black Friday sales. Now Black Friday madness is spreading all around the world.

In 2010, Amazon introduced Black Friday to online shoppers in the UK. Stores and shops were quick to copy Amazon and now Black Friday is the biggest shopping day in the UK – bigger than Boxing Day (26 December), the traditional sales day in the UK. Shoppers sometimes fight to get a bargain and stores have to call the police.

In China there are also November sales like Black Friday, called 'Singles Day' – a day that is aimed at young people who aren't married. In 2009, the Chinese online shop Alibaba turned Singles Day into a huge online sale. It is now bigger than Black Friday with sales of more than $30 billion dollars.

c Read the questionnaire and choose the answers (a, b or c) that are true for you.

SALES SEASON – CAN YOU SAY 'NO'?

Do our questionnaire. Can you say 'no' to a bargain?

1 Where are you most likely to buy something that is in the sales?
   a both in a shop and online
   b in a shop only
   c online only

2 Who makes you want to buy a sales item?
   a famous people on social media
   b the company that makes the product – you know they're good
   c family or friends

3 What makes you want to buy a certain product?
   a It looks good.
   b It is high quality.
   c It has a good discount price.

4 What are you likely to buy in the sales?
   a anything you see that you like
   b a mix of things you planned and didn't plan to buy
   c only things you planned to buy

5 How are you likely to pay for things you buy in the sales?
   a credit card only
   b a mix of cash and credit card
   c cash only

6 If you can't afford to buy a great bargain in the sales, do you … ?
   a borrow money from a bank
   b borrow money from family
   c save money and hope for more bargains next year

d 💬 Compare your answers with your partner's. Are they similar?

e 💬 Look at the results on p. 129. Do you agree with the description of yourself? Why / Why not?

UNIT 3

3 LISTENING

a ▶ 03.02 Listen to shop assistants Mike and Kathie talk to a radio journalist, Janie. Who did these things? Write Mike (*M*) or Kathie (*K*).

1 _____ worked on sales day for the first time.
2 _____ talked to people who were disappointed.
3 _____ helped someone who said they weren't feeling well.

b ▶ 03.02 Listen again. Are the sentences true (*T*) or false (*F*)?

1 Mike's day was much busier than in other years.
2 The guy who waited all night bought two expensive T-shirts.
3 Kathie put some sale items in the old lady's shopping basket.
4 Kathie helped the old lady get to the electronics department.
5 The man who wanted jeans queued at the wrong door.

c 💬 Work in pairs. Ask and answer the questions.

1 What do you think Mike and Kathie said to … ?
   a the guy who wanted a T-shirt
   b the old lady
   c the guy who wanted jeans
2 Do people do strange things during sales in your country? Think of a story you heard or make one up. Tell your partner. Can you guess if your partner's story is real or not?

4 GRAMMAR Present perfect or past simple

a ▶ 03.03 Complete the sentences with the verbs in the box. Listen and check your answers.

opened   met   worked (x2)   started   known

1 I've _____ on sales days three times before.
2 This morning, just before we _____ the doors …
3 I've never _____ someone to do that.
4 I've never _____ on a sales day before.
5 She's probably the cleverest customer I've ever _____.
6 He _____ queuing at about midnight last night.

b Which of the sentences in 4a are past simple? Which are present perfect?

☐☐ past simple   ☐☐☐☐ present perfect

c Underline the time expressions in the sentences in 4a. Complete the rules with the time expressions from the sentences.

> We can use the present perfect to talk about past experiences in our whole lives, not at a particular time. We often use adverbs like _____, _____ and _____.
>
> We use the past simple to talk about a particular time in the past. We often use time phrases like _____ and _____.

d ⏩ Now go to Grammar Focus 3A on p. 148.

Mike

Kathie

e ▶ 03.05 Complete the questions with present perfect and past simple forms of the verbs in brackets. Listen and check.

1 _____ you ever _____ to the sales when there were big crowds? (go)
  Where _____ you _____? (go)
2 _____ you ever _____ anything unusual in an online sale? (buy)
  What _____ you _____? (buy)
3 _____ you ever _____ up money for the sales? (save)
  How much _____ you _____? (save)

f 💬 Work in pairs. Ask and answer the questions.

5 SPEAKING

a 💬 You are going to find out about other students' money and shopping experiences. What questions can you ask with 'Have you ever … ?'

b Walk around the class and find someone who has done each thing in the grid. Ask more questions.

queue for the sales all night	ask for a discount when shopping
buy clothes online that are the wrong size	find a really good bargain
lend money to a friend	borrow money from someone in your family
spend a whole day shopping	buy something you already own
buy something that you couldn't really afford	take an item back to a shop
buy something online from another country	spend more money than you planned to spend

> Have you ever queued for the sales all night?

> Yes, I have. It was two years ago.

> What did you want to buy?

> A tablet computer that cost just £80. It was a really good bargain.

c 💬 What was the most interesting or unusual story you heard?

29

3B I'VE ALREADY GIVEN £25 TO CHARITY

Learn to talk about living with less
- **G** Present perfect with *already* and *yet*
- **V** *make* / *do* / *give* collocations

1 READING

a Work in pairs. Ask and answer the questions.
1. Does money make people happy? Why / Why not?
2. Can having a lot of money be a problem for some people? How?
3. If you give some money away, how can it help *you*, as well as the person or organisation you give it to?
4. What are some different ways to give money away in your country? What other things do people give away?

b Read the article. What does it say about question 3?

GET HAPPY — GIVE YOUR MONEY AWAY!

You know the old saying, 'Money can't buy you happiness'? Well, what if it could? Not by making it or spending it, but by giving it away.

Research tells us that if you give money away, you will feel much happier. In an experiment in Switzerland, researchers gave 50 volunteers 25 Swiss francs (about £20) each week for four weeks. Half the people spent the money on themselves and made a note of how they spent the money. But researchers asked the other half to spend the money on another person.

Afterwards, all 50 volunteers did the same task in a laboratory. Researchers asked them to think of a person they would like to give money to. Then they had to choose how much money, from £3 to £20, they wanted to give. While the volunteers thought about this, researchers studied their brain activity using an MRI machine.

The results showed two things. First, the 25 volunteers who gave their money away during the four weeks were more generous and chose larger amounts of money in the laboratory task. Second, those same people were much happier than the people who previously spent the money on themselves.

How did researchers know they were happy? When they studied the results of the MRI scans, they could see that the parts of the brain linked to being generous are also linked to being happy – and those parts of the brain were more active in the 25 people who gave their money away.

'OK,' I hear you say. 'That's great in theory, but does it work in the real world?' In the Swiss experiment, researchers told the volunteers they had to give money away. But what if you want to do this in your daily life? Can you really make yourself happy by giving? The answer is 'yes,' but it's important that you follow some simple rules.

First of all, don't start by giving away a lot of money. Give a pound to a homeless person or make a small donation to a charity. Maybe give just £5 from your wages, or try to change your habits so you save money to give away. To give an example, stop buying lunch at a café every day and take a packed lunch to work or school. You can then give your lunch money to charity.

Or perhaps you're the kind of person who does a lot of online shopping. So rather than looking at websites for shops, try looking at websites for charities. Which one do you think is important? Donate the money you were going to spend on a new T-shirt (that you probably don't need).

Learning to give money away is all about changing the way you behave. It's about living with less and being more generous. And research now tells us this will make you happy.

c Read the article again and answer the questions.
1. What did the two groups of volunteers in the Swiss experiment do with their 25 francs?
2. What did the volunteers have to decide in the laboratory?
3. What happened while they were doing this?
4. How did researchers know that one group was happier?
5. How can you begin to learn to be more generous?
6. What are two examples of changing your habits to save money and give it away?

d Does the article make you feel differently about giving your money away? Why / Why not? Who would you give money to?

UNIT 3

2 VOCABULARY
make / do / give collocations

a Look at the examples from the article. Notice the **bold** words that go with the underlined verbs. Underline one more example each of collocations with *give*, *make* and *do* in the last three paragraphs of the article.

1 If you **give** money **away**, you will feel much happier.
2 They **made a note** of how they spent the money.
3 All 50 volunteers **did** the same **task** in a laboratory.

b ▶ 03.06 Complete the collocations with the correct form of *make*, *do* or *give*. Listen and check.

1 When I joined the charity organisation, I _____ **a lot of friends**.
2 I called the charity shop yesterday and a woman _____ me **directions** to get there.
3 I'm going to _____ **some volunteer work** for a charity.
4 Last week, my cousin _____ me **good advice** on charities to donate money to.
5 His volunteer work was cleaning disabled people's houses, and he _____ **a good job**.
6 I didn't have any cash, so I _____ **a payment** by credit card to the charity.

c 💬 Look at the collocations in 2a and 2b. Which of these things did you do in the last year? Which would you like to do?

3 LISTENING

a ▶ 03.07 Listen to the radio programme *Ways of Life*. Daniel calls in and talks about his experience of living with less. Choose the correct words or phrases in *italics* to complete the notes.

1 Reason for living with less: Daniel felt *bored / annoyed / confused*.
2 Things given away: *IT equipment / furniture / clothes*
3 Lifestyle changes: *free time activities / food / transport*

b ▶ 03.07 Listen again and make more notes about these three points.

c 💬 What other changes might Daniel make if he wants to live with less?

4 GRAMMAR
Present perfect with *already* and *yet*

a Complete the sentences with the past participle form of the verbs in brackets.

1 I've already _____ away my tablet. (give)
2 I haven't _____ anyone who wants my desktop computer yet. (find)
3 Have you _____ your car yet? (sell)

b ▶ 03.08 Listen and check. Which tense is used?

c Look at the sentences in 4a. Then complete the rules with *already* and *yet*.

> Use _____ to say something is complete, often earlier than we expected.
>
> Use *not* + _____ to say something is not complete at this time.
>
> Use _____ to ask if something is complete at this time.

d ⟫ Now go to Grammar Focus 3B on p. 148.

e ▶ 03.10 **Pronunciation** Listen to how the following words spelled with *j* and *y* are pronounced. Then listen again and repeat.

/dʒ/	**j**ust	en**j**oy	**j**oin
/j/	**y**et	**y**ou	**y**oung

f ▶ 03.11 Put the adverbs in brackets in the correct places in the sentences. Then listen and check.

1 I emailed some information about our charity. Have you had a chance to read it? (yet)
2 I don't need my old DVDs. I've given them away. (already)
3 I haven't stopped using my car. Public transport isn't very good in this city. (yet)
4 I sold my car last week and I've bought a bike. (already)
5 Have you decided which books to give away? (yet)

g 💬 Write two present perfect sentences about yourself, one with *already* and the other with *yet*. Tell your partner your sentences. Ask each other questions about them.

5 SPEAKING

a Make notes on these questions.

> *Checklist for trying to live with less*
> 1 What things do you really need in your life? Why do you need them?
> 2 What things are less important? Why are they less important?
> 3 What things can you give to another person? Who can you give them to?
> 4 What habits can you change to spend less money?
> 5 What can you do with the money you save?

b 💬 Work in small groups. Discuss the questions. Do you think you can live with less? Why / Why not?

31

3C EVERYDAY ENGLISH
Do you have anything cheaper?

Learn to talk to people in shops
- P Sentence stress
- S Changing your mind

1 LISTENING

a Do you enjoy going shopping? Which of these things do you like shopping for? Why?
- food • gifts • clothes • books

> I like shopping for clothes. It's fun.

> I hate it. I think it's really boring, but I like buying books.

b Look at the pictures of Mark and Rachel shopping. What do you think they are shopping for?

c 03.12 Watch or listen to Part 1 and check your ideas.

d In pairs, look at the products 1–4. Answer the questions.
1. What do you think each product is used for?
2. Would you buy any of the products for someone you know?
3. Would you like to receive any of them as a present?

e 03.13 Watch or listen to Part 2. Which of the products in the pictures do they buy?

f 03.13 Watch or listen again. Answer the questions.
1. Why does Mark think 'Football in a tin' is a good present?
2. Why does Rachel disagree about the 'Football in a tin'?
3. Why doesn't Mark like the weather station?
4. Why does Mark decide not to buy the book money bank?

g Work in pairs. What do you think of the present they chose? Do you think Leo will like it?

2 USEFUL LANGUAGE
Talking to people in shops

a 03.14 Complete the phrases from Part 2 with the words in the box. Then listen and check.

| anything | sort | cheaper | looking |
| take | do | help | show |

1. Can I _____ you?
2. We're _____ for a present for a friend.
3. Are you looking for _____ in particular?
4. What _____ of thing does he like?
5. What does it _____?
6. Do you have anything _____?
7. Could you _____ us something else?
8. We'll _____ it.

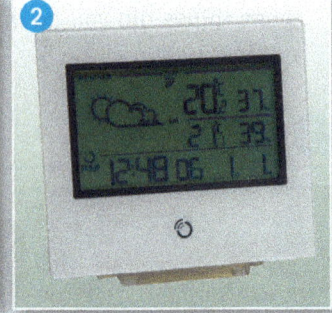

b Answer the questions about the phrases in 2a.
1. Which phrases did the shop assistant say?
2. Which phrase explains why they are in the shop?
3. Which phrases mean they want to see another product?
4. Which phrase asks for information about a product?
5. Which phrase means 'We want to buy this one'?

32

3 PRONUNCIATION
Sentence stress

a ▶ 03.15 Listen to the sentences. Notice the stress.
1 This looks perfect.
2 We're only here for Leo.

b ▶ 03.15 Listen again. Answer the questions.
1 How many syllables does each sentence have?
2 How many stressed syllables does each sentence have?
3 Do we say the unstressed syllables in sentence 2 quickly or slowly?

c ▶ 03.16 Listen and complete the sentences. The missing words are all unstressed.
1 I'd like ____ look ____ ____ different one.
2 Can you show ____ ____ first one again?
3 I'm looking ____ ____ present ____ ____ brother.
4 Do you have this ____ ____ different size?
5 It'll cost ____ ____ ____ money ____ fix.

4 USEFUL LANGUAGE
Paying at the till

a 📹 ▶ 03.17 Watch or listen to Part 3. What does Mark change his mind about?

b 📹 ▶ 03.17 Watch or listen again. Complete the questions with the words in the box.

| put your   receipt   enter your |
| you like   next, please |

1 Who's ____ ____?
2 How would ____ ____ to pay?
3 Can you ____ ____ card in, please?
4 Can you ____ ____ PIN, please?
5 Here's your ____.

c 💬 Practise the conversation from Part 3. Take turns to be the shop assistant and the customer (Mark).

5 CONVERSATION SKILLS Changing your mind

a Look at the underlined phrases in the sentences. Do the two phrases mean the same or are they different?

On second thoughts, I really think we should get something sporty.
Actually, I think I'll put it on my credit card.

b 💬 Work in pairs. Take turns to change your mind. Start with *I'd like*.
1 a coffee – a cup of tea
2 take the bus – get a taxi
3 a sandwich – a salad
4 go for a drive – go for a walk
5 watch TV – put some music on
6 a first-class ticket – a normal ticket

I'd like a coffee.
OK.
On second thoughts, I'd prefer a cup of tea.
Fine.

6 SPEAKING

Communication 3C Work in groups of three. Students A and B: You are buying a present – go to p.129. Student C: You are a shop assistant – go to p.127.

UNIT PROGRESS TEST
CHECK YOUR PROGRESS

You can now do the Unit Progress Test.

3D SKILLS FOR WRITING
We've successfully raised £500

Learn to write an update email

W Paragraphing

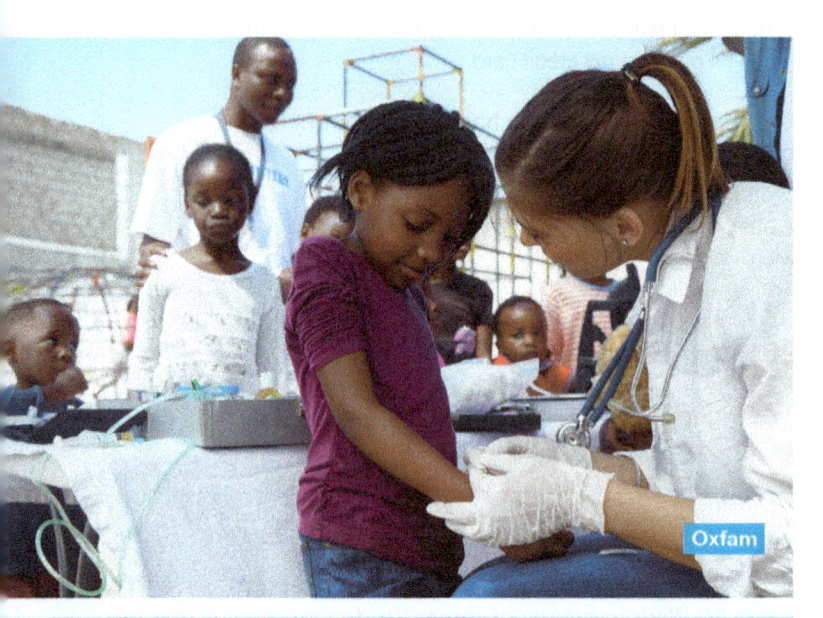

1 LISTENING AND SPEAKING

a 💬 Look at the names of the charities. What do you know about the charities? What do they do?

Match the charities with the sentences.
This charity … .
1 protects animals and the environment
2 protects cultural and natural places around the world
3 helps people in poorer countries

What other large charities do you know? What do they do?

b 💬 Work in pairs. How do people raise money for charity? Add ideas to the list.
  – collect money in the street
  – sponsor someone to do a sports event (e.g., run a marathon)
  – make and sell food (e.g., cakes at work or school)

c ▶03.18 Listen to four people talking about giving money to charity. Which charity, if any, do they support?
1 Shona 2 Jack 3 Jessica 4 William

d ▶03.18 Listen again. Why do/don't the people in 1c support a charity? How do they help? Listen and make notes.

e Work on your own. Make notes on these questions.
1 What charity do you prefer to give money to? Why?
2 Have you ever raised money for charity? What did you do? Who gave you money?

f 💬 Work in small groups. Talk about your answers to 1e.

Oxfam

UNESCO

Greenpeace

34

UNIT 3

2 READING

a Anita and her team at work support UNESCO. Read Anita's email. Why is she sending the email? Tick the correct reasons.
1. ☐ to say thank you
2. ☐ to apologise
3. ☐ to tell people how much money they have raised
4. ☐ to tell people about how the team raised money
5. ☐ to tell people about what UNESCO does
6. ☐ to ask people for money

Hello everyone,

(a) We'd like to thank everyone for their help over the past few months raising money for UNESCO. We've successfully raised £500.

(b) Most of you know one of the ways we raised money because you bought our cakes every Wednesday! But we'd just like to let you know about the different things we did. We also sold our old books, DVDs and clothes online. And every Friday, we each paid £1 to wear casual clothes to work.

(c) UNESCO uses the money to protect important cultural and natural places around the world. This includes places like the ancient pyramids in Teotihuacan in Mexico, Grand Canyon National Park in the USA, the Galápagos Islands in Ecuador and the ancient city of Pompeii in Italy. These places teach us about our cultures and the cultures of other people around the world. And learning about these cultures helps us to understand each other a little better.

(d) Thanks again for all your help. Please look out for our next event.
Anita Webb (and team)
Human Resources Manager

---

b Read the email again and answer the questions.
1. How did the team raise £500?
2. How will UNESCO spend the money?
3. Why is UNESCO's work important?

3 WRITING SKILLS Paragraphing

a Match the descriptions with paragraphs a–d in Anita's email.
1. ☐ closing the email
2. ☐ the introduction
3. ☐ how the team raised money
4. ☐ information about UNESCO

b What information does Anita include in the introduction? What does she mention in the closing paragraph?

c Put the paragraphs below in the correct order to make an email.

☐ Oxfam will use the money on projects around the world to help people have happier and healthier lives. Last year, they helped 13.5 million people. A small amount of money can make a big change. For example, just £15 can give free healthcare to a mother and her baby.

☐ Many of you have bought tickets to our 'Quiz and Pizza' nights. Others gave their unwanted clothes to the very successful 'Clothes Market' in March. We really hope you enjoyed these events. Your money and time will help Oxfam to continue their important work.

☐ Would you like to help us raise more money for Oxfam? Just email me and I'll tell you what we're planning next. Thanks again for all your help.

☐ This email is to say a big 'Thank you!' to everyone who has helped us to raise money for Oxfam over the last few months. We have now raised £750.

4 WRITING

a Choose one of these emails to write.
1. Write about a real experience of raising money for charity. Write to the people who gave you money to thank them. Tell them about how much money you raised, how you raised the money and about the charity.
2. You and some friends have raised £1,000 for a charity at work/school. Write to everyone who helped you to say thank you. Tell them about how much money you raised, how you raised the money and about the charity.

b Plan the email. Use four paragraphs. What information will you put in each paragraph?

c Write the email.

d Swap emails with a partner. Read your partner's email. Are there four paragraphs in the email? What information is in each paragraph?

35

UNIT 3
Review and extension

1 GRAMMAR

a Put the words in the correct order to make questions.
1. you / bought / ever / have / something you didn't need ?
2. given / you / a stranger / have / ever / money / to ?
3. ever / to / a very expensive restaurant / have / you / been ?
4. ever / driven / you / an expensive car / have ?
5. lost / ever / you / money / have / on the street ?

b Ask and answer the questions in 1a.

c Complete the text with the present perfect forms of the verbs in the box.

do   have   help   raise   run   spend

My colleague Andrea is really generous. She ¹_____ a lot of work for charity. She ²_____ two marathons, and from that she ³_____ a lot of money for different charities. She ⁴_____ some time in foreign countries – she went to India to help build a school. At work, she ⁵_____ me a lot when I ⁶_____ problems.

d Put the adverbs in brackets in the correct places.
- A Have you spoken to John? (yet)
- B Yes, he's called me. (already)
- A Have you asked him about the party? (yet)
- B Yes, he's bought the food. (already)
- A Great. I haven't been to the shops. (yet)
- B Have you decided what music to play? (yet)
- A Yes, I've made a list. (already)

e Practise the exchange in 1d.

2 VOCABULARY

a Complete the sentences with the words in the box.

directions   advice   note   something   volunteer

1. My teacher gave me good _____ about my essay.
2. I gave the woman _____ to the tourist office.
3. I want to do some _____ work for a charity this summer.
4. He made a _____ of the charity's phone number.
5. I always try to do _____ fun at the weekend.

b Match questions 1–5 with answers a–e.
1. ☐ Can you lend me ten euros?
2. ☐ How did you afford your new car?
3. ☐ What are you saving up for?
4. ☐ Did you get a discount on your new bike?
5. ☐ Have you got the money you owe me?

a. A new laptop. I want to buy one in the sales.
b. Sorry, no. I just spent it on my electricity bill.
c. I got a loan!
d. No, you won't pay me back!
e. Yes, there was a special offer.

3 Wordpower just

a Look at the different meanings of *just* in 1–4. Read the example sentences. Match the meanings of *just* in sentences a–d with meanings 1–4.

1 ☐ = *a short time ago*
I've **just** got home from work. I need a rest!
2 ☐ = *only*
He doesn't understand money. He's **just** a child.
3 ☐ = *almost not*
I ran to the station, and I **just** caught my train.
4 ☐ = *soon*
Hang on! I'm **just** arriving at the station now.

a. The tickets cost **just** a few dollars.
b. I'm **just** finishing this email – I'll be ready in one minute.
c. Sorry, he's **just** left – he was here a minute ago.
d. You can **just** see the sea from my window, but it's very far away.

b Match sentences 1–5 with replies a–e.
1. ☐ She looks **just like** her sister.
2. ☐ I think the books cost **just under** £20.
3. ☐ The flight is three hours long.
4. ☐ I've **just about** finished my work.
5. ☐ Look at that rain.

a. Yes, they're £19.95. I checked.
b. Yes – we got home **just in time**!
c. That's good. We need to leave in five minutes.
d. Really? It was **just over** two hours when I went.
e. Of course – they're twins!

c Complete the sentences with expressions from 3b.
1. Michelle leaves home at 8 am and arrives at work at 8:25. It takes her _____ half an hour to get there.
2. Steven looks _____ his brother – they're both tall and they both have black hair.
3. I usually arrive _____ when I get a train or plane. I never arrive early!
4. My electricity bill is always _____ €80. This time it's €86.75.
5. The new university building is _____ ready – we'll have our classes there next month.

d Work in pairs. Make sentences about your life with the expressions in 3b.

⟳ REVIEW YOUR PROGRESS

How well did you do in this unit? Write 3, 2 or 1 for each objective.
3 = very well   2 = well   1 = not so well

I CAN ...	
talk about money and shopping experiences	☐
talk about living with less	☐
talk to people in shops	☐
write an update email.	☐

CAN DO OBJECTIVES

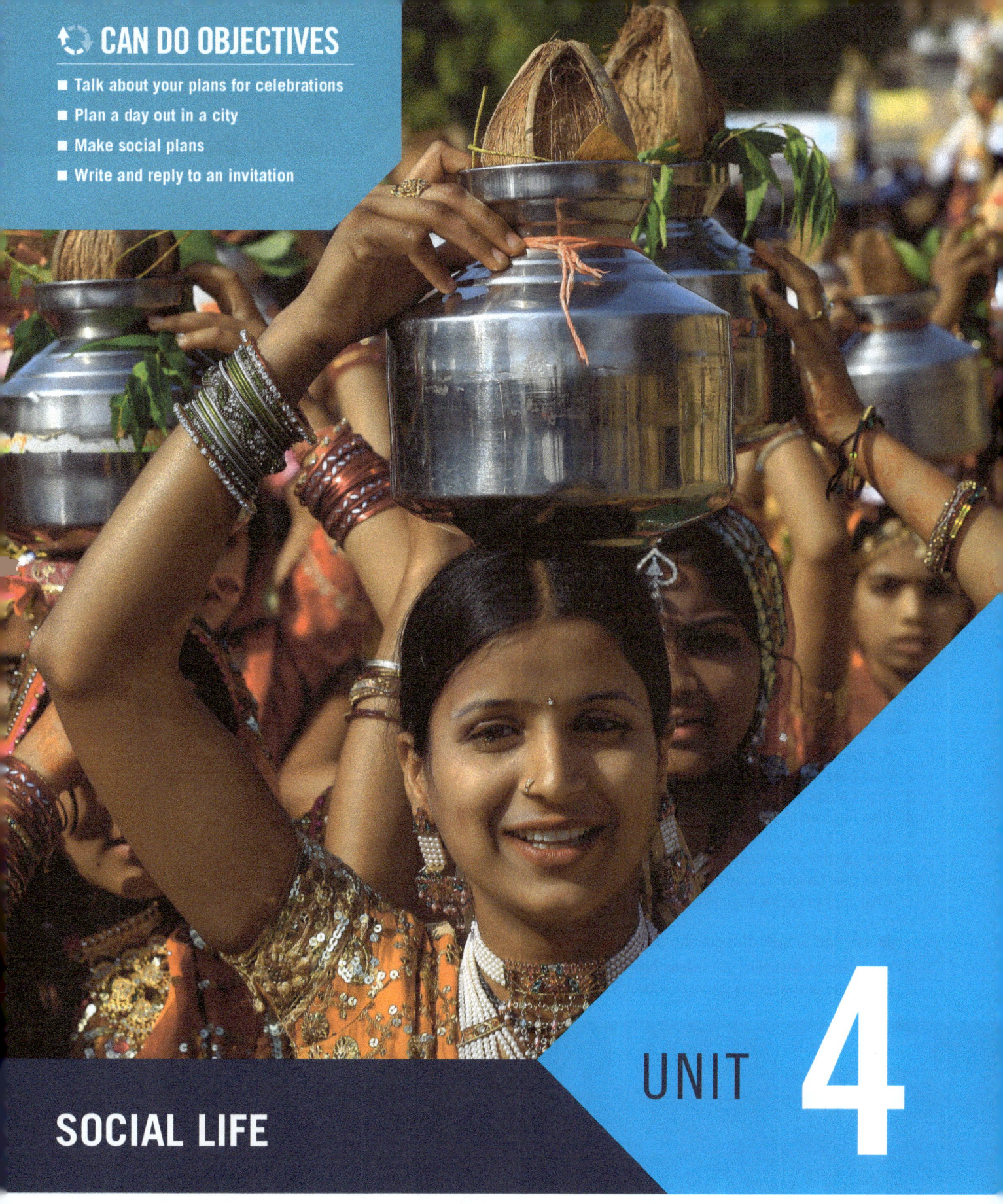

- Talk about your plans for celebrations
- Plan a day out in a city
- Make social plans
- Write and reply to an invitation

SOCIAL LIFE

UNIT 4

GETTING STARTED

a Look at the picture and answer the questions.
1 What are the people doing? What are they carrying? How do you think they feel?
2 What activities do you think they'll do on this day?

b Think of a celebration you know that involves food. Tell your partner about it. You could talk about:
- types of food
- special traditions
- activities people do

4A I'M GOING TO THE HAIRDRESSER'S TOMORROW

Learn to talk about your plans for celebrations
- **G** Present continuous and *be going to*
- **V** Clothes and appearance

1 VOCABULARY Clothes and appearance

a Look at the pictures on these pages. Answer the questions with a partner.
1 What clothes and accessories can you see?
2 Would you like to wear any of the clothes?
3 Are there any clothes that you would never wear? Why?

b Now go to Vocabulary Focus 4A on p. 136.

2 LISTENING

a Look at the pictures of Marta and Craig below. What events are they at? What are they doing in the pictures?

b 04.03 Work in pairs. Read sentences 1–6. Do you think Marta (*M*) or Craig (*C*) is speaking? Listen and check.
1 ☐ We're going to stay the whole night – until they serve breakfast!
2 ☐ This year, one of my favourite DJs is playing.
3 ☐ They're going to make a special cream from turmeric.
4 ☐ I'm not going to see Monisha until the ceremony begins.
5 ☐ I'm meeting the others at 7 pm so we can start queuing.
6 ☐ My friends are arriving early tomorrow to help me get ready.

c 04.03 Listen again and answer the questions.
1 Why does the college organise the May Ball?
2 What does Marta say about her dress?
3 Why is Marta going to stay at home on Saturday?
4 What happens at the end of the May Ball?
5 What are Craig's guests going to do with the special cream?
6 When do the wedding day celebrations start and finish?
7 How does Craig describe the clothes he's going to wear?
8 What happens at the beginning of the wedding day?

d Ask and answer the questions.
1 What's the biggest party you've ever been to?
2 What's the best wedding you've ever been to?

3 GRAMMAR Present continuous and *be going to*

a Read the sentences. Are Craig and Marta talking about the present or the future?
1 My friends **are arriving** early tomorrow.
2 **I'm not going to leave** the house on Saturday.
3 We**'re going to stay** the whole night.
4 A beautician **is doing** our make-up.

b Look at the verb forms in **bold** in the sentences in 3a. Answer the questions with present continuous or *be going to*.
1 Which sentences are about future plans with other people?
2 Which future plans are just ideas, not already arranged?

c Now go to Grammar Focus 4A on p. 150.

d 04.05 **Pronunciation** Listen to five speakers. Does each speaker say *going to* or *gonna*?

e Answer questions 1 and 2 for each future time in the box.

> today   this week   this weekend
> this summer   this month   next year

1 What are your plans? Who are they with?
2 Have you arranged anything yet?

f Tell your partner about your plans.

> I'm travelling to Brazil this summer.

> When are you going?

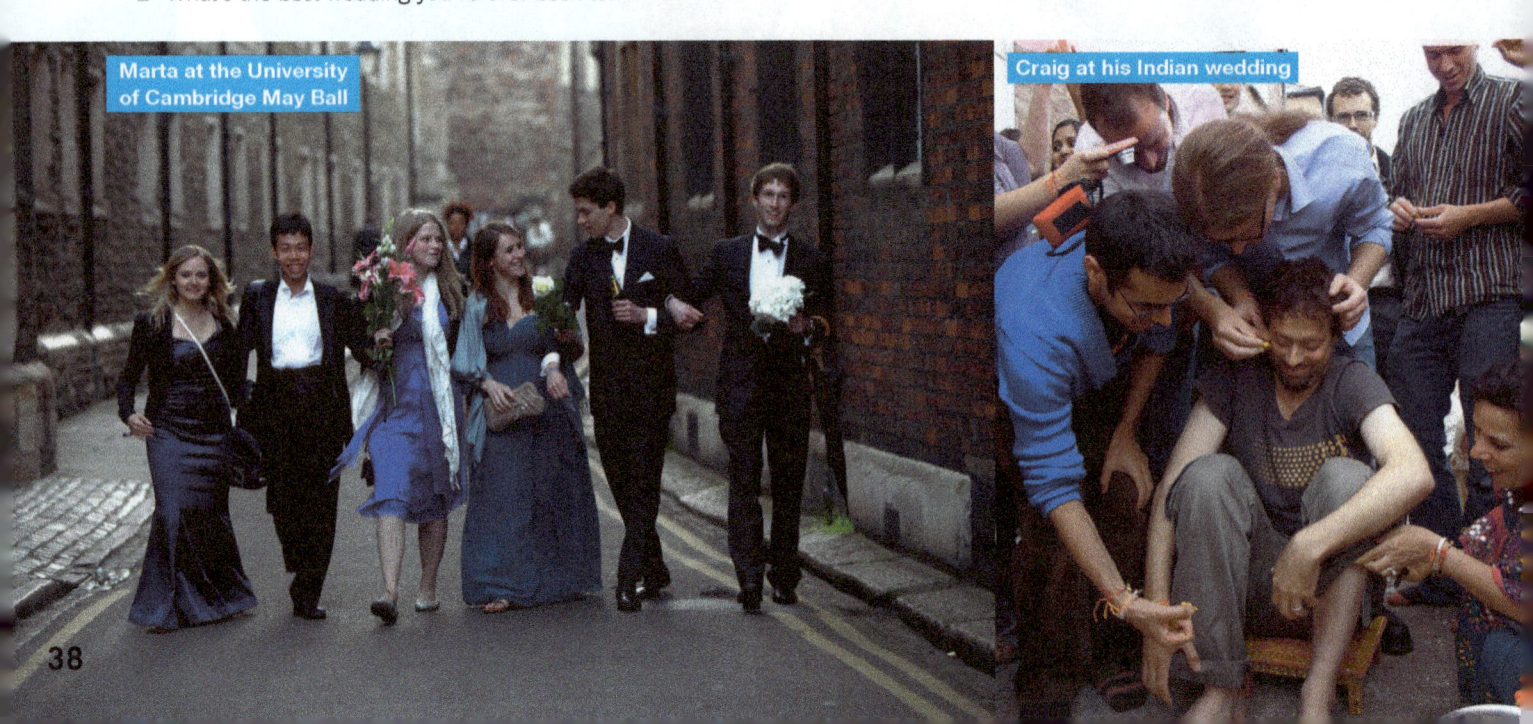

Marta at the University of Cambridge May Ball

Craig at his Indian wedding

38

LIFE in NUMBERS

VIETNAM — 1

Imagine sharing your birthday with the whole country! That's exactly what happens every year in Vietnam. The Vietnamese don't celebrate on the day they were born. Instead, everyone gets one year older on the same day – *Tet,* or Vietnamese New Year's Day. People don't give birthday presents, but children receive red envelopes with money inside. Children greet older people with the phrase, 'Long life of 100 years!'

Tet is the biggest celebration of the year in Vietnam – and it can last for a week. Everyone takes to the streets to make as much noise as they can, and there are fireworks and lion dances.

LATIN AMERICA — 15

Becoming an adult is a very special day for girls in Latin America, and it happens on their fifteenth birthday – the *quinceañera*.

In some places, such as parts of Mexico, the father or another relative gives the girl a doll or teddy bear as her last toy before becoming a woman. In other countries, the birthday girl, or quinceañera, gives a candle to each of the fifteen most important people in her life.

Then there is a meal and dancing. The quinceañera's first dance is always with her father. They practise for weeks before the big day.

JAPAN — 20

In Japan, everyone has a day off to celebrate the world's biggest twentieth birthday party.

The second Monday of January every year is Coming of Age Day, or *Seijin no Hi* – the day all twenty-year-old Japanese become adults.

Men wear suits and women dress in beautiful kimonos, which they often have to rent or borrow because they're so expensive. A ceremony is held in the local government office, and afterwards the new adults can party with their friends and family.

THE UK — 100

Your 100th birthday is an important day in any country, but it's even more special in the UK – you get a card from the Royal Family! You don't need to apply - someone will get in touch around six weeks before the big day.

Each card contains a personal greeting – when twins reach 100 years old together, each one gets a slightly different message. The oldest person to receive a royal birthday card lived to 115 years old.

4 READING

a Ask and answer the questions.
1. Do you celebrate your birthday? What do you do?
2. Do people in your country celebrate any specific ages? Which ones?

b Read the article. What do the numbers refer to? (Sometimes there is more than one possible answer.)
1. 15   20   100

c Read the article again and answer the questions.

For which celebration do people … ?
1. wear clothes they can't afford to buy
2. not need to request something
3. both give and receive something
4. have a party that goes on for several days
5. receive a toy
6. not go to work or university, so they can celebrate

d Work in pairs. Answer the questions.
1. Which celebration in the article did you find the most interesting? Why?
2. What other celebrations are important in your country? Which is your favourite?
   - weddings
   - local festivals
   - family celebrations
   - work/school/university events
   - birthdays
   - national holidays and New Year's Eve

5 SPEAKING

a Work on your own. Write down three events you are going to go to in the future. Use the list in 4d for ideas.
1. my best friend's wedding in August
2. 21st September – grandfather's 80th birthday

b Now work in a small group. Ask each person questions. Try to guess the three events they are going to. (You can't ask *What is the event?*)

- When is the event happening?
- It's in August.
- Who are you going with?
- I'm going with my friend.
- What are you going to wear?

4B SHALL WE GO TO THE MARKET?

Learn to plan a day out in a city
- **G** will / won't / shall
- **V** Adjectives: places

TOKYO HIGHLIGHTS

1 Go to the top of **Tokyo Skytree** for a great view of the city

1 LISTENING

a Ask and answer the questions.
1. What do you know about Tokyo? Have you ever been there? Would you like to go? Why / Why not?
2. Look at places 1–5 in *Tokyo Highlights*. Which would you like to visit?

b 04.06 Mike is visiting his friend Harry in Tokyo for one day. Listen and answer the questions.
1. Which places in *Tokyo Highlights* do they decide to visit?
2. Which three other places do they decide to visit?

c 04.06 Listen again and answer the questions.
1. Why do they decide not to go to the Imperial Palace?
2. How does Harry describe the noodle restaurant?
3. What happens at Yoyogi Park?
4. Why is Akihabara a good place for Mike's shopping?
5. Where will they do karaoke?
6. Why does Harry want to go to the market in the early morning?

d Do you think they chose good places to visit? Did they choose any places you would not like to visit?

2 GRAMMAR
will / won't / shall

a 04.07 Listen to the sentences. Complete the sentences with the words in the box.

> 'll   won't (x2)   shall (x2)

1. So we _____ go to Disneyland then!
2. _____ we start with something to eat?
3. **M** I want to look for a new camera.
   H I _____ take you to Akihabara, then.
4. Don't worry – you _____ miss your flight!
5. _____ I come to your hotel in about an hour?

b Are Mike and Harry talking about the present or the future? What are the full forms of *'ll* and *won't*?

c Match the sentences in 2a with the uses of *will* and *shall*. Write the numbers.

> We use *will* and *won't* to:
> ☐ make promises
> ☐ ☐ make decisions while we are speaking.
> We use *shall* to:
> ☐ make offers
> ☐ make suggestions.

d Now go to Grammar Focus 4B on p. 150.

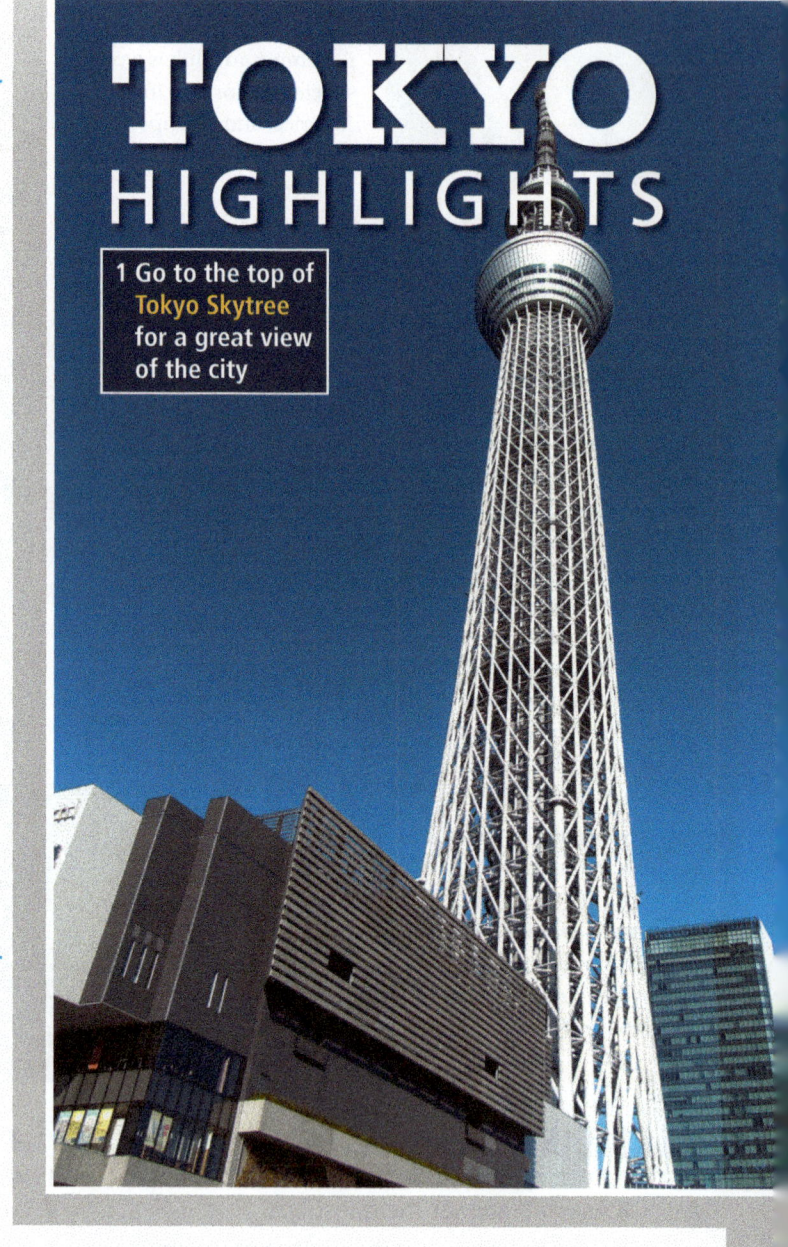

e 04.10 **Pronunciation** Listen to the sentences. Is the vowel in **bold** pronounced /ɒ/ or /əʊ/?
1. I w**a**nt to visit the museum.
2. We w**o**n't have time to see everything.

f 04.11 Listen to the sentences. Choose the correct answers.
1. We *want to / won't* come back next year.
2. They *want to / won't* stay in the same hotel again.
3. I *want to / won't* go for a walk in the park.
4. They *want to / won't* see the market.
5. You *want to / won't* find a table at that restaurant.
6. I *want to / won't* take you to see the castle.

g 04.11 Listen again and repeat.

h **Communication 4B** Work in pairs. Student A: Go to p. 128. Student B: Go to p. 130.

2 Enjoy a day out at **Tokyo Disneyland**

3 Walk around beautiful **Yoyogi Park**

4 Visit Kōkyo – the **Imperial Palace**

5 Go shopping in **Akihabara**

3 LISTENING

a ▶ 04.12 Listen to Mike and Harry's conversation. What was Mike's favourite part of the day?

b ▶ 04.13 Listen to the last part of the conversation. What is the problem? What does Harry suggest?

c 💬 Would you stay another day? Why / Why not?

d 💬 Are there any cities in another country that you would like to visit? Is there any city you would like to live in? Which?

4 VOCABULARY Adjectives: places

a Look at the sentences. What are the opposites of the highlighted adjectives? Choose the adjectives in the box.

tiny   empty   ugly

1 The palace is nice, but it's so crowded. _____
2 It's a huge park, and it's always really nice. _____
3 Everyone goes to look at the pretty flowers. _____

b Match the opposite adjectives.

1 ☐ modern   a peaceful
2 ☐ high   b wide
3 ☐ indoor   c ancient
4 ☐ magnificent   d outdoor
5 ☐ narrow   e low
6 ☐ noisy   f ordinary

c ▶ 04.14 Listen and check. Underline the stressed syllables.

d ▶ 04.14 Listen again. Repeat the words.

e 💬 Work in a small group. Think about places you all know. Can you think of one place for each adjective in 3b?

> There's an outdoor swimming pool near the river.

> The market in the town centre is really noisy.

5 SPEAKING

a Your partner is going to visit you for one day in a city you know well. Make notes on:

- places to visit
- where to eat
- what to do at night.

b 💬 Student A: Describe the places to your partner. Student B: Choose which places you want to visit. Agree on a plan for the day. Then swap roles.

> Shall we go to an art gallery first?

> OK – I'll take you to the National Film Museum. It's huge.

> I don't really like art galleries.

> That sounds good.

c 💬 Describe each day out to the class. Vote for the day out you like the most.

UNIT 4

41

4C EVERYDAY ENGLISH
Are you doing anything on Wednesday?

Learn to make social arrangements
- **P** Sentence stress
- **S** Making time to think

1 LISTENING

a 💬 Do you make arrangements with people by phone? What kind of things do you arrange?

b 🎥 ▶ 04.15 Watch or listen to Part 1. Why does Annie call Rachel?

c 🎥 ▶ 04.15 Watch or listen again. Answer the questions.
1. Why can't Rachel come on Wednesday?
2. What is she doing on Thursday?
3. Which day do they agree to have the meal?
4. What time do they decide?
5. What does Annie want Rachel to bring?

2 USEFUL LANGUAGE
Making arrangements

a Look at the phrases. Which phrases are for inviting? Which are for responding to invitations? Write inviting (*I*) or responding (*R*).
1. ☐ Would you like to come round for a meal?
2. ☐ Are you doing anything on Wednesday?
3. ☐ We can't do Wednesday.
4. ☐ How about Thursday? Is that OK for you?
5. ☐ This week's really busy for us.
6. ☐ What are you doing on Monday?
7. ☐ What time shall we come round?
8. ☐ Would you like us to bring anything?

b ▶ 04.16 Listen to how Rachel and Annie replied to each question. Make notes. What different replies could you give?

c ▶ 04.17 Complete the gaps with words from the box. Listen and check.

| how about   shall I   are you doing (x2) |
| is that OK   would you like   can't do   busy |

A ¹_____ anything tomorrow? ²_____ to come round for a coffee?
B I ³_____ tomorrow. ⁴_____ the weekend? ⁵_____ for you?
A No, the weekend's really ⁶_____ for me. What ⁷_____ on Monday next week?
B Nothing – I'm free. What time ⁸_____ come round?
A Any time in the morning.

d 💬 Work in pairs. Practise the conversation in 2c. Change the details.

> Are you doing anything on Friday? Would you like to go to the cinema?

> I can't do Friday.

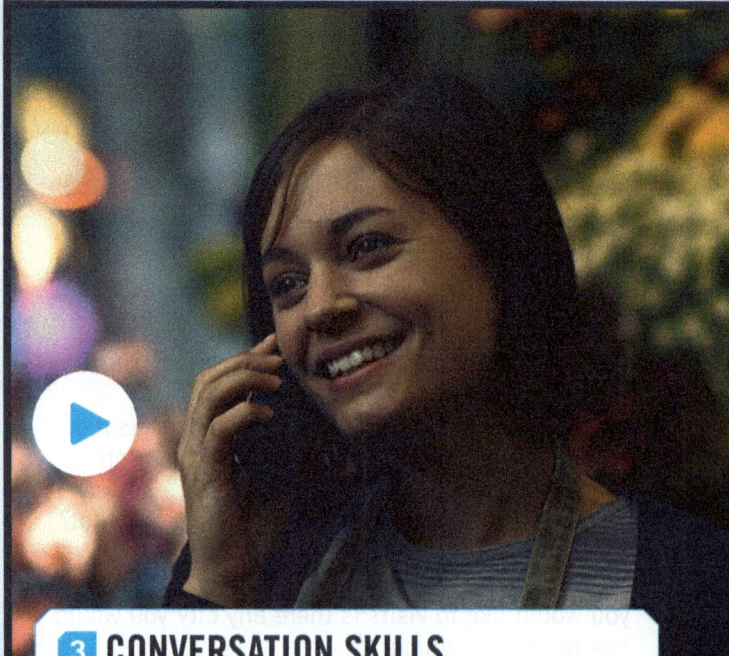

3 CONVERSATION SKILLS
Making time to think

a Look at the examples from Part 1. <u>Underline</u> the phrases Rachel uses to give herself time to think.
1. Oh, that sounds nice. I'll just check. No, we can't do Wednesday. Sorry.
2. Thursday … hang on a minute … no, sorry.
3. Just a moment … Nothing! We can do Monday.

b ▶ 04.18 Listen and repeat the phrases in 3a.

c 💬 Work in pairs. Take turns to make an invitation. Check your phone/diary before you reply. Use the phrases in 3a.

> Do you want to come to the cinema on Saturday?

> Saturday … hang on a minute … yes, that would be great!

42

UNIT 4

4 LISTENING

a ▶ 04.19 Look at the pictures. Where are they? Do you think Leo likes his present? Watch or listen to Part 2 and check your ideas.

b ▶ 04.19 Watch or listen again. Answer the questions.
1 Why does Mark want to go for a run tomorrow?
2 What does Rachel find out about Leo?
3 What do Mark and Leo arrange to do and when?

c 💬 Ask and answer the questions.
1 Do people in your country usually open their presents when the giver is there? Why / Why not?
2 Do you ever receive presents you don't like?
3 Do you think you are good at choosing presents for people?

5 PRONUNCIATION Sentence stress

a ▶ 04.20 Listen to two sentences from Part 1. Answer the questions.
We can do Monday.
We can't do Wednesday.
1 Which word is stressed more – *can* or *can't*?
2 Is the vowel in *can't* long or short?

b ▶ 04.21 Listen to the sentences. Complete the rule.
I don't really like sport.
I can't stand football.
You really didn't need to.

Negative auxiliary forms are *sometimes* / *always* stressed.

c ▶ 04.22 Listen and repeat.
1 I can't do next week.
2 We don't have time.
3 I won't be late.
4 I could see you tomorrow.
5 We didn't go to the party.
6 We can come at six o'clock.

6 SPEAKING

a ⟫ Communication 4C Work in pairs. Student A: Go to 6b below. Student B: Go to p.130.

Student A

b You want to invite Student B for dinner one evening. Look at your diary. Complete your diary with plans for three evenings. Decide what you want Student B to bring to the dinner.

Wednesday
_____

Thursday
_____

Friday
_____

Saturday
_____

Sunday
_____

Need guests to bring:

c 💬 Call and invite Student B to dinner. Arrange an evening for dinner. Try to arrange it this week. If you can't, arrange it for next week. Tell Student B what to bring.

✓ UNIT PROGRESS TEST

→ CHECK YOUR PROGRESS

You can now do the Unit Progress Test.

43

4D SKILLS FOR WRITING
Are you free on Saturday?

Learn to write and reply to an invitation

W Inviting and replying

1 SPEAKING AND LISTENING

a How often do you do the things on this list? Who do you do them with?
- have a party
- go out for coffee or a meal
- go out and do something (e.g., see a film)
- do sport (e.g., go swimming or play football)
- invite people for a meal at your home
- go for a walk

b Which of the activities in 1a do you do to … ?
- celebrate a birthday
- celebrate the end of the school year
- meet new friends
- spend time with old friends
- spend time with colleagues

c 04.23 Listen to three people. What is each person going to do this weekend?
1 Susanna
2 Barbara
3 Sven

d 04.23 Listen again and answer the questions.

Susanna
1 Why doesn't Susanna like parties at home?
2 Where is she going to celebrate her 21st birthday?
3 What is she going to wear?

Barbara
4 Why doesn't Barbara like cooking for people at home?
5 Why does she prefer cooking things together?
6 What's Barbara going to make for the barbecue on Saturday?

Sven
7 What does Sven say people do at parties?
8 What does he prefer to do with friends? Why?
9 What is he going to do at the lake?

e Which person are you most similar to? Why?

2 READING

a Barbara sent emails inviting people to her barbecue. Read the emails and answer the questions.
1 Has Barbara seen Isabella recently?
2 When is the barbecue?
3 What do Isabella and Bill need to bring to the barbecue?

b Who do you think Barbara sees more often? How do you know?

Hi Isabella,

How are you? We haven't seen you for ages! Hope you're well and are enjoying your new job. This is just to say that we're having a barbecue at the weekend. Are you free on Saturday, and if so, would you like to come? People are going to arrive around eight o'clock. Everyone's bringing something for the barbecue. Do you think you could bring something?

It would be lovely to see you and have a chance to chat.

Best wishes,

Barbara

Hi Bill,

How are things? I hope the cycling trip went well – you had good weather for it!

Are you doing anything on Saturday evening? We're having a barbecue and inviting a few people. Can you come? It'd be great to see you!

Everyone is bringing something. We'll make some salads, but could you bring some meat for the barbecue?

Love,

Barbara

3 WRITING SKILLS Inviting and replying

a Look at the emails in 2a again and complete the chart.

Type of phrase	Email to Isabella	Email to Bill
Asks how the other person is	1 How are you?	5 How _____?
Asks if they are free	2 Are you _____ on Saturday?	6 Are you _____ on Saturday?
Invites them	3 _____ to come?	7 _____ come?
Says she wants to see them	4 It _____ to see you.	8 It'd _____ to see you!

b Read the replies to Barbara's emails. Which is from Isabella and which is from Bill? How do you know? Who is coming to Barbara's barbecue?

Hi Barbara,

Nice to hear from you. Yes, I'm fine, but I'm very busy. The job's great, but I have to work very long hours. Thanks for inviting me on Saturday. I'm free that evening, and I'd love to come. Is it OK if I bring my daughter, Stephanie? We don't eat meat, but we'll bring some vegetables for the barbecue.

I'm looking forward to seeing you and catching up.

All the best,

Hi Barbara,

Yes, we had a great time, but my legs still hurt!

I'm really sorry. The barbecue sounds great, but I'm afraid I can't come. Thanks for asking. I'd love to, but I'm staying with my sister at the weekend.

See you soon anyway. Hope you have a nice time!

Take care,

---

c Underline the phrases in the replies that each person uses to:
1 say thank you
2 say yes to an invitation
3 say no to an invitation
4 give a reason
5 talk about the next time they'll meet.

d Correct the mistakes in each of the sentences. Use the emails in this lesson to help you.
1 You like to come to my birthday party?
2 Thanks that you invited me to your wedding.
3 It's afraid I can't go to the cinema with you.
4 I love to come, but I'm busy that weekend.
5 I'm looking forward to see you tomorrow.

4 WRITING

a Work in pairs. You are organising an activity this weekend. Write an invitation to another pair of students. Include these points:
- ask them how they are
- invite them to come
- say where and when the event is
- tell them what they need to bring

b Swap invitations with another pair. Write a reply to the invitation. Include these points:
- say thank you
- decide if you can go (If you can't go, give a reason.)
- add a comment or a question

c Give your reply back to the other pair. Look at their invitations and replies. Have they included these points?
- said clearly where and when the event is
- used the correct language for the invitation
- used the correct language to reply to the invitation

45

UNIT 4
Review and extension

1 GRAMMAR

a Complete the sentences with the correct forms of *be going to* and the verbs in the box.

buy   go   travel   meet   not take   watch

1 I _____ a film soon.
2 They _____ around South America this summer.
3 Gina and Sean _____ on holiday by the sea next summer.
4 I _____ an English exam this year.
5 She _____ something from the shops after work.
6 We _____ some friends for lunch tomorrow.

b Complete the conversation with the present continuous forms of the verbs in brackets.

A ¹_____ (you / do) anything this Saturday?
B I ²_____ (go) to my sister's in the evening. She ³_____ (have) a party. I ⁴_____ (not do) anything in the afternoon.
A Great! I ⁵_____ (have) a barbecue. Do you want to come? Tina and Matt ⁶_____ (come).
B Sounds good! Do you want me to bring anything?
A Well, I ⁷_____ (make) vegetarian food. Is that OK?
B Yes, that's great.

c 💬 Practise the conversation in 1b.

d Complete the text messages with *will*, *won't* or *shall*.

> Hi! I'm almost at the cinema. ¹_____ (I / get) the tickets when I arrive. ²_____ (I / get) you something to eat or drink? Try to be on time …

> Hi. ³_____ (I / have) a lemonade, please. ⁴_____ (I / eat) something later. ⁵_____ (we / go) for a coffee after the film? I promise ⁶_____ (I / be) late!

2 VOCABULARY

a Where do these clothes and accessories go on the body? Write the correct numbers.

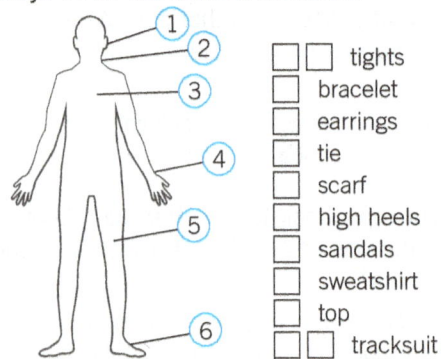

- [ ] tights
- [ ] bracelet
- [ ] earrings
- [ ] tie
- [ ] scarf
- [ ] high heels
- [ ] sandals
- [ ] sweatshirt
- [ ] top
- [ ] tracksuit

b 💬 Talk about the clothes and accessories you are wearing.

3 WORDPOWER *look*

a Match the words in **bold** 1–4 with definitions a–d.

1 We're really **looking forward to** our holiday in Florida.
2 I didn't know the address, so I **looked** it **up** online. 
3 He doesn't **look** very well – maybe he's got a cold. 
4 I was only in the city for an hour, so I didn't have time to **look around**. 

- a ☐ visit a place and see the things in it
- b ☐ appear, seem
- c ☐ feel happy and excited about a future event
- d ☐ try to find information in a book or on a computer

b Choose the correct answers.

1 I'm really looking *up / forward* to the weekend.
2 I always look *up / out* a film online before I see it.
3 I spend too much time looking *at / to* social media.
4 I always look *for / to* special offers when I go shopping.
5 I *look / look like* tired when I don't get much sleep.
6 I love looking *around / up* clothes shops.

c 💬 Work in pairs. Which of the sentences in 3b are true for you?

🔄 REVIEW YOUR PROGRESS

How well did you do in this unit? Write 3, 2 or 1 for each objective.
3 = very well   2 = well   1 = not so well

I CAN …	
talk about plans for celebrations	☐
plan a day out in a city	☐
make social arrangements	☐
write and reply to an invitation.	☐

46

CAN DO OBJECTIVES
- Talk about what people do at work
- Talk about the future of work
- Make offers and suggestions
- Write a job application

UNIT 5
WORK

GETTING STARTED

a Look at the picture and answer the questions.
1 What is the man's job?
2 How safe do you think he is? Why?
3 How do you think the man feels about his work? Why?

b Ask and answer the questions.
1 How would you feel about doing this man's job?
2 What kinds of jobs would you find … ?
- exciting
- scary
- dangerous

47

5A I HAVE TO WORK LONG HOURS

Learn to talk about what people do at work
- G must / have to / can
- V Work

1 VOCABULARY Work

a Work in pairs. Talk about a job you would like to do and a job you would not like to do. Explain your answers.

b Make a list of as many jobs as you can in one minute.

c Look at the lists of jobs you made in 1a and 1b. Match them to the categories below. Compare with your partner.
1 Works long hours: _____
2 Needs several years of training: _____
3 Deals with people every day: _____
4 Often works on a team: _____

d Now go to Vocabulary Focus 5A on p. 137.

2 READING

a Read the introduction to *The Coolest Jobs* and match the jobs 1–4 in **bold** to the photos.

b What do you think people with these jobs do every day?

c Read the job descriptions in the article and match them to the jobs in bold in 2a.

the COOLEST JOBS

The job website *Job Hunter* asked people what they thought were the coolest jobs – the kind of jobs that don't seem like work at all because they're a lot of fun! Meet some of the people who do these jobs:

Megan was once an accountant and a banker. Now she's a ¹**private island caretaker**.

Ethan was once a lawyer. Now he's a ²**bed tester**.

Greg was once a scientist. Now he's a ³**chocolate taster**.

Alisha was once an IT worker. Now she's a ⁴**video game designer**.

	What kind of person is good for this job?	What are their qualifications or training?	What do they do?	Are there any negative things about this job?
A	This job is for someone who is good at tasting and smelling food and giving a clear opinion.	None – companies will probably give you training when you start the job.	They try a lot of food to understand differences in the taste. They decide if it is good or bad quality, but they don't usually swallow the food.	They sometimes taste some really bad food!
B	Someone who is creative, has a good imagination, and is good at drawing is good for this job.	A degree in art or design is necessary, and it's also a good idea to understand some computer programming language.	They create characters, stories and situations. They work together with computer programmers and other developers. Teamwork is important.	It's difficult to find a job because lots of people want to do this. Sometimes people work for a few months with no pay before they are offered a job.
C	This is a good job for an independent person – someone who likes to be outside and loves the sea.	None – your boss will explain the things you'll be doing.	They make sure everything is always ready for the owners. They often do gardening and fix things that are broken.	It can be very lonely, so it's good for someone who likes to spend a lot of time alone.
D	This job is good for someone who likes a very relaxed life. If you don't like getting up in the morning, this is the job for you!	None – but companies may give you training in the kinds of things you need to do.	You spend the day resting or sleeping while the company changes the conditions of the room – they make it hot or cold or they change the light. Then you write a review.	It's not really a permanent job, and there's only work when companies or hotels want you.

UNIT 5

d Read the article again and answer the questions.
1 Which job would be good for someone who has experience in these jobs?
   a a gardener   c a furniture salesperson
   b a chef   d a cartoonist

2 Which jobs are these sentences about? Sometimes more than one job is correct.
   a You don't get any training.
   b You decide if something is good or not.
   c You will work with a lot of people.
   d You will have a lot of free time.

e 💬 Which of these cool jobs would you like to do? Which wouldn't you like to do? Why?

3 LISTENING

a ▶ 05.03 Listen to Alisha, Jason and Megan. Why did they change jobs?

Jason

b ▶ 05.03 Listen again and make notes on:
1 the speakers' qualifications for their jobs
2 why they like their jobs.

c 💬 Work in pairs. What would be a cool job for you? Talk about one of the jobs in the lesson or another job you think is cool.

4 GRAMMAR *must / have to / can*

a Look at the sentences. Match the underlined words with the meanings.
1 You have to have good exam results and a good degree.
2 You don't have to do the same thing every day.
3 My students can't have a lesson if they're not wearing a helmet.

a _____ = this is not necessary
b _____ = this is not allowed or not possible
c _____ = this is necessary

b Compare rules from two workplaces. Notice who is speaking. Complete the rules below.

> Designers mustn't make copies of their artwork and remove them from the office.
> *boss to designer*

> You can't make a copy of your artwork and take it away from the office.
> *designer to colleague*

> Architects must wear helmets at all times.
> *safety officer to architect*

> You always have to wear a helmet when you're on site.
> *architect to colleague*

If the speaker is in charge, they use:
_____ to say that something is necessary
_____ to say that something is not allowed or not possible.

c ⟫ Now go to Grammar Focus 5A on p. 152.

d 💬 What do you have to do if you work in these places? What can't you do?
• office   • restaurant   • bank   • school

> In a school, you can't leave children on their own.

> Yes, and you have to be on time.

e Write rules for the people who work in each place in 4d. Use *must* and *mustn't*.
Teachers mustn't leave children on their own.
Teachers must be on time.

5 SPEAKING

a 💬 Choose five of the jobs from the list. Think of three advantages and three disadvantages for each job.
• scientist   • lawyer   • accountant   • electrician
• IT worker   • engineer   • nurse   • pilot
• police officer   • receptionist   • secretary   • teacher

b 💬 Which job do you think is the hardest? Which job is the most interesting?

> Receptionists don't have to have a university degree, and they can find a job quite easily.

> But they have to deal with people, and they don't earn a good salary.

49

5B I MIGHT GET A JOB TODAY!

Learn to talk about the future of work
- **G** *will* and *might* for predictions
- **V** Jobs

1 SPEAKING

a What can you do if you need a job? Where can you go? Who can you speak to?

b Match the worries 1–3 with the situations in the pictures.
1. ☐ I'll say something stupid on my first day.
2. ☐ I won't find a job I'll enjoy.
3. ☐ They'll ask me really difficult questions.

a looking for a job
b having a job interview
c starting a new job

c Have you ever had any of the worries in 1b? Tell a partner.

2 LISTENING

a 05.07 Listen to three people talking about finding work. Where are they? Who is the most positive about finding work? Who is the least positive?

Sara   Marco   Kate

b 05.07 Read the predictions each speaker makes. Listen again. What reasons do they give for each prediction?

Sara
1. It won't be easy to find a job I'll enjoy.
2. I don't think I'll get an interview.

Marco
3. I'm sure I'll make some really useful contacts.
4. I might get a job today!

Kate
5. I might not get my perfect job.
6. I'm sure I'll find some kind of work.

c Have you ever been to a careers fair? What was it like?

3 GRAMMAR
will and *might* for predictions

a Look at the sentences in 2b again. Then underline the correct word to complete the rule about *will* and *might*.

> We use *will* and *might* to make predictions about the future.
> *Will* and *won't* are *more / less* sure than *might* and *might not*.

b Now go to Grammar Focus 5B on p. 152.

c Write a positive response to each worry in 1b. Then compare with other students. Whose responses are the most positive?

I won't find a job I'll enjoy. → You might find something really interesting.

d Communication 5B If your partner has a job, go to p. 129. If your partner does not have a job, go to p. 128.

50

4 VOCABULARY Jobs

a 💬 Find the jobs in the photos on the page.
☐ builder ☐ computer programmer
☐ shop assistant ☐ taxi driver ☐ carer

Do you know anyone who does one of these jobs?

b ≫ Now go to Vocabulary Focus 5B on p. 137.

c ▶ 05.11 **Pronunciation** Listen to the words. How does the speaker say the consonant sound /ʃ/ in the part of the words in **bold**?

mu**si**cian poli**ti**cian **sh**op assistant

d ▶ 05.12 Listen to the words. Which words have the /ʃ/ sound? Underline the letters.

qualification   question   information
machine   experience   change

e Practise saying the words in 4c and 4d.

5 READING

a 💬 Look at the jobs in the photos. Answer the questions with a partner.
1 Which jobs do you think might disappear in the future?
2 Which jobs do you think there will be more of in the future?

b Now read the article and check your ideas in 5a.

c Read the article again and look at the things below. What will happen to jobs in the future because of these things?
- online shopping
- paying without cash
- driverless cars
- 3D printers
- using renewable energy
- living longer
- using robots

6 SPEAKING

a 💬 Work in small groups. Look at the predictions. Do you think these things will happen in your lifetime? Why / Why not?
1 3D printers will make parts of buildings or whole buildings.
2 We will stop using coal and oil for energy.
3 There won't be many shops.
4 There won't be any huge offices. People will mostly work from home.
5 Companies will pay the bosses less and other staff more.
6 A normal work week will have four days, not five.

b Work alone. Write three new predictions.

c 💬 Read your predictions to your group. Do they agree?

UNIT 5

PLANNING A SAFE FUTURE CAREER

Choose your future career carefully – experts are predicting big changes in the jobs we'll do in the next 10 to 20 years. Some jobs might disappear, but others will become more important.

The Internet is having a big effect. People already choose to do a lot of their shopping online, so there won't be as many shops, and there won't be many jobs for shop assistants. Bank clerks and other bank employees might also lose their jobs, as people may stop using cash altogether.

Another job that might disappear is taxi drivers. In the future, it will become normal to travel in cars without a driver, including taxis. Also, there may not be as many jobs for builders as there are today. Soon, 3D printers will make complete parts of buildings in just a few hours, and they might one day make whole buildings.

SO WHICH JOBS ARE SAFE?

■ **Computer programmers** – A hundred years ago, there were none, but now there are a lot of them. And there will be even more in the future because almost all jobs will need computers.

■ **Carers** – People will live longer, and we'll need carers to look after us in our old age.

■ **Robot specialists** – We will use robots for many everyday jobs, but they will need a team of human workers to support them – designers, developers, programmers and salespeople.

■ **Solar and wind power engineers** – Over the next 20 years, it will become more important to use clean energy. There are now 10 million jobs in this area, but by 2050 it might be 30 million.

And of course, we will still need **actors** and **musicians** to entertain us, **lawyers** to argue and **politicians** to make the big decisions.

51

5C EVERYDAY ENGLISH
I'll finish things here, if you want

Learn to make offers and suggestions
- P Stressed/unstressed modals: vowel sounds
- S Reassurance

1 LISTENING

a When was the last time someone asked you for help? Who was it? What did they ask?

b Look at the picture of Rachel and read the text message. How is she feeling? Who is the text from? What's the problem?

c ▶ 05.13 Watch or listen to Part 1. Answer the questions.
1 What does Tina think Rachel should do for Annie?
2 What does Tina offer to do?
3 Why is Rachel worried about leaving early?
4 How are they going to deal with the problem?

d What would you do in Rachel's situation? Would you call Annie or go and see her? Why?

2 CONVERSATION SKILLS Reassurance

a ▶ 05.13 Watch or listen again. Match the sentences with the responses.
1 ☐ But I can't leave you here on your own.
2 ☐ We've still got so much to do.
3 ☐ It means you won't be able to leave early today.
4 ☐ OK, well if you're sure.

a **Never mind**.
b Of course. **It's no problem**.
c I'll be fine! **Don't worry about it**.
d Oh, **it doesn't matter**.

b ▶ 05.14 Why do you think Tina uses the expressions in **bold** in a–d? Listen and repeat the phrases.

c In pairs, look at situations 1–6. Take turns to apologise for the problems. Respond with expressions a–d in 2a.
1 You can't help your partner this weekend.
2 You lost your partner's book.
3 You have to cancel the dinner party.
4 You don't have the money you owe your partner.
5 You can't come to the cinema tonight.
6 You're going to be late for the party.

> I'm really sorry, but I can't help you this weekend. I have to work.

> Oh, it doesn't matter.

3 LISTENING

▶ 05.15 Watch or listen to Part 2. Which jobs will Tina do before she goes home?
1 ☐ finish off the flowers
2 ☐ start the order for Mrs Thompson
3 ☐ start the order for the birthday party
4 ☐ put the alarm on
5 ☐ take out the rubbish
6 ☐ take the order for the wedding

4 USEFUL LANGUAGE
Offers and suggestions

a ▶ 05.16 Listen and complete the sentences.
1 ☐ _____ finish things here, if you want.
2 ☐ Why _____ you tell me what we still need to do?
3 ☐ _____ I finish off those flowers?
4 ☐ Would you _____ me to prepare some of the orders for tomorrow?
5 ☐ You _____ start with that order for Mrs Thompson.
6 ☐ Maybe you _____ start on the order for that big birthday party.
7 ☐ Do you want _____ to take out the rubbish when I leave?
8 ☐ How _____ taking her some flowers?
9 ☐ Why _____ I deal with this?

b Look at the sentences in 4a again. Mark them offer (O) or suggestion (S).

c Work in pairs. What offers and suggestions could you make in situations 1–4? Use the phrases and your own ideas.

> I'll …   Why don't I / you … ?   Shall I … ?
> Would you like me to … ?   Maybe you should …
> How about … ?   Do you want me to … ?

1 It's raining. Your friend has to walk to the station, but doesn't have an umbrella.
2 Your colleague has to write a report for her boss before the end of the day. There's not enough time.
3 Your friend wants to go for a meal. You don't like the restaurant he suggests.
4 You see a tourist. She's lost her bag and doesn't have any money.

> Why don't I drive you to the station?

> How about getting a taxi?

5 PRONUNCIATION
Stressed/unstressed modals: vowel sounds

a ▶ 05.17 Listen to the phrases from 4a. Are the highlighted modal verbs stressed?
1 Shall I finish off those flowers?
2 Would you like me to prepare some of the orders for tomorrow?
3 You could start with that order for Mrs Thompson.
4 Maybe you should start on the order for that big birthday party.

b ▶ 05.17 Listen again. Which vowel sound do you hear in each of the modal verbs?

c Practise saying the sentences in 5a.

6 SPEAKING

a Work in groups of four. Choose one of the two events to organise.

A work meeting
- book meeting room
- arrange hotel for guest from advertising company
- book taxis for colleagues from other office
-
-
-

A surprise birthday party for a friend
- buy food and drink
- make and send invitations
- book somewhere for the party
-
-
-

b Work with a partner in your group. Look at the list of things to do for the event you chose. Add three more things.

c Work in your group again. Now you have to organise the event. Make offers and suggestions to decide which person in your group will do which job.

> Shall I book a meeting room?

> OK, why don't you call a hotel?

> Would you like me to buy the food?

> Sure. How about going to the supermarket?

UNIT PROGRESS TEST
CHECK YOUR PROGRESS

You can now do the Unit Progress Test.

5D SKILLS FOR WRITING
I am writing to apply for a job

Learn to write a job application
W Organising an email

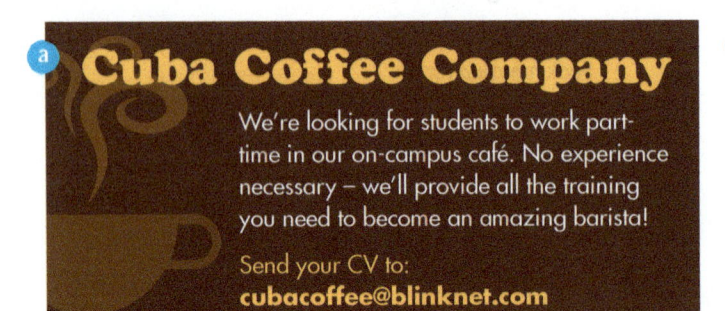

a Cuba Coffee Company
We're looking for students to work part-time in our on-campus café. No experience necessary – we'll provide all the training you need to become an amazing barista!

Send your CV to:
cubacoffee@blinknet.com

b OWLS The University Bookshop
Part-time jobs for students
Shop assistants and general helpers are needed. Good pay and benefits … and big discounts on the books you buy!

Email the bookshop at:
owlsjobs@xyzmail.com

c Babysitters required
Good with kids? Work as a babysitter for university staff. Great pay – earn up to £10 an hour!

Contact Veronica at:
veronicaparks@mymail.net
(students only)

d Get a job as an EVENTS ASSISTANT
Help out with dances, concerts, plays and social events on campus. You can earn good money …
and you get to see the events for free!

To apply, contact John at:
jdownes@listmail.net

1 SPEAKING AND LISTENING

a Have you ever had a summer job or a part-time job? What was it? Did you enjoy it?

b Look at the online job adverts. Where can you do these jobs? Who can apply for them?

c Which jobs in the adverts could these sentences describe? Sometimes more than one answer is possible.
1 ☐☐ You need to work fast at busy times.
2 ☐ You may have a chance to do some studying.
3 ☐☐ You may have to work late in the evenings.
4 ☐ You can earn extra money from tips.
5 ☐ You can pay less for things you buy.
6 ☐☐☐ It's a good way to meet people.

d Work in pairs. Answer the questions about the jobs.
1 Which job would you most like to do? Why?
2 Which job would you least like to do? Why?
3 Which job would you do best? Why?

e ▶05.18 Listen to two students, Penny and John, talking about jobs on campus. Answer the questions.
1 Which job in the adverts are they talking about?
2 Do they like the jobs they've had? Why / Why not?

f ▶05.18 Listen again and choose the correct answers.
1 John *has / hasn't* worked in the café before.
2 John *likes / doesn't like* working in a team.
3 John makes £20 in tips *every day / on some days*.
4 Penny *has / hasn't* worked in a café before.
5 Penny *is / isn't* going to apply for the job.

2 READING

Read Penny's job application. Are sentences 1–4 true (*T*) or false (*F*)? Correct the false sentences.
1 She tells them she has worked in cafés before.
2 She saw the ad in the campus magazine.
3 She can start work immediately.
4 She wants to know how much she will earn.

---

1 Dear Sir/Madam,

2 I am writing to apply for the job of barista at the Cuba Coffee Company, which you advertised online.

3 I am a second-year student at this university, and I am available to work from next term.

4 A job at your café would be an exciting opportunity for me to learn new skills, and I would really love to be part of your team. I'm a very quick learner, and I am sure I'll be successful in your training programme. I already have a lot of experience working in a team and helping customers in my job at Owls university bookshop, where I worked last term. I am sure my experience of working in a busy bookshop will be very useful for this job.

5 I attach a copy of my CV, with details of my past employment.

6 Could you please send me information about the pay and working hours and also more details about your training programme?

7 I look forward to hearing from you.

Yours faithfully,
Penny Longwell

54

UNIT 5

3 WRITING SKILLS Organising an email

a Penny's email in 2 has seven parts. What does each part of the letter do?

- [ ] says why she's writing
- [ ] asks for more information about the job
- [ ] describes documents she's sending with the email
- [ ] opens the email
- [ ] closes the email
- [ ] says why she wants the job and describes her experience
- [ ] says what she's doing now and when she can work

b Look at sentences 1–5. Which ones are about … ?

- what you are doing now
- past jobs
- skills

1 I am good at working in a team.
2 I have experience of working in a restaurant.
3 I am currently working as a shop assistant in a bookshop.
4 I am studying engineering in Madrid.
5 I speak fluent English.

c What are the missing prepositions? Complete the sentences.

1 I am writing to apply _____ the job _____ barista.
2 I am a second-year student _____ this university.
3 I have a lot _____ experience _____ working _____ a team.
4 I look forward _____ hearing from you.

d Put the parts of the email below in the correct order.

- I attach a copy of my CV.
- I look forward to hearing from you. Yours faithfully,
- I am writing to apply for the job of shop assistant.
- Dear Sir/Madam,
- I am currently working as a shop assistant in a clothes shop.
- I would like to work for your company because it would be a good opportunity for me to improve my communication skills. I have three years' experience in sales.
- Could you please send me more information about the working hours?

4 WRITING A job application

a Read the adverts on Jobsearch.com. Choose one and write an email applying for the job. Include these parts:

- open the email
- say why you are writing
- say what you are doing now
- say why you want the job
- describe documents you are sending
- ask for more information
- close the email

b Work in groups. Read the applications together. Which student would you give each job to? Why?

Jobsearch.com

Home | New Jobs | Advice

Use your English … and your local knowledge!
Get a summer job as a guide for English-speaking tourists to your town.
You will need:
- a good level of English
- knowledge of your local town or area.

VIEW JOB

Work with children and have a holiday
We're looking for people to work at an international summer camp for children aged 7–12. You will help organise activities and trips and speak English with the children. We prefer someone with experience working with children.

VIEW JOB

Part-time receptionist
We're a small hotel and many of our guests are from the UK and other countries. We're looking for a part-time receptionist to work evenings and some weekends. No experience is necessary, but you will need to be able to speak and write English.
Contact: *interhoteljobs@xyzmail.com*

VIEW JOB

55

UNIT 5
Review and extension

1 GRAMMAR

a Choose the correct answers.

1 Employees mustn't use their computers to send personal emails.
   'We _____ use our computers to send personal emails.'
   a have to   b don't have to   c can't

2 Employees can leave the building at lunch time.
   'We _____ stay in the building at lunch.'
   a must   b don't have to   c can't

3 Employees _____ use social media.
   'We can't use social media at work.'
   a mustn't   b must   c don't have to

4 _____ make local phone calls on company phones.
   'We don't have to use our own phones to make local calls.'
   a can   b can't   c must

5 _____ wear identification.
   'We have to wear identification.'
   a can   b mustn't   c must

b Match sentences 1–5 with meanings a–c.

1 ☐ It won't be difficult for me to find a job.
2 ☐ I think I'll finish university next year.
3 ☐ I might work for a bank one day.
4 ☐ I'll find a good job in the USA.
5 ☐ I might not find a job I like in my home town.

a completely sure   b fairly sure   c not sure

c 💬 Which of the sentences in 1b are true for you?

2 VOCABULARY

a Choose the best jobs for each person 1–7.

accountant   carer   hairdresser   IT worker
journalist   politician   vet

1 I really like working with animals. _____
2 I enjoy helping older people. _____
3 I want to tell people what's happening in the world. _____
4 I'm good with numbers. _____
5 I like meeting people and helping them look good. _____
6 I want to make my country a better place. _____
7 I enjoy working with computers. _____

b 💬 Which jobs would you like and not like in 2a?

c Match the sentence halves.

1 ☐ In my job, I have to work
2 ☐ My job's interesting because I have to make
3 ☐ I don't have a boss because I'm
4 ☐ I enjoy being in my office. We're lucky that we have
5 ☐ I'm tired at the end of the day because I deal with

a self-employed.
b very long hours.
c a nice working environment.
d important decisions every day.
e lots of serious problems.

3 WORDPOWER *job* and *work*

a Look at the sentences. Which word (*job* or *work*) is countable? Which is uncountable?

1 I have a really interesting **job**.
2 I'm looking for **work** at the moment.

b Match the uses of *work* and *job* 1–4 with the meanings a–d.

1 ☐ Most gardeners feel their **work** is important and useful.
2 ☐ We spend most of our time at **work**.
3 ☐ I've got a lot of **jobs** to do at home this weekend.
4 ☐ I enjoy my course, but it's hard **work**.

a when you use lots of energy to do something
b the activity or activities you do for your job
c activities you have to do, often without getting money
d the place where you work

c Match sentences 1–3 with replies a–c.

1 ☐ Why isn't my email **working** on this computer?
2 ☐ Is the medicine from the doctor **working**?
3 ☐ I can't **work out** this morning. Are you free later?

a I am. Let's go jogging this afternoon instead.
b I don't know. Maybe there's a problem with the Internet.
c Definitely. I feel much better.

d Complete the sentences with *work* or *job*.

1 I'm painting my flat at the moment. It's a lot of hard _____.
2 I'm starting a new _____ soon.
3 My phone doesn't _____ when I'm inside this building.
4 I've got an important _____ to do at home this weekend.
5 I leave _____ early on Fridays.
6 The education system in my country doesn't _____ well.
7 I know a lot of people who are trying to find _____.
8 I can't _____ out with weights because I've hurt my shoulder.

e Complete these sentences with your own ideas.

1 I can't work out …
2 I would like to get a job …
3 Two jobs I need to do this week are …
4 … makes me happy at work.
5 I need do some hard work …
6 … doesn't work very well.

f 💬 Compare your sentences in 3e with another student.

🔄 REVIEW YOUR PROGRESS

How well did you do in this unit? Write 3, 2 or 1 for each objective.
3 = very well   2 = well   1 = not so well

I CAN …	
talk about what people do at work	☐
talk about my future career	☐
make offers and suggestions	☐
write a job application.	☐

CAN DO OBJECTIVES
- Give advice for common problems
- Describe extreme experiences
- Ask for and give advice
- Write an email giving advice

PROBLEMS AND ADVICE

UNIT 6

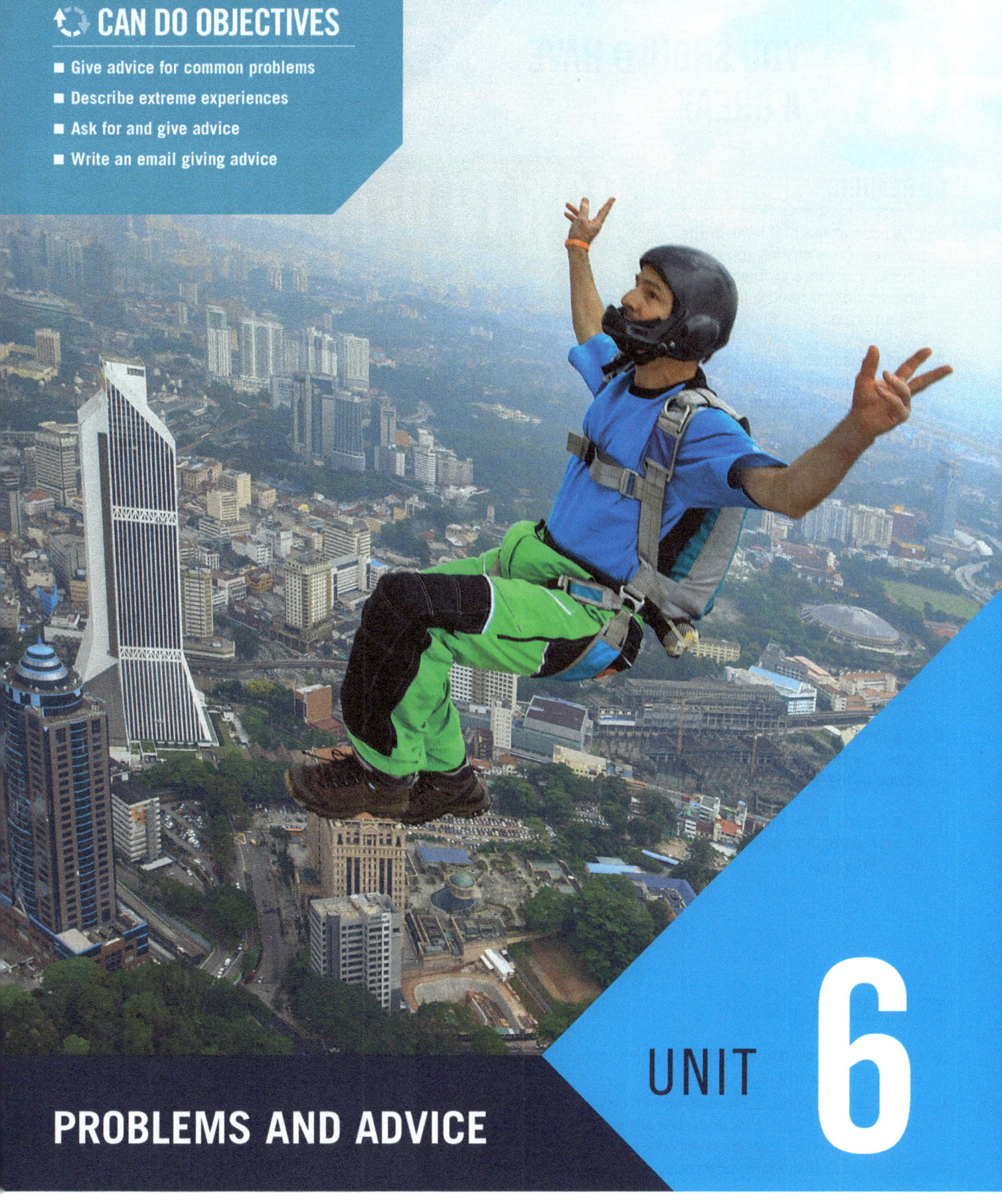

GETTING STARTED

a Look at the picture and answer the questions.
1 What is the man doing?
2 How do you think he is feeling?

b Write down three words or phrases to describe his feelings before, during and after this experience.

c Ask and answer the questions.
1 How does the picture make you feel?
2 Why do you think some people are afraid of heights?
3 What are some other things people are often afraid of?
4 What can people do to stop feeling afraid of these things?

57

6A YOU SHOULD HAVE A BREAK

Learn to give advice for common problems
G Imperative; *should*
V Verbs with dependent prepositions

1 READING

a Look at the problems in the pictures. Does anyone you know have any of these problems? How would you handle them? Tell a partner.

b Read the advice. Which four problems in the pictures is it for? Complete headings 1–4.

c Read the advice again. What is the advice about these things? Make notes.
  1 • music
    • 15 minutes
  2 • rules
    • a pile
  3 • breaks
    • rewards
  4 • screens
    • milk

d Cover the article. Use your notes. Try to remember the advice in the article.

e Do you think the advice in each paragraph is useful? Why / Why not?

HOW TO DEAL WITH LIFE'S LITTLE PROBLEMS

You don't have any money, you never finish anything you start, your house is dirty, you can't find a good job and your whole life is terrible. Well, maybe it's not that bad! If you'd like to improve things, we can help. Here are our top ways to deal with some of life's little problems.

I'm addicted to my phone.

I can't concentrate on my work.

My home is a mess.

I don't sleep well.

2 GRAMMAR Imperative; *should*

a Complete the sentences with the correct verbs. Check your answers in the article.
  1 Turn on the TV or _____ to music while you clean.
  2 You should _____ to drink less coffee and eat less fast food, too.
  3 You shouldn't _____ for hours without a break.
  4 Don't _____ devices with bright screens before you go to sleep.

b Match the sentences in 2a with the rules.

To give advice, we use:
☐ infinitive
☐ *don't* + infinitive
☐ subject + *should* + infinitive
☐ subject + *shouldn't* + infinitive

c Now go to Grammar Focus 6A on p. 154.

d 06.03 **Pronunciation** Listen to the sentence. Is the vowel sound /uː/ or /ʊ/ in the words *shouldn't* and *use*?

You sh**ou**ldn't **u**se your mobile phone before you go to sleep.

e 06.04 Listen to the sentences. Do the letters in **bold** have the long vowel sound /uː/ or the short vowel sound /ʊ/?
  1 You sh**ou**ldn't **u**se your comp**u**ter all day.
  2 L**oo**k for n**ew** ways of d**o**ing exercise.
  3 Find a g**oo**d time of day to study.
  4 Ch**oo**se the healthiest f**oo**d.
  5 Read a b**oo**k before you go to sleep.

f Practise saying the sentences in 2e.

58

UNIT 6

Speech bubbles in photos:
- I have too much work to do.
- I don't have enough money.
- I'm always late.
- I feel tired all the time.

1 _____
Learn to enjoy cleaning and tidying. People who enjoy this usually have clean homes. Turn on the TV or listen to music while you clean. Start by cleaning every day, but only for 15 minutes. When the 15 minutes are finished, you should stop. Don't worry if things aren't perfectly clean. Do a little bit of cleaning every day, and in a week your place will look great.

2 _____
It's important to give yourself rules. When you go out with friends, decide how many times you will look at your phone – maybe only two or three times in an evening. Ask your friends about how they feel. If they have the same problem as you, put all of your phones together in a pile out of the way. That way, no one can look at their phone, and you can all enjoy each other's company.

3 _____
The machine we use so much for work – our computer – is the same machine we often use to have fun. So control how you use your computer. If your problem is that you check your email every five minutes, you can get apps that stop the Internet from working for a period of time you choose. Use this time to focus on your work. But you shouldn't work for hours without a break. Work for half an hour and then take a five-minute break. Rewards are really important, too. Have a snack or get some fresh air every hour or so.

4 _____
First, think about your body. Exercising regularly will help you to fall asleep more easily. You should try to drink less coffee, and eat less fast food, too. These bad habits keep you awake. Don't use devices with bright screens (for example, your mobile phone) before you go to sleep. They make your brain think that it is daytime instead of night time. Read a book and drink a cup of warm milk or herbal tea in the evening. Then you'll feel ready for sleep.

3 VOCABULARY
Verbs with dependent prepositions

a Complete the sentences with the correct prepositions from the box.

at   about (x2)   with   to   on

1 What is a problem you have to deal _____ every day?
2 Do you listen _____ music while you clean?
3 How often do you look _____ your phone?
4 What stops you from concentrating _____ your work?
5 Do you think _____ your work or school at weekends?
6 Who can you talk to _____ problems at school or work?

b 💬 Work in pairs. Ask and answer the questions in 3a.

c Match the sentence halves to make advice for two problems.

1 ☐ Don't **borrow** money
2 ☐ Only **spend** money
3 ☐ Don't **pay**
4 ☐ You should **wait**
5 ☐ You should **ask**
6 ☐ **Talk**
7 ☐ You should **think**
8 ☐ Eat a good breakfast, so you **arrive**

a **for** the sales to buy expensive things.
b **for** friends' meals when you go out.
c **on** things you really need.
d **from** friends, because it creates problems.
e **of** ways to save energy.
f **for** a few days off.
g **at** work or school full of energy.
h **to** a doctor about how you feel.

d ▶ 06.05 Listen and check your answers in 3c. Which two problems is the advice for?

e Cover the second half of the sentences in 3c. Try to remember the advice.

4 SPEAKING

a ≫ Communication 6A Student A: Go to p. 129. Student B: Go to p. 130.

b 💬 Work in pairs. Choose one of the problems and write some advice.
- I feel really stressed before exams.
- I'm not creative enough at work.
- I don't laugh very often.
- I never finish anything I start.
- I always lose important things.

c 💬 Work in small groups. Present the problems and your advice. Whose advice is the most useful for you?

6B I WAS VERY FRIGHTENED

Learn to describe extreme experiences

G Uses of *to* + infinitive
V *-ed* / *-ing* adjectives

1 VOCABULARY *-ed* / *-ing* adjectives

a 💬 Look at the pictures on these pages. How do you think the people are feeling? Make a list of words.

b Read the sentences and answer the questions.
Johan's day at the beach was very <u>relaxing</u>.
After a day at the beach, Johan was completely <u>relaxed</u>.

   a Which adjective describes how he feels?
   b Which adjective describes the thing that makes him feel like that?

c ≫ Now go to Vocabulary Focus 6B on p. 138.

2 READING AND LISTENING

a 💬 Have you tried scuba diving? Would you like to? How do you think you would feel if you saw a shark?

b 💬 Match the words with pictures a–f. Use the words to describe the scene.

☐ scuba diver ☐ shark ☐ reef
☐ the surface ☐ breathe ☐ air

c Read *Sharks Saved My Life*. Which sentence is true about Caroline's experience in Egypt?
1 She went scuba diving to deal with her fear of sharks.
2 She was afraid because she went scuba diving in very deep water.
3 She got lost when she was scuba diving.

d Read the article again. Answer the questions with a partner.
1 Why did Caroline go to Egypt?
2 Why did she ask the instructor how deep the water was?
3 How did she feel when they got to the reef? Why?
4 Why didn't Caroline go back up to the surface of the water fast?

e 💬 What do you think happened next? How do you think sharks saved Caroline's life?

f ▶ 06.08 Listen to the rest of the story and check your ideas in 2e.

g ▶ 06.08 Listen again and answer the questions.
1 What happened after Caroline saw the sharks?
2 How did Caroline feel when she was back on the fishing boat?
3 How has the experience changed Caroline?

h 💬 Ask and answer the questions.
1 Were you surprised by anything in the story?
2 Do you think you would feel the same way as Caroline if this happened to you?

SHARKS SAVED MY LIFE

I started scuba diving because I was interested in sharks. I learned how to dive in England, but English waters were very disappointing. So I decided to try the Red Sea in Egypt.

The diving there was much more interesting. I saw so many beautiful fish, including sharks. After a few days, my instructor suggested a trip to the Shaab Shagra reef to swim with the sharks there.

We went out in an old fishing boat, and I asked the instructor, 'How deep is the water?' 'Not deep. Only 30 metres,' he said. I thought, 'Good, I can do that, but I can't go below 30 metres.' I didn't have any experience of deep diving, and I knew that below 30 metres people often feel strange. Some people suddenly feel very happy. Other people get confused, and they don't know which way is up or down.

I jumped in and followed my instructor. When we got down to the reef, I looked at my diving watch to see how deep we were. I was shocked to see we were at 40 metres! I was scared, and I was breathing very quickly. I thought to myself, 'Don't use all your air. Breathe slowly.' But I was really frightened, and I couldn't slow my breathing down.

I was really worried about my air. How much did I need? Did I have enough? I remember looking up at the light. I felt terrified, and I just wanted to go back up to the surface fast. But I knew that if you go up too fast, you can get 'the bends' and die in terrible pain. I was thinking, 'Don't go up. You'll die.' But my heart was saying, 'Go up! Go up!' I looked for my instructor. But I couldn't get his attention.

3 GRAMMAR Uses of *to* + infinitive

a Look at the sentences. Complete the sentences with the words in the box.

| to see   to do   to be   to get |

1 I didn't really know what _____.
2 I just wanted _____ out of the water.
3 I was happy _____ alive.
4 I looked at my diving watch _____ how deep we were.

b ▶06.09 Listen and check.

c Match the sentences in 3a with the rules.

> We use *to* + infinitive:
> ☐ to give a reason   ☐ after adjectives
> ☐ after certain verbs   ☐ after question words

d ▶06.09 **Pronunciation** Listen to the sentences from 3a again. Which part of the infinitive is stressed: *to* or the verb?

e Look at the article in 2c again. <u>Underline</u> another example for each use of the infinitive in 3c.

f ≫ Now go to Grammar Focus 6B on p. 154.

g Choose one topic to talk about in each pair of topics 1–4 below. Think about what you will say about …
  1 • an interesting place you've visited. Why did you go there? (to …)
    • an important course you've done. Why did you do it? (to …)
  2 • a time when you decided to do something, but then changed your mind. What was it?
    • a time when you tried to do something difficult. What happened?
  3 • a time when you didn't know what to do or where to go. What did you do?
    • a problem that you didn't know how to deal with. What happened?
  4 • someone you were surprised to see somewhere. Who was it? Where did you see the person?
    • some information you were shocked to hear. What was it?

h Work in pairs. Talk about your ideas in 3g.

4 LISTENING

a You are going to hear about another experience. Look at the words in the box. What do you think happened?

| parachute   6,000 metres   wind (n.)   get stuck |
| hang   free (v.)   pull along   lucky |

b ▶06.11 Listen to the interview and check your ideas in 4a.

c ▶06.11 Look at the interviewer's questions below. Listen again and make notes on Aaron's answers.
  1 What happened to you?
  2 How did it happen?
  3 What went wrong?
  4 How did you feel?
  5 Did the others help you?
  6 Did that experience stop you from jumping?

d Tell Aaron's story with a partner. Use your notes to help you.

5 SPEAKING

a Do you know of a person who has had an experience like the situations in this lesson? Try to think of a time when someone:
  • had a dangerous or frightening experience
  • had a lucky experience
  • learned something from a difficult situation
  • changed a lot because of an experience
  • had an experience that made them very happy.

b Prepare some notes about one experience you talked about in 5a. Use the questions to help you.
  • What was the person's situation at the time?
  • What exactly was the experience?
  • How did the person feel?
  • What did other people do?
  • How did the experience change the person?

c Work in new pairs. Tell your partner about the experience. Choose the best story to tell to the whole class.

UNIT 6

61

6C EVERYDAY ENGLISH
What do you think I should do?

Learn to ask for and give advice
- P Main stress
- S Showing sympathy

1 LISTENING

a When you have a problem, who do you prefer to talk to about it?

b Look at the picture. Annie is telling Rachel about some bad news. What do you think the news might be?

c 06.12 Watch or listen to Part 1 and check your ideas.

2 CONVERSATION SKILLS
Showing sympathy

a 06.12 Which of the phrases did Rachel use to show she feels sorry for Annie? Watch or listen again and check.

1 How awful.
2 That's terrible.
3 What a pity.
4 I'm really sorry to hear that.
5 That's a shame.

b Look at the two phrases in 2a that Rachel didn't use. Would you use them in a similar situation or in a less serious situation?

c 06.13 Listen and repeat the phrases in 2a.

d Work in pairs. Take turns to give bad news. Respond with the best phrases from 2a.
- your best friend forgot your birthday
- you broke your leg playing football
- you missed your train and waited two hours for the next one
- you spent hours preparing dinner and then burnt the food
- someone stole your phone and money when you were on holiday

3 LISTENING

a 06.14 Watch or listen to Part 2. What advice does Rachel give about … ?
1 Annie's boss
2 Annie's colleagues
3 Mark
4 changing jobs

b 06.14 Watch or listen again. Which piece of advice in 3a does Annie disagree with? Why?

c Which of Rachel's pieces of advice do you think is most useful? What else could Annie do?

4 PRONUNCIATION Main stress

a 06.15 Listen to the sentences. Underline the word in each sentence that Rachel stresses the most.
1 Did you ask when you're going to lose your job?
2 Maybe there'll be other jobs there.
3 You work in marketing, right?
4 Mark works in marketing, too.
5 Changing jobs could be a good thing.

b Why does Rachel stress the words you underlined in 4a? Choose the best answer.
1 to show more sympathy
2 none of the other words are important
3 the underlined words are the most important

c 06.15 Listen to 4a 1–5 again and repeat.

d Practise the dialogues with a partner. Stress the underlined words.
1 A We're meeting at 4 pm.
   B I know. But I don't know where!
2 A I'm really busy at work at the moment.
   B You work in a bank, right?
3 A I used to work for IBM.
   B Really? I used to work for IBM, too!
4 A I don't think it's a good time to change jobs.
   B I'm not sure. I think there are lots of interesting jobs out there.

62

5 USEFUL LANGUAGE
Asking for and giving advice

a ▶ 06.16 Listen and complete the phrases.

Asking for advice
1 _____ do you think I should do?
2 Do you _____ I should speak to him about it?

Giving advice
3 _____ get all the details first.
4 I think you _____ speak to your boss again.
5 I think it's a _____ _____ to ask.
6 I _____ worry too much.

b Look at Annie's responses to Rachel's advice. Which phrases show that Annie doesn't agree with the advice?
1 I don't think that's a good idea.
2 I suppose so.
3 I don't think I should do that.
4 You're right.

c ▶ 06.17 Listen and repeat the phrases in 5a and 5b.

d Complete the dialogue. Then practise the dialogue with a partner.

A I just heard I didn't get that job. I'm really disappointed. What do you ¹_____ I should do?
B I'm really sorry to ²_____ that. But I wouldn't ³_____ too much – you'll find something soon.
A I ⁴_____ so. But I'm surprised. I thought the interview went very well.
B Well then, I think you ⁵_____ write to the company. ⁶_____ them for some information about your interview.
A I don't think ⁷_____'s a good idea. They won't want to give me information like that.
B I think it's a good ⁸_____ to ask. I've done that before and the information can be really useful.
A You're ⁹_____. I'll send them an email tomorrow.

6 LISTENING

a 🎥 ▶ 06.18 Annie is worried about Leo. Watch or listen to Part 3 and answer the questions.
1 Why is Annie worried about Leo?
2 What explanation does Rachel give?

b 💬 Ask and answer the questions.
1 What other reasons could there be for Leo's behaviour?
2 Do you think Annie is right to worry?

7 SPEAKING

a You are going to tell your partner about something bad that happened to you. Read the cards 1–4 and choose a problem. Think about what you want to say.

1 Someone stole your bag in a café.
- What was in the bag?
- What were you doing when the person stole it?
- Who do you think stole it?
- How did you feel?
- What problems will you now have without your bag?

2 You failed an important exam.
- What was the exam?
- Why was it important?
- Did you think you would pass?
- Who else will be upset that you failed?

3 You had an argument with your best friend.
- Do you normally argue with your best friend?
- What was the argument about?
- How did it start?
- Do you want to contact your friend again?

4 Your boss said your work wasn't good enough.
- What work was it?
- What did your boss say exactly?
- How did you feel?
- Do you think this will create problems for you in the future?

b 💬 Student A: Tell your partner about what happened. Student B: Show sympathy and give Student A some advice.

c 💬 Now swap roles.

d 💬 Did your partner show sympathy? Was their advice helpful?

UNIT PROGRESS TEST
CHECK YOUR PROGRESS

You can now do the Unit Progress Test.

6D SKILLS FOR WRITING
I often worry about tests and exams

Learn to write an email giving advice

W Linking: ordering ideas and giving examples

1 LISTENING AND SPEAKING

a Are these situations connected to work or study? Write work (*W*), study (*S*) or both (*B*).
1. ☐ doing exams or tests
2. ☐ doing a presentation
3. ☐ managing other people
4. ☐ making business decisions
5. ☐ learning to communicate in a foreign language
6. ☐ reading all the books on a reading list

b 💬 What problems do people sometimes have in the situations in 1a?

c ▶ 06.19 Listen to Chloe, Bob and Marisa talking about problems with work and study. Complete the first row of the table.

	Chloe	Bob	Marisa
What's the main problem?			
What are the details of the problem?			
How do they feel?			
What advice have they had from friends or family?			

d ▶ 06.19 Listen again and complete the table.

e 💬 What advice would you give to Chloe, Bob and Marisa?

2 READING

a Eliza teaches English. She has a wiki for her class, where students can write and ask for advice. Read Sevim's message. What does Sevim want help with?

b Read Eliza's reply on p. 65. How many suggestions does Eliza make?

c Read the text again. Are sentences 1–5 true (*T*) or false (*F*)? Correct the false sentences.
1. Eliza always felt relaxed about speaking Turkish.
2. Eliza thinks language learners should try not to make mistakes.
3. Eliza says Sevim should use English with the students in her class.
4. Sevim can pay extra to go to a chat group at the study centre.
5. Eliza thinks you can practise speaking on the Internet.

Sevim — Monday 12:21 p.m.

Dear Eliza,
I think my reading and listening are all right for my level, but I'm worried about my speaking. I don't feel very relaxed when I speak English, and I want to improve.
Do you have any ideas?
Thank you,
Sevim

64

UNIT 6

3 WRITING SKILLS Linking: ordering ideas and giving examples

a Eliza uses words and phrases to order information in her reply. Notice the underlined example.

First of all, don't worry about making mistakes.

Underline three more words in the message that order Eliza's ideas.

b Read the advice on studying vocabulary for an exam. Add words and phrases where you see ⌃ to order the information.

> ⌃ you can study vocabulary lists at the back of the course book. There are also some practice exercises there to help you. ⌃ you should test yourself on the words you have studied. For example, you can try writing down all the words you can remember about a particular topic. ⌃ you can work with another student and test each other. If you both speak the same language, you can translate words from your language into English. ⌃ it's a good idea to try and think about the words you've learned and use them in a conversation the same day. This is a very active way of studying vocabulary.

c Read the text in 2b again. Notice the highlighted expressions Eliza uses to give examples. Cover the text and complete the sentences.
  1 _____, it's a good idea to use only English in class.
  2 You can join a conversation group, _____ the chat groups in the study centre.
  3 _____, there are a lot of websites where you can find speaking partners from all around the world.

d Match the sentence halves.
  1 ☐ You can download apps to help you study. For
  2 ☐ There are a lot of ways to practise listening, such
  3 ☐ It's easy to get extra reading practice. For

  a as podcasts and online videos.
  b instance, there are a lot of books and magazines in the study centre.
  c example, I use the *Cambridge Advanced Learner's Dictionary* on my phone.

Eliza Monday 2:08 p.m.

Hi Sevim,

Thanks for your message. I'm glad that you wrote to me for ideas.

I remember when I was learning Turkish, I felt embarrassed about speaking. I could remember a lot of words and I knew grammar rules, but speaking was difficult. I now feel a lot more relaxed about speaking, so here are some ideas that I've taken from my own experience.

First of all, don't worry about making mistakes. Other people will still understand you, and they probably won't notice your mistakes. Secondly, remember that the only way to learn to speak a language is by speaking it. Use every chance you get to speak. For example, it's a good idea to use only English in class and not speak to other students in Turkish. You should also try practising the new vocabulary and grammar we learn in class by repeating it at home.

Next, you should think about extra speaking practice outside the classroom. You can join a conversation group, such as the chat groups in the study centre. They are free to join. Finally, you can also practise speaking online. For instance, there are a lot of websites where you can find speaking partners from all around the world.

I hope this helps you, and please feel free to talk to me after class next week.

Best wishes,

Eliza

4 WRITING

a Work in pairs. Read the ideas for Sevim about how to improve her writing. Add three more ideas to the list.

> • plan your ideas before you write
> • ask another student to check your grammar
> •
> •
> •

b Work in pairs. Write a message giving advice to Sevim. Make sure you order your ideas clearly and give examples.

c Work in groups of four. Read the other pair's message to Sevim. Does it contain similar ideas to your message? Are the ideas ordered clearly? Are there examples?

65

UNIT 6
Review and extension

1 GRAMMAR

a Complete the exchanges with *should* or *shouldn't*.

1 **A** I can't sleep.
   B You _____ drink coffee in the afternoon.
2 **A** My desk is messy.
   B I think you _____ tidy it at the end of every day.
3 **A** I'm addicted to TV.
   B You _____ watch more than two hours a day.
4 **A** I don't have time to exercise.
   B You _____ try to walk for ten minutes every day.
5 **A** I don't have much money.
   B I don't think you _____ buy so many clothes.
6 **A** I don't know many people where I live.
   B I think you _____ join a club or a sports team.

b Change the advice in 1a into imperatives.

1 *Don't drink coffee in the afternoon.*

c Complete the sentences with the correct forms of the verbs in the box.

do   drive   find   go   learn   meet

1 Do you think people in your country should _____ more exercise?
2 Is it difficult _____ parking where you live?
3 Do you need _____ to the shops today?
4 Do you think everyone should _____ a foreign language?
5 Is it easy _____ new people where you live?
6 Do you know how _____ ?

d 💬 Ask and answer the questions in 1c.

2 VOCABULARY

a Complete the sentences with the correct forms of the verbs in the box.

arrive   ask   borrow   concentrate   deal   spend

1 Sometimes I find it hard to _____ on my work.
2 What time did you _____ at the airport?
3 She _____ the waiter for the bill.
4 We _____ a car from a friend for the day.
5 They _____ too much money on food last month.
6 I _____ with a lot of different people in my job.

b Choose the correct answers.

1 I felt so *relaxed / relaxing* during my holiday.
2 The news was really *shocked / shocking*.
3 I needed to rest after my *tired / tiring* day.
4 I had a really *amazing / amazed* time in the city.
5 It's very *annoyed / annoying* when you have to queue.
6 I was *embarrassed / embarrassing* when I fell down.

c 💬 Talk about when the situations in 2b have been true for you.

3 WORDPOWER Verb + *to*

a Match sentences 1–2 with replies a–b.

1 My chair at work isn't very comfortable.
2 I can't afford to go to the cinema tonight.

a ☐ I think you should stop **lending** money **to** your friends.
b ☐ I think you should **explain** the problem **to** your boss.

b Which verb + *to* combination in **bold** in 3a is a way of giving? Which is a way of communicating?

c Look at the sentences. Add the verb + *to* combinations to the table.

1 You have to **pay** a lot of money **to** the government when you start a new business.
2 She **wrote to** the newspaper to tell them what happened.
3 I **sold** my car **to** my brother-in-law.
4 I always **read to** my children before they go to sleep.
5 She **described** the building **to** her friend, but he couldn't find it.
6 She **brought** flowers **to** her mother to say she was sorry.

Communicating	Giving
explain to	lend to

d Where does *to* come in the sentences? Tick the correct answer.

1 ☐ before the object of the verb
2 ☐ after the direct object and before the indirect object

e Put *to* in the correct places in the sentences.

1 They sold their house some friends from another country.
2 When Steve described his holiday his friends, they were amazed.
3 Please bring something to drink the party.
4 I read the joke my friend because it was funny.
5 Tara lent an umbrella her neighbour because it was raining.
6 Did you write the letter the bank like I told you?
7 I explained the problem the company, but they didn't help me.
8 I paid the money for my course the school last week.

f Write five sentences about your life using the verbs + *to* from the chart in 3c.

🔄 REVIEW YOUR PROGRESS

How well did you do in this unit? Write 3, 2 or 1 for each objective.
3 = very well   2 = well   1 = not so well

I CAN ...	
give advice for common problems	☐
describe extreme experiences	☐
ask for and give advice	☐
write an email giving advice.	☐

66

CAN DO OBJECTIVES

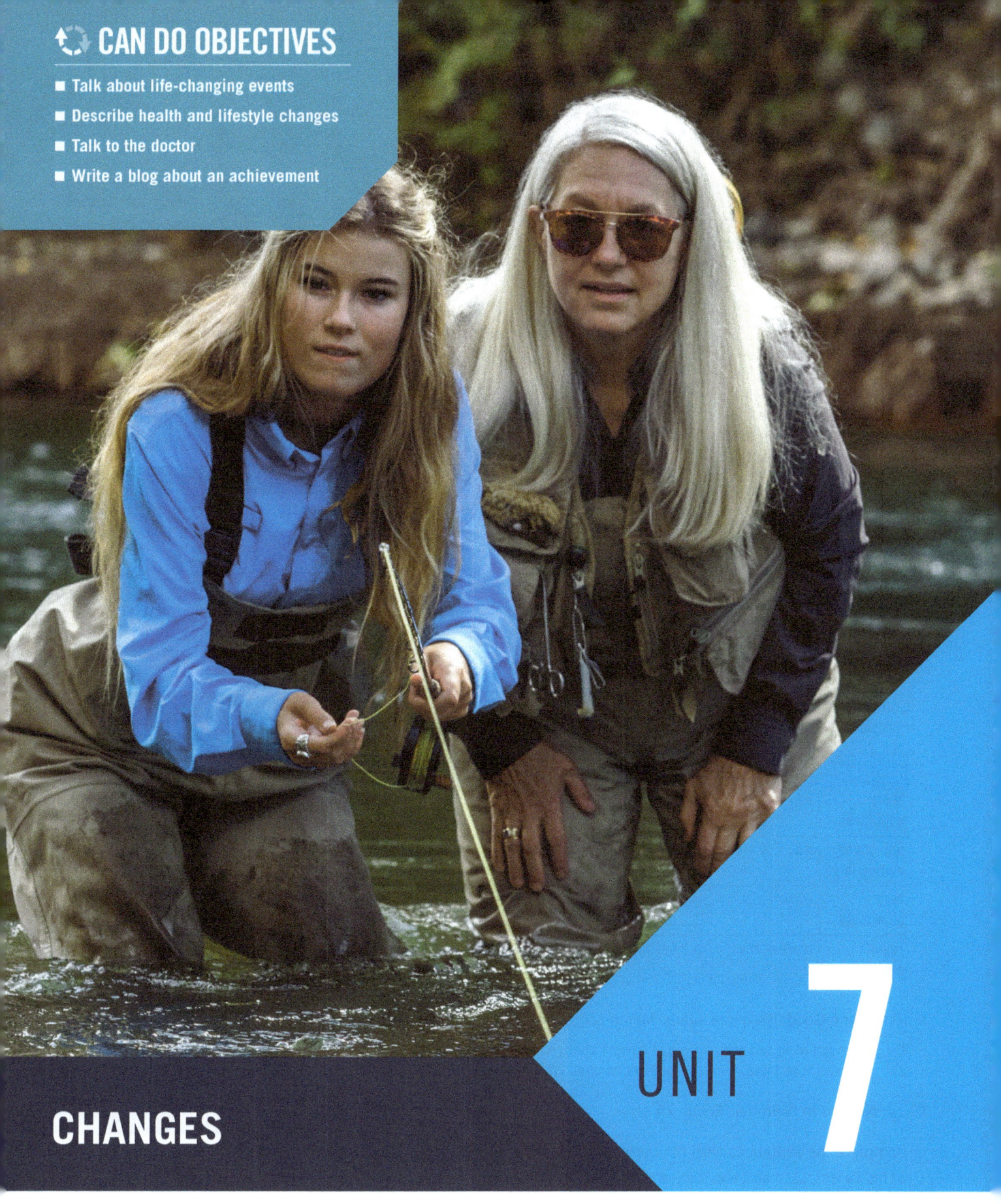

- Talk about life-changing events
- Describe health and lifestyle changes
- Talk to the doctor
- Write a blog about an achievement

UNIT 7

CHANGES

GETTING STARTED

a Look at the picture and answer the questions.
1. Who are the two people? What are they doing?
2. How do you think each of them is feeling? Who is having more fun? Why?

b Ask and answer the questions.
1. Think of a time you learned from someone with experience. Who did you learn from? What did you learn?
2. What can younger people teach older generations?

67

7A I'M THE HAPPIEST I'VE EVER BEEN

Learn to talk about life-changing events
- **G** Comparatives and superlatives
- **V** *get* collocations

1 READING

a 💬 Look at the pictures. Which of the people are famous in your country? What do you know about them?

b Read the quotes. Which person a–f is talking about these life events?
1. ☐ setting goals
2. ☐ the body getting older
3. ☐ how nature can tell you how to live life
4. ☐ a healthy lifestyle
5. ☐ taking advantage of what life offers you
6. ☐ becoming a parent

c Read the quotes again. Which quotes talk about the following?
1. the way the person lives their life
2. some kind of change in the person's life

d 💬 Which quotes do you like the most? Why?

a Michelle Obama
❝ I can't say this enough – the food that you put into your bodies can actually help you get better grades. And it can also affect your performance in sports and other activities, too. You see, when you give your body the best possible fuel, you have more energy, you're stronger, you think **more quickly**. ❞

b Chris Hemsworth
❝ I almost feel **more anxious** lately about, 'Here's your opportunity, now you've got to make something of it.' ❞

c Jane Goodall
❝ I get back twice a year and sometimes I see the chimps, and sometimes I don't … I'm not as fit as I was, so if they're way up at the top of the mountain, it's difficult. ❞

2 GRAMMAR Comparatives and superlatives

a Complete the table with the highlighted comparative and superlative forms from the quotes.

	Comparative	Examples	Superlative	Examples
short adjectives	adj. + -er	shorter ¹_____	*the* adj. + -est	the kindest ² the _____
adjectives ending in *y*	adj. – -y + -ier	funnier healthier	*the* adj. – -y + -iest	the silliest ³ the _____
long adjectives	*more* + adj.	more important ⁴_____	*the most* + adj.	the most interesting ⁵ the _____
regular adverbs	*more* + adv.	more easily ⁶_____	*the most* + adv.	the most carefully the most politely

b Read Jane Goodall's quote again. Match sentences 1–2 with the meanings a–b.
1. ☐ I am not as fit as I was.
2. ☐ I am as fit as I was.
   a. I haven't changed. I'm equally fit now.
   b. I've changed. I'm less fit now.

c ≫ Now go to Grammar Focus 7A on p. 156.

d Complete the sentences with the correct forms of the adjectives and adverbs in brackets.
1. My life is _____ than it was five years ago. (good)
2. I'm the _____ I've ever been. (confident)
3. I learn _____ than when I was younger. (slowly)
4. I'm not as _____ as I was a year ago. (busy)
5. This is the _____ town I've ever lived in. (large)
6. My home is _____ these days. (tidy)
7. I work _____ now than I did five years ago. (hard)
8. I speak English _____ than I did a year ago. (good)

e ▶ 07.02 Listen and check. Practise the sentences.

f 💬 Are the sentences in 2d true for you? Why?

> My life is better than it was five years ago.

> Why?

> Well, I have my own flat, but I still see my friends and family all the time.

68

UNIT 7

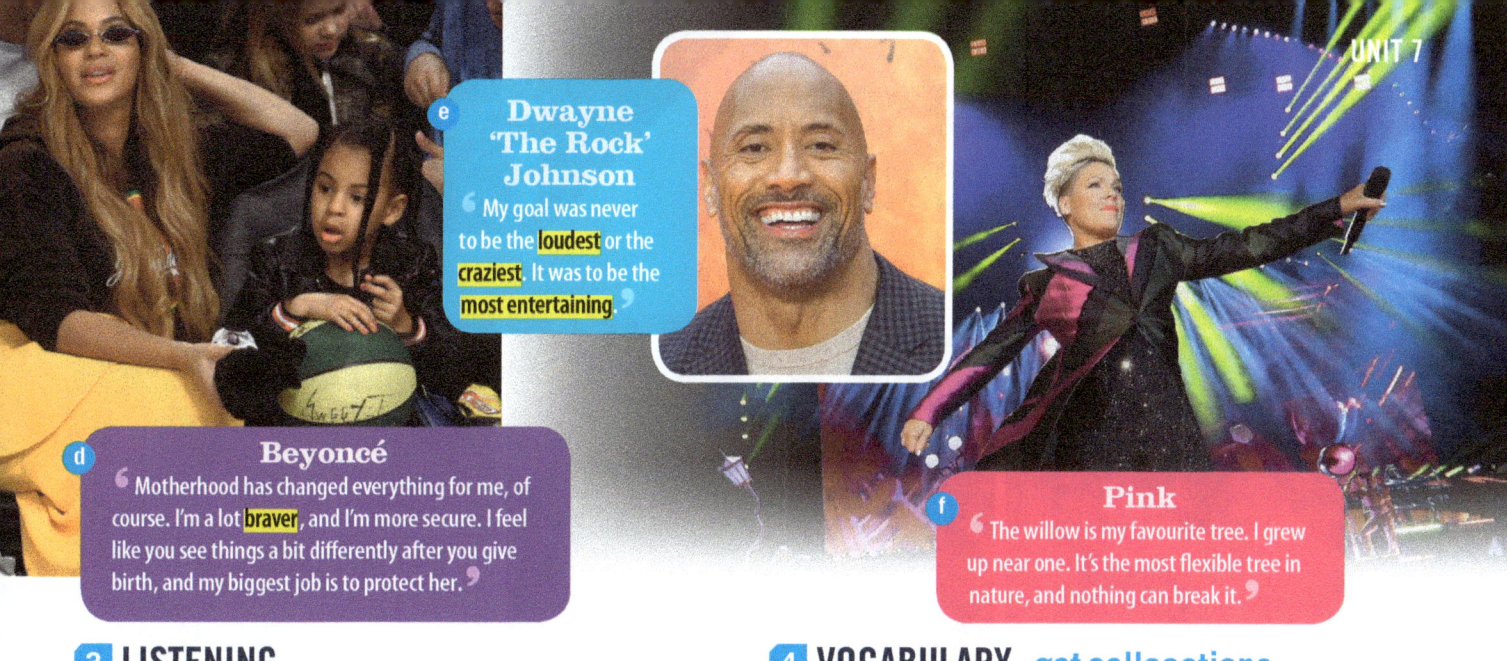

e Dwayne 'The Rock' Johnson
"My goal was never to be the **loudest** or the **craziest**. It was to be the **most entertaining**."

d Beyoncé
"Motherhood has changed everything for me, of course. I'm a lot **braver**, and I'm more secure. I feel like you see things a bit differently after you give birth, and my biggest job is to protect her."

f Pink
"The willow is my favourite tree. I grew up near one. It's the most flexible tree in nature, and nothing can break it."

3 LISTENING

a Read about two famous people. Do you know anything about them? How do you think their lives were different before they became famous?

Steven Adams
Born: 20 July, 1993, Rotorua, New Zealand.
Steven Adams is a professional basketball player and is the first New Zealander to be selected for the National Basketball Association (NBA) in the USA. He is 2.11 metres tall and plays for Oklahoma City Thunder.

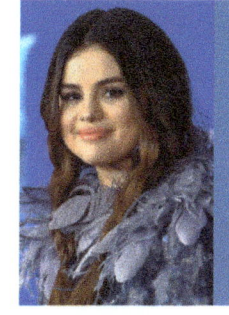

Selena Gomez
Born: 22 July, 1992, Grand Prairie, Texas, USA
Selena Gomez is an American singer and actress. She has starred in a TV series and a number of films. As a singer, she has had top-ten hit songs and has sold millions of albums.

b 07.03 Listen to the stories of the two people. Who do you think had the most difficult time when they were young? Why?

c 07.03 Listen again and write Steven (*SA*), Selena (*SG*) or both (*B*).

1. ☐ He/She was happy as a small child.
2. ☐ He/She couldn't afford healthy food.
3. ☐ He/She got help from his/her family.
4. ☐ He/She had problems after a sad event.
5. ☐ He/She stopped going to school.
6. ☐ He/She didn't become famous easily.
7. ☐ He/She moved to a new city.
8. ☐ He/She is not only interested in money.

d Ask and answer the questions.
1. What do you think is the most important thing that helped Steven and Selena during their difficult times? Why?
2. What other people do you know about who had a difficult start in life but became successful?

4 VOCABULARY *get* collocations

a 07.04 Complete the sentences with the correct forms of the phrases in the box. Listen and check.

get support   get paid   get divorced   get work   get an offer

1. Selena Gomez's parents _____ when she was five years old.
2. Selena's mother found it hard to _____ as an actress.
3. Selena _____ from her mother at the beginning of her career.
4. In June 2012, Steven _____ of a place from the Pittsburgh Panthers.
5. He _____ more than $20 million a year.

b Now go to Vocabulary Focus 7A on p. 139.

5 SPEAKING

a Think of a person you know and put their most important and interesting life events in order on the timeline. Use expressions with *get* and any other events you like.

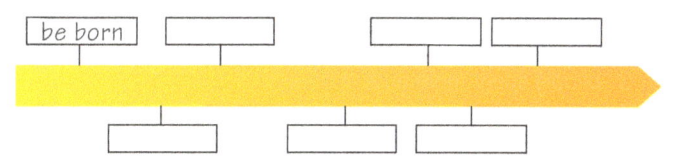

| be born | | | |

b Work in pairs. Tell your partner about the person you chose.

When she was 20, my mother got a place at university in London. She met my father …

c Ask and answer the questions. Look at the life events in the box.

get a place at university   get engaged   get married
have children   get rich   get a job   get old

1. Which of the life events have you experienced? When do you think you will experience the other events?
2. Which life events do you think change people the most? How do people change?

69

7B I DIDN'T USE TO EAT HEALTHY FOOD

Learn to describe health and lifestyle changes

G used to
V Health collocations

1 READING

a Look at the photographs from the 1970s. How do you think daily life was different back then? Think about the following categories.
- lives of men, women and children
- food and drink
- medicine and healthcare
- healthy living and exercise

b Read sentences 1–4 about the 1970s. Do you think they are true (*T*) or false (*F*)? Compare your answers with your partner.

In the 1970s, …
1 people didn't worry so much about the food they ate.
2 people didn't live as long as they do today.
3 people spent more time at the gym.
4 people didn't spend time in front of computers.

c Read the article. Check your answers to 1b.

d Read the article again. Answer the questions.
1 Why is eating too much red meat a problem?
2 What is a change in eating habits in the UK?
3 What two improvements in medical treatment have helped people to live longer?
4 What health problem has not improved since the 1970s?
5 Why has exercise and fitness become popular since the 1970s?
6 What is different now about people's everyday activity?
7 In what ways can computer use be bad for our health?
8 What can we now use to find out if we are getting enough exercise?

Health: 1970s and TODAY

People are often shocked by the unhealthy lifestyles shown in TV programmes and films from the 1970s. But are we really any healthier than we were 50 years ago?

Food and drink

People didn't use to worry so much about the food they ate. Back then, people used to eat a lot more red meat. However, since then we've learned that too much red meat can be bad for your health. In the UK, people used to prefer white bread, but sales of white bread have dropped by 75% and British people now prefer wholemeal bread. In general, British people now eat a healthy diet, but they still love chips!

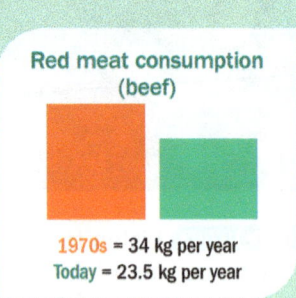

Red meat consumption (beef)
1970s = 34 kg per year
Today = 23.5 kg per year

Healthcare

People in the UK didn't use to live as long as they do today. Advances in drugs and technology have helped people to live longer lives. For example, drugs such as statins, which lower cholesterol in the blood, mean that fewer people suffer from heart disease. In hospitals, there are now MRI machines that can see inside a person's body. This means doctors can have a better understanding of health problems. One area that has become worse is allergies. These days more people are allergic to various foods than they were in the 1970s. One possible reason for this is a lack of Vitamin D because we spend less time in the sun.

Average age at death
1970s = 73 years
Today = 78 years

UNIT 7

Exercise

It was in the 1970s that people began doing exercise regularly. In the beginning, there weren't many fitness centres, but the number grew because people decided they wanted to keep in shape and get fit. Since then, gyms and fitness centres have become more popular and more than 10 million British people go regularly to a gym. However, in general, they are less active in their normal day-to-day lives than they were in the 1970s. For example, more people own a car, so they do a lot less walking. These days people go to a gym because they need to include a fitness programme into their comfortable lifestyles.

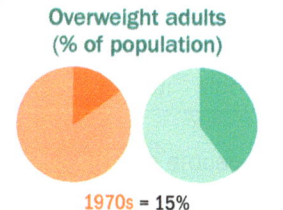

Overweight adults (% of population)
1970s = 15%
Today = 40%

Technology

There is no doubt that developments in technology have helped improve healthcare. However, they have also had a negative effect on people's health. In the 1970s people didn't use to spend time in front of a computer, but now they do. This means they are sitting for long periods of time and they don't get enough exercise. Too much computer use can also mean people have problems with their neck, shoulders and back because they don't sit properly. The blue light from computer screens can cause lack of sleep, so people suffer from stress. But it's also worth remembering that people can go online to watch and follow fitness workouts, most smartphones have health apps and many people wear fitness trackers that allow them to check they're getting enough exercise.

2 VOCABULARY Health collocations

a Work in pairs. Look at the highlighted phrases. Which do you think are about the following topics? Some can go in more than one category.
  1 food   2 exercise   3 health problems

b ▶ 07.07 Complete the sentences with phrases from the article. Then listen and check.
  1 I have problems walking upstairs these days – I really need to _____.
  2 I often have sleeping problems – the next day the _____ makes me feel exhausted.
  3 In my family we have a low-cholesterol diet – I don't think we'll ever _____.
  4 When I joined my gym, I got _____ from a trainer.
  5 They all work 10 to 12 hours a day and they all _____.
  6 We _____ to nuts and eggs – we get ill if we eat them.
  7 I _____, but sometimes I eat food that's bad for me – like chips or chocolate.
  8 He stayed inside all summer and suffered from _____.
  9 I don't want to put on weight, so I walk to work each day to _____

c 💬 Which of the ideas in 2b are common in your country? Do you think people are generally healthy in your country? Why / Why not?

3 GRAMMAR used to

a Look at the sentences about the 1970s. Are these things the same or different today?

People **used to eat** a lot more red meat.
People **used to prefer** white bread.
People **didn't use to worry** so much about the food they ate.
People in the UK **didn't use to live** as long as they do today.

b Look at the sentences in 3a again and complete the rules.

> To talk about something that was different in the past, we use _____ + infinitive. The negative is _____ + infinitive.

c ▶ 07.08 **Pronunciation** Listen to the sentences in 3a. Notice the pronunciation of *used to*. Does the pronunciation change in negative sentences?

d ≫ Now go to Grammar Focus 7B on p. 156.

e Complete the sentences with *used to* and the verbs in the box.

walk   be   think   spend   not be   not eat

  1 When I was a child, I _____ to school every day.
  2 When I was a teenager, my parents _____ I was lazy.
  3 I _____ allergic to seafood, but now I am.
  4 People in my country _____ a lot of fast food, but they do now.
  5 I _____ more time outdoors than I do now.
  6 Healthcare in my country _____ better than it is now.

f 💬 Change the sentences in 3e so they are true for you. Compare your answers with a partner.

4 SPEAKING

≫ **Communication 7B** Work in pairs. Go to p. 133.

71

7C EVERYDAY ENGLISH
It hurts all the time

Learn to talk to the doctor
- P Intonation for asking questions
- S Showing concern and relief

1 VOCABULARY At the doctor's

a Look at the health problems in the box. Which have you had in the last six months?

> backache   a cold   a temperature   a broken leg
> a serious stomach ache   the flu   a rash

b What do people in your country do for each of the health problems in 1a? Choose ideas from the list and add more of your own ideas.
- get a prescription from a doctor
- take pills or other medicine
- have some tests
- go to the hospital
- go to the chemist's
- have an operation
- put on cream

2 LISTENING

a 07.10 Watch or listen to Part 1. Answer the questions.
1 Why has Leo gone to the doctor?
2 When did the problem start?

b 07.10 Watch or listen to Part 1 again. What other information does the doctor get from Leo about his back problem? Compare your notes with a partner.

c Ask and answer the questions.
1 Do you ever suffer from the same health problem as Leo?
2 What causes it?
3 What treatments would you recommend?

3 USEFUL LANGUAGE
Describing symptoms

a 07.11 Complete the phrases with the words in the box. Then listen and check.

> exhausted   all the time   back   painful   get to sleep

1 My _____ hurts.
2 It's very _____.
3 I can't _____.
4 It hurts _____.
5 I feel _____.

b 07.11 Listen again and repeat.

c Make eight more phrases with 1–5 in 3a and the words in the box below.

> when I walk   uncomfortable   concentrate
> arm   run   terrible   itchy   sick

d When do people get the symptoms in 3a and 3c? Talk about your ideas with a partner.

> People feel sick when they eat bad food.

> Some people feel sick on car journeys.

4 LISTENING

a 07.12 Which treatments do you think the doctor will suggest for Leo? Put a ✓ or a ✗. Then watch or listen to Part 2 and check your ideas.
1 ☐ stay in bed
2 ☐ do the things you normally do
3 ☐ stay in the same position for a long time
4 ☐ do some exercise
5 ☐ take pills for the pain

b 07.12 Watch or listen again. Are sentences 1–6 true (T) or false (F)? Correct the false sentences.
1 ☐ Leo is going to the gym a lot at the moment.
2 ☐ Leo sits down a lot for his job.
3 ☐ Leo isn't taking anything for the pain.
4 ☐ Leo has to take two pills every two hours.
5 ☐ Leo shouldn't take more than 24 pills in a day.
6 ☐ Leo might need to see the doctor again in a week.

5 CONVERSATION SKILLS
Showing concern and relief

a Look at the underlined phrases in the conversations. Which phrases show that Leo is … ?
1 happy with what the doctor says
2 worried about what the doctor says

Doctor	I don't think it's anything to worry about.
Leo	Phew. That's good to hear.
Doctor	But you shouldn't stay in bed – that's not going to help.
Leo	Oh dear. Really?
Doctor	I really don't think it's anything to worry about.
Leo	What a relief!

b ▶07.13 Listen to the phrases in 5a. How do we pronounce *phew*? Repeat the phrases.

c Work in pairs. Take turns to say the sentences. Respond using the phrases in 5a.

Student A
1 I don't think it's serious.
2 I think you'll need to see another doctor.
3 You should feel better in 48 hours.

Student B
1 I need you to take a few tests.
2 Your foot's definitely not broken.
3 I think it's just a cold, not the flu.

6 USEFUL LANGUAGE
Doctors' questions

a ▶07.14 Match the doctor's questions with Leo's answers. Then listen and check.
1 ☐ So, what's the problem?
2 ☐ When did this problem start?
3 ☐ Where does it hurt?
4 ☐ Can I have a look?
5 ☐ Do you do any exercise?
6 ☐ Are you taking anything for the pain?
7 ☐ Do you have any allergies?

a About three or four days ago.
b Here. This area.
c Yes, I've taken some aspirin.
d No, I don't think so.
e Sure.
f Well, I usually go to the gym, but I haven't been recently.
g Well, my back hurts.

b ▶07.15 Listen to the doctor's questions. Choose the best answer (a or b) for each question.
1 a Yes, I've taken some tablets. b My leg hurts.
2 a No, not often. b Yes, of course.
3 a I go running. b I work in an office.
4 a Not much. b I can't eat fish.
5 a I feel tired all the time. b No, nothing.
6 a All day. b About a week ago.
7 a It hurts a lot. b Here – under my arm.

7 PRONUNCIATION
Intonation for asking questions

a ▶07.16 Listen to the questions. Does the doctor's voice go up (↗) or down (↘) at the end of each question?
1 So, what's the problem?
2 When did this problem start?
3 Where does it hurt?
4 Can I have a look?

b Which question in 7a does the doctor already know the answer to? Complete the rule.

- In questions where the speaker doesn't know the answer, the voice usually goes **up / down**.
- In questions where the speaker knows the answer, the voice usually goes **up / down**.

c Listen to the questions in 7a again and repeat.

8 SPEAKING

a Work in pairs. Student A: You are a doctor. Listen to your partner's health problem and give advice.
Student B: Choose a health problem from the pictures and explain the problem to your partner. Give details.

What's the problem?
I have a stomach ache.
When did this start?
Yesterday. After dinner. But it happens quite often.
I see …

b Swap roles. Student A: Choose a new health problem.

UNIT PROGRESS TEST
CHECK YOUR PROGRESS

You can now do the Unit Progress Test.

7D SKILLS FOR WRITING
After that, I decided to make a change

Learn to write a blog about an achievement
W Linking: ordering events

1 LISTENING AND SPEAKING

a What kinds of things do people sometimes want to change about themselves? Think of one example for each area.
- diet
- education
- money
- exercise
- bad habits
- relationships

b 07.17 Listen to Jeff, Silvia and Lucas. What change did each person try to make? Were they successful?

c 07.17 Listen again. Complete the table.

	Jeff	Silvia	Lucas
What was their problem?			
How did the problem happen?			
What did they change?			
What was the result of the change?			

d Think of something you would like to change in your life. Make notes about the questions.
1. What is the change?
2. Why do you want to make the change?
3. How could you make the change?
4. What do you hope the result will be?

e Work in pairs. Talk about the changes you would like to make.

> I think I should eat less fast food.

> How often do you eat it?

2 READING

a Sam wrote about a change he made for the *Living to Change* blog. Read the blog and answer the questions.
1. What was Sam like before he made a change?
2. What kind of exercise did he start doing?
3. What was the result?

b Are these sentences about Sam true (*T*) or false (*F*)? Correct the false sentences.
1. Sam felt much fitter just after he gave up smoking.
2. He started exercising before he stopped smoking.
3. He chose running because he liked it when he was younger.
4. He found it difficult to run when he started.
5. When he hurt his foot, he was happy to have a break from running.
6. He now thinks he might enter a race.

LIVING to CHANGE
TALKING ABOUT HOW YOU GOT EVEN BETTER!

About three years ago I used to smoke and I didn't do much exercise. I was really unfit and I didn't feel very good about myself, so I decided to make a change.

¹To begin with I had to give up smoking, which wasn't too difficult. But then I started eating too much fast food instead and I wasn't doing any exercise. I could breathe a bit more easily but I still found it difficult to walk upstairs or run for a bus.

²After that I thought I really have to do some exercise. When I was at secondary school I used to enjoy running so I thought that would be an easy way for me to get fit. ³At first I could only run for about thirty seconds and then I had to walk. It was terrible. So that's how I got started – I went for walks and every

3 WRITING SKILLS
Linking: ordering events

a Complete the rules with the words in the box. Use the highlighted words in Sam's blog to help you.

to begin with   after that   at first
after a while   soon   then   in the end

> To show the order of events we use …
> _____ or _____ to talk about the first thing that happened.
> _____ or _____ or _____ or _____ to mean *next*.
> _____ for the final action, event or result.

b Which word or phrase in 3a means … ?
1 after a short time
2 after a longer time period

c Complete the text with the words and phrases in 3a.
I stopped drinking coffee.
1 _____, I got headaches and really missed it.
(This is the first thing that happened.)
2 _____, I started drinking just one cup a day.
(This is what happened next.)
3 _____, the headaches stopped.
(This is what happened a short time later.)
4 _____, I started drinking green tea during the day.
(This is what happened after a longer period of time.)
5 _____, I forgot to make coffee in the morning one day.
(This is what happened next.)
6 _____, I realised I didn't need coffee at all.
(This is the last thing that happened.)

Home | News | Articles | Contact us   log in

few days I made the walk a bit longer. ⁴**After a while** I began feeling fitter and that's when I started to run and walk. But ⁵**then**, one day I fell over and hurt my foot when I was running and I had to stop for about two weeks. I was surprised how much I missed it!

However, when I started again, it was much easier than I thought. ⁶**Soon** I found I didn't need to walk any more and I found I could run further and further. ⁷**In the end** I was able to go for a 10 kilometre run without problems. I feel so much better and I'm now planning to run a marathon next year. And instead of spending all my money on cigarettes and fast food, I spend money on going out or buying things.

---

d Complete the text with the time linkers in the box. Use each linker once.

after that   soon   in the end   at first
to begin with   after a while   then

About a year ago, I was walking near a river and I slipped and fell in. I couldn't swim and I was really frightened. I was lucky because a friend was there and she helped me. So I decided that I needed to learn to swim.

1 _____, I hated getting into the water at the swimming pool. My teacher told me to take a shower before getting in, so I was already wet. This was a good idea. 2 _____, I found it easier to get into the water. 3 _____, I started with very easy exercises, like putting my head underwater. I felt a bit stupid. But my teacher made it fun and we laughed a lot. 4 _____, I found it easy to put my head underwater.

Learning how to breathe out underwater was difficult, and it took a long time. 5 _____, it got easier and I made good progress. 6 _____, I learned how to swim. I'm not a great swimmer, but I'm not afraid of the water like I used to be. And I'm a lot more careful near the river now!

4 WRITING

a You are going to write an article for the *Living to Change* blog. Think about a difficult change you made or something difficult you tried to do. Choose one of these topics or your own idea.
- health
- education
- work
- money
- bad habits
- relationships

b Make notes on your ideas. Use questions 1–5 to help you.
1 What did you want to do?
2 How did you start? Did your plan change?
3 What was difficult? What was easy?
4 Did anything you didn't expect happen?
5 What happened in the end? How do you feel about it?

c Use your notes to write an article about the change you made. Use time linkers to show the order of events.

d Work in pairs. Read each other's articles. Did you write about similar topics? Did your partner use time linkers?

UNIT 7

75

UNIT 7
Review and extension

1 GRAMMAR

a Complete the sentences using the comparative and superlative forms of the words.

1. Top speed: Kawasa 130 km/h, Shumika 140 km/h, TTR 150 km/h
   The Shumika is <u>faster than</u> the Kawasa, but the TTR is <u>the fastest</u>. (fast)
2. Room price: Grand Hotel €130, Hotel Central €200, Hotel Europe €260
   The Hotel Central is _____ the Grand Hotel, but the Hotel Europe is _____. (expensive)
3. Speakers: Soundgood ***, MusicPro ****, iListen *****
   The MusicPro is _____ the Soundgood, but the iListen is _____. (good)
4. Number of fans in the USA: New York Yankees 24 million, Chicago Cubs 18 million, Pittsburgh Pirates 4 million
   The Chicago Cubs are _____ the Yankees, but the Pittsburgh Pirates are _____. (popular)

b Complete the text with the correct form of *used to* and the verbs in the box.

plan   not be   buy   not open   not have   see

Thirty years ago, we ¹_____ any big supermarkets in my town. There were some small shops, and I ²_____ everything there. I liked it because I always ³_____ people I knew, so it was very friendly. But it wasn't perfect – there ⁴_____ a lot of different products. And the shops ⁵_____ on Sunday or late in the evening, so I ⁶_____ my week carefully.

2 VOCABULARY

a Complete the sentences with the words or phrases in the box.

a place   in touch   on well   paid   to know

1. I'm going to get _____ with an old friend this week.
2. I get _____ much more now than in my old job.
3. I'd like to get _____ at a university in a different city.
4. When I was younger, I wasn't very close to my parents, but now we get _____.
5. I got _____ most of my close friends when I was in school.

b Match the sentence halves.

1. ☐ I go running twice a week to keep
2. ☐ I'm healthy now, but I used to be
3. ☐ I prefer to exercise than go
4. ☐ I don't like cats because I'm
5. ☐ When I study a lot, I often put on

a overweight.
b on a diet.
c fit.
d weight.
e allergic to them.

3 WORDPOWER *change*

a Is *change* a verb or a noun in sentences 1–8? Write noun (*N*) or verb (*V*).

1. ☐ I just want to **change** into something more comfortable.
2. ☐ I have a difficult journey to work – I have to **change** trains twice and take a bus.
3. ☐ You've given me the wrong **change** – I gave you $10, not $5.
4. ☐ I've **changed my mind** – I'm going to stay in tonight.
5. ☐ I always keep some **change** in the car to pay for parking.
6. ☐ We usually go shopping on Saturdays, but we're playing football **for a change**.
7. ☐ Before my trip to Mexico, **I changed** some euros into pesos.

b Match the words in **bold** in 3a with meanings a–g.

Verbs
a ☐ get off a train, bus or plane and get on a different one
b ☐ put different clothes on
c ☐ exchange money for different notes or coins
d ☐ make a different decision

Nouns
e ☐ because you want a new experience
f ☐ coins
g ☐ the money a shop assistant returns to you

c Complete the sentences with the words or phrases in the box.

change trains   change my mind   change into
keep some change   the right change
for a change   change some money

1. I always _____ in my pocket.
2. I usually _____ comfortable clothes when I get home in the evening.
3. I have to _____ on my way home.
4. I usually go to the mountains, but this year I'm going on a beach holiday _____.
5. I think it's better to _____ before you go abroad.
6. I don't often _____ after I've made a decision.
7. When I buy things, I always check that the shop assistant gives me _____.

d 💬 Which of the sentences in 3c are true for you?

🔄 REVIEW YOUR PROGRESS

How well did you do in this unit? Write 3, 2 or 1 for each objective.
3 = very well   2 = well   1 = not so well

I CAN ...	
talk about life-changing events	☐
describe health and lifestyle changes	☐
talk to the doctor	☐
write a blog about an achievement.	☐

CAN DO OBJECTIVES

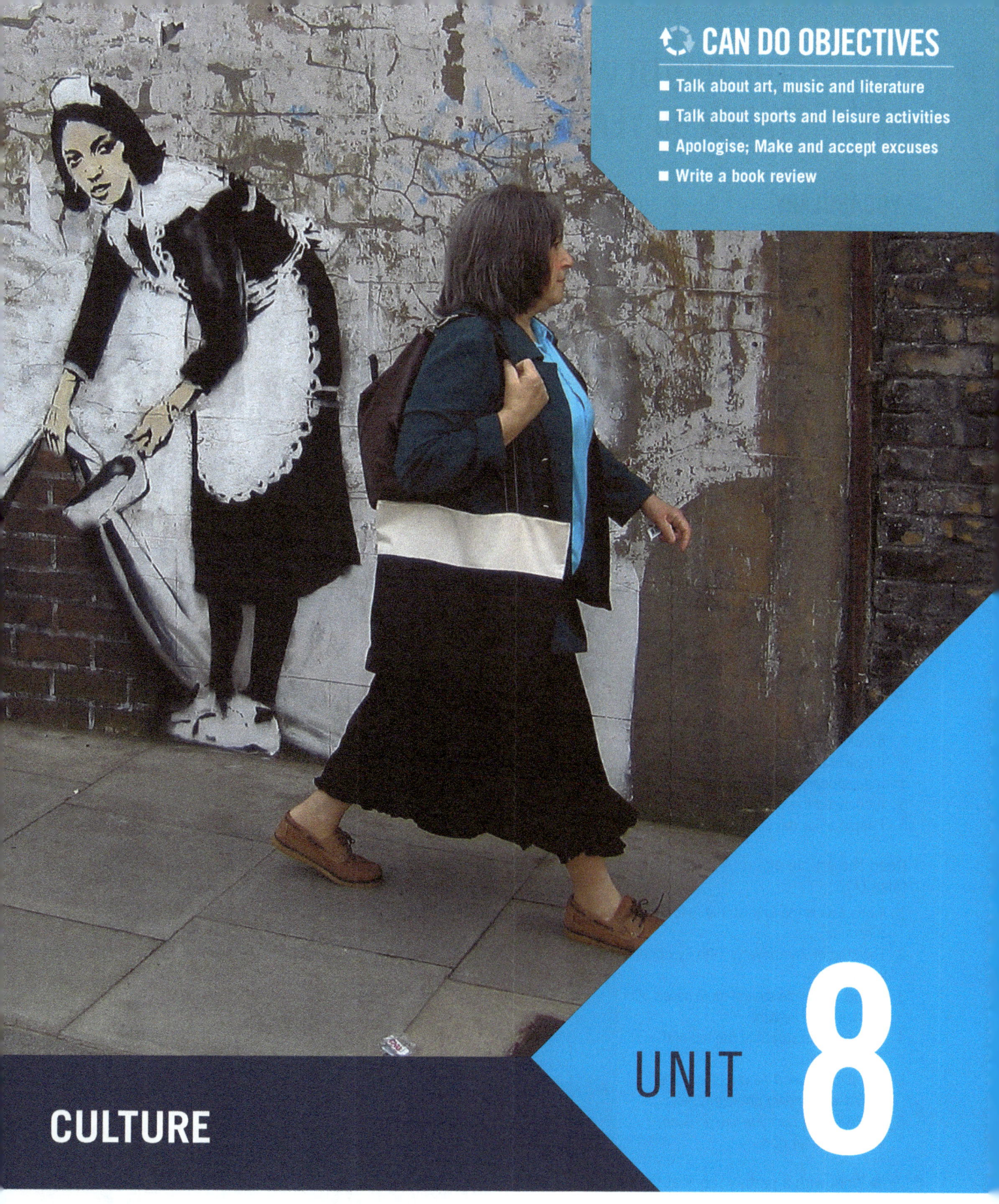

- Talk about art, music and literature
- Talk about sports and leisure activities
- Apologise; Make and accept excuses
- Write a book review

UNIT 8

CULTURE

GETTING STARTED

a Look at the picture and answer the questions.
   1 Where do you think this was painted?
   2 What do you think this painting means?
   3 Do you think this is art or graffiti? Why?

b Ask and answer the questions.
   1 What is your opinion of street art?
   2 Where are the best places to see art in your city or country?

77

8A THE PHOTO WAS TAKEN 90 YEARS AGO

Learn to talk about art, music and literature
- **G** The passive: present simple and past simple
- **V** Art, music and literature

1 VOCABULARY Art, music and literature

a Match pictures 1–8 with the words below.
- ☐ architecture
- ☐ a novel
- ☐ classical music
- ☐ a poem
- ☐ a photograph
- ☐ an album
- ☐ a painting
- ☐ a sculpture

b ▶08.01 Look at the words in 1a again. Underline the stressed syllable. Then listen and check.

c 💬 Which kinds of art, music or literature are you interested in? Why do you like them?

2 READING

a 💬 Look at the pictures and titles in the article. Which of these things do you know about? Which of them have you read, seen or listened to? Do you like them? Why / Why not?

b Read the article. Which things do the comments describe? Sometimes there is more than one answer.
1 'You can have an expensive dinner and enjoy the view.'
2 'It looks natural, but it was planned.'
3 'It took some time to become popular.'
4 'It disappeared for two years.'
5 'It changed the way people think.'
6 'People enjoy dancing to it.'

c Read the article again. Are the sentences true (*T*) or false (*F*)?
1 *Mona Lisa* is the English name for the painting *La Gioconda*.
2 The start of Beethoven's Fifth Symphony is well known today.
3 Harper Lee wrote several more novels after *To Kill a Mockingbird*.
4 There's a restaurant at the top of the Burj Khalifa.
5 The photo *Lunch Atop a Skyscraper* is by a well-known photographer.
6 ABBA's song *Dancing Queen* is no longer popular now.

d 💬 Work with a partner. Look at the highlighted words in the article. What do they mean?

e Which of the things in the article do you think is the most interesting? Why?

SIX of the BEST, BIGGEST and MOST POPULAR

Read about some of the most iconic books, music, art, and buildings of all time.

ABBA Greatest Hits

Since 70s pop group ABBA released the album *Gold: Greatest Hits* in 1992, it has sold over 30 million copies, which makes it one of the most popular albums of all time. Their hit single from 1976 'Dancing Queen' is still played everywhere, and many other bands have made their own versions of it.

Beethoven's FIFTH SYMPHONY

When Beethoven was alive, his Fifth Symphony wasn't his most popular piece of music, but now most people recognise the famous four-note introduction. These opening notes are sometimes used by other musicians to make electro dance, hip-hop, rock and roll and disco music.

LA GIOCONDA

Leonardo da Vinci's painting *La Gioconda* (it is called the *Mona Lisa* in English-speaking countries) was not always as famous as it is today. It only became really well known when it was stolen from the Louvre in Paris in 1911. It was taken by Vincenzo Peruggia, an Italian who wanted to return it to Italy. The painting was found two years later, and it is now kept under tight security.

78

UNIT 8

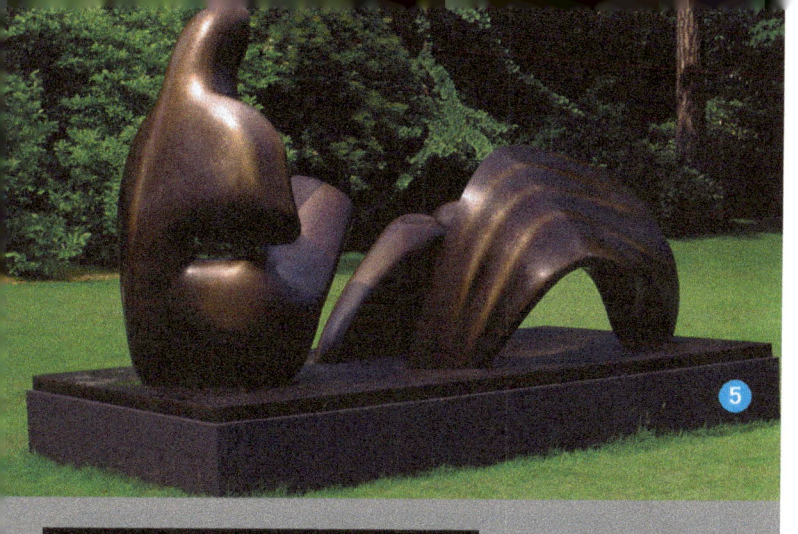

Lunch Atop a SKYSCRAPER

This iconic photo shows 11 construction workers having lunch and chatting 260 metres above Manhattan during the construction of the Rockefeller Center in New York in 1932. No one knows exactly who took the photo, nor even who the men in the photo are. In fact, the photo was set up by the photographer, who planned to use it in advertisements for the new skyscrapers.

To Kill a Mockingbird by Harper Lee

This novel examines the subject of racism in the southern states of the USA through the eyes of a young girl. It is one of the most influential books of all time. To Kill a Mockingbird was written by Harper Lee in 1957. After it was published in 1960, Harper Lee didn't publish any other books until Go Set a Watchman in 2015. Part of the reason that To Kill a Mockingbird has become so well known is that it is read in schools all over the world. It was also made into a film.

THE BURJ KHALIFA, Dubai

The Burj Khalifa in Dubai is 829 metres high, making it the tallest building in the world. It also has the most floors (163), the world's highest restaurant (on the 122nd floor) and the world's highest nightclub (on the 144th floor). Building the Burj Khalifa took six years: they started building it in 2004 and it was finished in 2010, at a cost of $1.5 billion.

3 GRAMMAR The passive: present simple and past simple

a Look at the sentences and answer the questions.
ACTIVE
Harper Lee **wrote** To Kill a Mockingbird in 1957.
PASSIVE
To Kill a Mockingbird **was written** by Harper Lee in 1957.

1 Is the information in the active and passive sentences the same or different?
2 Which sentence is about the book? _____
   Which sentence is about the writer? _____
3 How does the verb change in the passive? What are the two parts of the verb form?
   b____ + p____ p____

b ⟫ Now go to Grammar Focus 8A on p. 158.

c Underline five more examples of the passive in the article. (There are 12 in total.)

d Complete the sentences using the correct form of the verb be and the past participle forms of the verbs in the box.

| build | paint | sell | play |
| publish | write | take | enjoy |

1 The songs on Gold: Greatest Hits _____ around 45 years ago, but they are still popular now.
2 When Beethoven's Fifth Symphony _____ for the first time, the audience didn't like it very much.
3 Postcards of the Mona Lisa _____ in the museum shop at the Louvre.
4 The Burj Khalifa _____ between 2004 and 2010.
5 Today, Harper Lee's novel To Kill a Mockingbird _____ by readers all over the world.
6 The photo Lunch Atop a Skyscraper _____ in 1932.
7 Harper Lee's second book _____ 55 years after her first.
8 La Gioconda _____ by Leonardo da Vinci.

e Write down the name of two things you know about, such as books, buildings, music or paintings. For each one, write a sentence using a passive verb from 3d or from the article.
   It was built in 1750.   It is sung by Beyoncé.
Read your sentences out without naming the things you chose. Can other people guess them?

4 SPEAKING

a Complete the sentences so they are true for you.
   My favourite album is …
   A painting I like is …
   The best book I've ever read was …
   A TV series / film I've seen more than once is …
   A song I sometimes sing is …
   A poem I studied at school was …
   A sculpture/building which is famous in my country is …

b 💬 Talk about your answers to 4a in small groups.

8B I'VE BEEN A FAN FOR 20 YEARS

Learn to talk about sports and leisure activities
G Present perfect with *for* and *since*
V Sports and leisure activities

1 LISTENING

a Who do you think is an interesting sportsperson? What do you know about this person? Why are they interesting?

b Read the Fact Files about two successful football players. Do you know them?

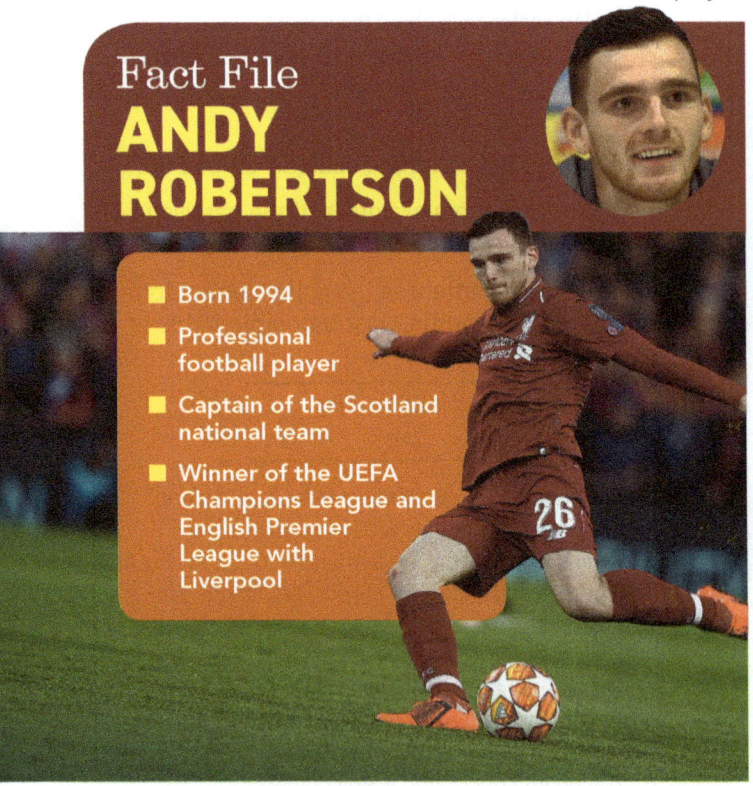

Fact File
ANDY ROBERTSON
- Born 1994
- Professional football player
- Captain of the Scotland national team
- Winner of the UEFA Champions League and English Premier League with Liverpool

Fact File
SAM KERR
- Born 1993
- Professional football player
- Captain of the Australian women's national team
- Winner of the Cup of Nations 2019

c ▶08.03 Listen to Michael, a contestant on the radio competition 'Superfans', and answer the questions.
1 What does Michael know about Andy Robertson?
2 Does he get his question correct?

d ▶08.03 Listen again. Complete the notes and underline the correct answer to the competition question.

Michael (fan)
Football fan for [1]_____
In local team for [2]_____
Andy Robertson (football player)
Playing style: [3]_____, gets up and down [4]_____, determined [5]_____
Background: started career in [6]_____, had no [7]_____, worked hard, got dream move
Activities outside football: a lot of [8]_____ work
Competition question: big fan of [9]*Celtic / Liverpool* as a boy

e ▶08.04 Listen to Kelly, another contestant on 'Superfans', and answer the questions.
1 What does Kelly know about Sam Kerr?
2 Does she get her question correct?

f ▶08.04 Listen again. Complete the notes and underline the correct answer to the competition question.

Kelly (fan)
Played football at [1]_____
Big football fan since [2]_____
Sam Kerr (football player)
Playing style: scores lots of goals; she's really [3]_____, exciting to [4]_____
Personality: a [5]_____ person, helps [6]_____ talks about [7]_____ and [8]_____
Background: started playing football when she was [9]_____
Competition question: her mother played [10]*football/volleyball/basketball*

g Think of a famous person you know a lot about. Tell your partner some facts about the person.

UNIT 8

2 GRAMMAR Present perfect with *for* and *since*

a Look at a sentence Michael said. Is he still in the team now?

I've played with my local team **for about ten years** now.

b Complete the rule with the words *present* and *past*.

> We can use the present perfect to talk about something that started in the _____ and continues in the _____.

c Look at two more sentences from the listening. Choose the correct words. Then complete the rules.
  1 I've been a fan *for / since* about 20 years.
  2 I've only been a really big fan *for / since* 2019.

> With the present perfect:
> • we use _____ to say the time period,
>   e.g., *ten minutes, three years*
> • we use _____ to say when something started,
>   e.g., *yesterday, a year ago*.

d ▶▶ Now go to Grammar Focus 8B on p. 158.

e Complete the sentences with the past participles of the verbs in brackets and a time phrase with *for* or *since*. Write four true sentences and two false ones.
  1 I've _____ (live) in my house/flat …
  2 I've _____ (be) a student here …
  3 I've _____ (have) my phone …
  4 I've _____ (know) _____ …
  5 I've _____ (want) _____ …
  6 I've _____ (own) my _____ …

f 💬 Read your sentences to a partner. Can your partner guess which two sentences are false?

3 VOCABULARY Sports and leisure activities

a Look at the pictures on the page. Which sports and leisure activities can you see? Make a list.

b 💬 Have you ever tried any of the sports in the pictures? Would you like to?

c ▶▶ Now go to Vocabulary Focus 8B on p. 139.

4 SPEAKING

a You are going to talk about sports and leisure activities. Make notes about 1–4 first.
  1 A sport or activity you do.
     • when you do it
     • who you do it with
     • why you like it
  2 A sport you are a fan of.
     • why you like it
     • how long you've been a fan
     • any teams or players you like
  3 A sport or activity you've tried, but you didn't like.
     • when you tried it
     • why you didn't like it
  4 A sport you hate watching.
     • why you don't like it
     • when you started hating it

b 💬 Work in small groups. Compare your interests and experiences. Which person in your group are you most similar to?

> Yoga is very dull. I tried it once and I fell asleep.

> I've been a tennis fan since I saw Rafael Nadal win his first French Open.

> But I love yoga. It's relaxing. Maybe you went to a bad class.

> I love tennis, too.

81

8C EVERYDAY ENGLISH
I'm really sorry I haven't called

Learn to apologise; Make and accept excuses

P Intonation for continuing or finishing

1 LISTENING

a Do your friends sometimes do any of these things?
- not call you back
- visit unexpectedly
- not reply to text messages or emails

If yes, does it annoy you? Do they do anything else that annoys you?

b ▶ 08.07 Look at the pictures. What do you think is happening? Watch or listen to Part 1 and check your ideas.

c ▶ 08.07 Watch or listen again. Answer the questions.
1 What excuse does Leo give first for not calling?
2 Is Annie happy with Leo's first excuse? What does she ask him?
3 What excuse does Leo give next?
4 What did Annie think the problem was?
5 Why does Leo say he was working so much?
6 Does Annie think this was a good idea?

d Work in pairs. Answer the questions.
1 When was the last time you apologised to someone? What happened?
2 Do you think it's necessary to apologise if … ?
   - you're ten minutes late when you meet someone
   - you don't reply to someone's text message the same day
   - you forget someone's birthday
   - you have to cancel because you're ill

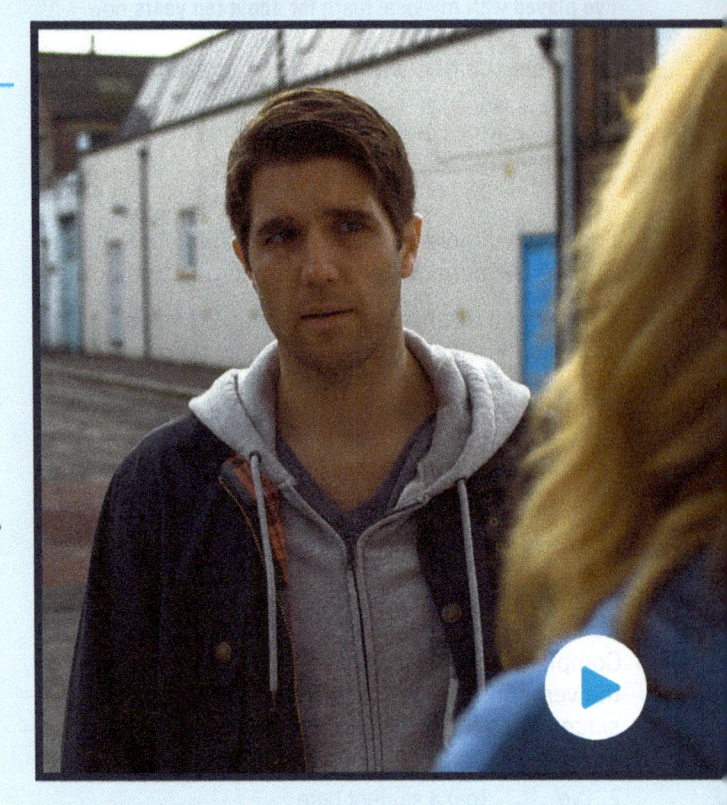

2 USEFUL LANGUAGE Apologies and excuses

a ▶ 08.08 Listen and complete the sentences from Part 1.
1 I'm _____ _____ I haven't called you.
2 I _____ call or send you a message.
3 I _____ _____ to call you, but I couldn't find my mobile.
4 I _____ _____ to make you worry.
5 I _____ to call you after I went to the doctor.
6 I _____ _____ work that much.
7 No, _____ no excuse.

b In which of the phrases in 2a is Leo … ?
1 apologising
2 giving an excuse

c ▶ 08.08 Listen and repeat the phrases in 2a.

d Complete the excuses with words from 2a.
1 I _____ going to text you, but I didn't have my phone.
2 I _____ to tell you, but I forgot.
3 I _____ work at the weekend, because my boss asked me.
4 I _____ to be so rude.
5 I _____ come to your party, because I was ill.

e ▶ 08.09 Complete the phrases Annie uses to accept Leo's apologies. Then listen and check.
1 It doesn't _____.
2 Well, it's not your _____.
3 Don't _____ about it.
4 No really, it's _____.

f ▶ 08.09 Listen and repeat the phrases in 2e.

g Work in pairs. Take turns to apologise for the situations and to give an excuse. Respond and accept your partner's apologies. Use ideas from the boxes or your own ideas.

Situations
- being late for a meeting
- not answering an email
- forgetting to pay back some money

Excuses
- lots of traffic
- very busy
- didn't get paid
- missed the bus/train

UNIT 8

3 PRONUNCIATION Intonation for continuing or finishing

a ▶ 08.10 Listen to two sentences. Does the voice in the underlined parts (1–4) go down then up (↘↗) or down (↘)?

I was going to call you, but my phone was dead.
　　　1　　　　　　　　2

I meant to call you, but I had to work a lot.
　　3　　　　　　　　　　4

b Complete the rule.

> When a speaker wants to show that they have something more to say, their voice often goes **down then up / down**.
> When a speaker wants to show the information they're giving has finished, their voice often goes **down then up / down**.

c ▶ 08.11 Listen to four sentences. Do you think each speaker has finished or has something more to say?
1　I didn't see John
2　I won't have time tomorrow
3　I was going to tell you what happened
4　I didn't call her

4 LISTENING

a 🎥 ▶ 08.12 Watch or listen to Part 2. What does Leo agree to do?

b 🎥 ▶ 08.12 Watch or listen again. What are the three other suggestions Annie makes? Why doesn't Leo like them?

Suggestion 1: _____
Leo's response: _____
Suggestion 2: _____
Leo's response: _____
Suggestion 3: _____
Leo's response: _____

c 💬 What do you think of Annie's suggestions? Can you think of anything else to suggest?

5 SPEAKING

a 💬 Work in pairs. Look at the sentences. Who might say each one?

'You still haven't given me the report I asked you to do.'

'You were driving 70 km an hour. The speed limit is 50 km an hour.'

'I'm at the café. Where are you? Is everything OK?'

'You can't sit here unless you order something.'

'Why didn't you get a ticket before you got on?'

'You forgot to buy milk again.'

'Do you know you can't park here?'

'There's a queue here!'

b 💬 What excuses could you give for each situation in 5a?

c 💬 Swap partners. Take turns saying the sentences from 5a to your partner. Apologise and give an excuse. Whose excuses are better?

> You still haven't given me the report I asked you to do.

> I'm sorry. I was at a meeting all morning. I just didn't have time.

> That's OK. It's not your fault. But I need it this week.

✓ UNIT PROGRESS TEST

➤ CHECK YOUR PROGRESS

You can now do the Unit Progress Test.

83

8D SKILLS FOR WRITING
I couldn't put the book down

Learn to write an online book review

W Positive and negative comments; *although*, *however*

1 LISTENING AND SPEAKING

a 💬 Look at the book covers. What do you think the stories are about?

b Read the summaries of the stories and match them with the book covers. Are they similar to your ideas in 1a?
1. ☐ One winter evening in Budapest, John Taylor sees a man who looks exactly like himself. But then the man runs away. Why? Over the next year, he discovers that the man has something very important to tell him.
2. ☐ A man in Florida is out in his fishing boat, and a hurricane is coming. His daughter must tell him before it's too late.
3. ☐ In Scotland, a woman is murdered. A man has just escaped from prison, and the police think he is the murderer … but is he?

c ▶ 08.13 Listen to three people talking about the books. Answer the questions.
1. Who has finished the book and who is still reading?
2. What do they think about the stories?

d ▶ 08.13 Listen again and answer the questions.

How I Met Myself
1. How does John Taylor first meet the other man?
2. What does he decide to do?

Eye of the Storm
3. Did everything in this story happen in real life?
4. What does the girl do to try to save her father's life?

A Puzzle for Logan
5. Why do the police think the prisoner is the murderer?
6. What does Inspector Logan try to do?

e Think of a book you are reading or a book you remember. What happens in the story? Make notes about:
- the characters
- the kind of story it is
- what happens / the main points
- what you think / thought about it.

f 💬 Work in small groups. Talk about your book and say if you liked it. Have any other students read it? Would they like to read it now?

84

2 READING

a Read the online reviews. Match them with the books in the pictures.

b 💬 The first reviewer gave the book three stars (= quite good). How many stars do you think the other reviewers gave?

REVIEWS

1 EDUARDO ★★★☆☆

This book is quite exciting. Even after the first few pages, you want to know who killed the woman, and you don't know until the end. It's well written, and the characters are really interesting and realistic. However, the story is quite hard to follow because there are so many different people, so I didn't enjoy it as much as I expected.

2 KATIE ☆☆☆☆☆

This is a wonderful story, although it's also very sad at the end. At first, you can't guess who the other man is, so you want to keep reading. The two men are both very interesting characters, and they are described well. I definitely recommend it!

3 TINA ☆☆☆☆☆

This book is OK, but it's not brilliant. The story is quite interesting, and it's easy to read. However, it's not very exciting because you know from the start that the girl and her friend will save the girl's father from the storm, and they will all live happily ever after. I also thought the characters were a bit dull. In real life, people are not good and kind all of the time!

4 WOO-JIN ☆☆☆☆☆

I really enjoyed this book. It was interesting to read and it describes Edinburgh very well, so you can really imagine what the city and the people are like. Although the story is quite complicated, you should keep going because the ending is very surprising. You can't guess who killed the woman until the very last page. I couldn't put the book down until I got to the end! I can recommend it.

3 WRITING SKILLS Positive and negative comments; Linking: *although*, *however*

a Look at the highlighted phrases in the book reviews. Are they positive or negative? Make two lists.

b Look at the examples and answer the questions.

The characters are really interesting and realistic. **However**, the story is quite hard to follow.

The characters are really interesting and realistic, **although** the story is quite hard to follow.

1 Do the words *however* and *although* … ?
 a connect similar ideas
 b contrast two different ideas
2 Which word … ?
 a begins a new sentence _____
 b connects two ideas in the same sentence _____

c Underline four examples of *however* and *although* in the reviews.

d Where can *although* come in the sentence?
1 only in the middle
2 at the beginning or in the middle

e Look at the two sentences in comments 1–4. Connect the two sentences in each comment using *however* or *although*. There is more than one possible answer.
1 I can recommend the book. It's difficult to read.
2 The story is a bit boring. The characters are interesting.
3 It's an exciting story. It's not the best story I've ever read.
4 It's fiction. It's based on a true story.

4 WRITING

a Think of a book you've read. (Use the one you chose in 1e or a different one.) You're going to write a review of the book. Answer the questions.
1 What are the good and bad points? Think about:
 • the characters • the story
 • the descriptions
2 What phrases in 3a can you use to describe the story?
3 How can you use *however* or *although* to connect your ideas?

b Use your ideas in 4a to write a review of the book and give a star rating (1–5).

c Work in pairs. Read your partner's review. Check their work. Does it do all these things? Tick (✓) each box.
☐ tell you about the characters
☐ give a description of the story
☐ use *however* and *although* correctly

d Read other students' reviews. Choose a book you would like to read and tell the class why.

UNIT 8
Review and extension

1 GRAMMAR

a Complete the text with present simple or past simple passive forms of the verbs in the box.

| record | direct | draw | put | write | do | use |

Studio Ghibli is one of the most famous animation studios in the world. Between 1985 and 2014, it produced over 20 animated (or cartoon) films. Most of the films ¹_____ by Hayao Miyazaki and Isao Takahata. Ghibli is famous for using traditional animation methods. Most modern animation ²_____ using computers. However, at Ghibli, every frame (or picture) ³_____ by hand. There are thousands of frames in a film! First, a script (or story) ⁴_____, and this ⁵_____ to create a storyboard. Then, artists draw the scenes. Speaking parts ⁶_____ as well as music. Finally, all the pieces ⁷_____ together by the director. It's a long process!

b 💬 Do you like animated films? Why / Why not?

c Complete the sentences with the active or passive forms of the verbs in brackets.

1 This sculpture _____ in 1870. (create)
2 He _____ some very famous photographs. (take)
3 The film _____ on a true story. (base)
4 Ash Johansen _____ the film while he was still a student. (direct)
5 The author _____ the story in a single day while he was on holiday. (write)
6 The car _____ by a company in Milan. (design)

d Correct the mistakes in these sentences.

1 We live here since 2014.
2 She's studied English since two years.
3 I've had my job from 2018.
4 They're been football fans all their lives.
5 We've been married for 2012.
6 I loved their music since I saw them at a concert.

2 VOCABULARY

a Complete the sentences with the words in the box.

| poem | sculpture | classical music | novels | architecture |

1 There's a famous _____ in an art gallery near where I live.
2 Stephen King is a great author. I love all his _____.
3 I like to listen to _____ by Mozart.
4 I can still remember a _____ I wrote when I was a child.
5 I don't really like the _____ in my town.

b 💬 Which of the sentences in 2a are true for you?

c Complete the names of the sports and leisure activities.

1 sn__b_____g   5 j_____g
2 g_____s   6 s_____h
3 wi_____g   7 g___
4 s_____d_____g   8 y___

3 WORDPOWER by

a Match the sentences that use by 1–4 with the meanings a–d.

1 Have you heard the new song **by** Drake?
2 Can I pay **by** credit card?
3 You need to bring the car back **by** eight o'clock.
4 He was standing **by** the window looking at the rain.

a near or next to
b using
c created or written
d not later than

b Match questions 1–5 with replies a–e.

1 ☐ Are you going to read your speech from a card?
2 ☐ Can I borrow a pen?
3 ☐ I didn't understand your text message.
4 ☐ Can you recommend a good Italian restaurant here?
5 ☐ Can I put this jacket in the washing machine?

a There are a few, but I think Leonardo's is **by far** the best.
b No, I'm going to learn it **by heart**.
c Yes, of course. Oh, **by the way**, did you speak to Silvia?
d No, you need to wash it **by hand**.
e Sorry, it was for someone else. I sent it to you **by mistake**.

c Which phrase in **bold** in 3b do we use to start talking about something different?

d Match the other phrases in **bold** in 3b with the meanings 1–4.

1 without wanting to _____
2 without using a machine _____
3 much more than anything else _____
4 so you can remember it without reading _____

e Complete the sentences with expressions from 3b.

1 Hello! Are you enjoying the party? My name's Mark, _____.
2 I'm sorry, I turned on the washing machine _____ and now I can't stop it.
3 This form doesn't work on the computer, so I'll have to complete it _____.
4 I think that is _____ the best film at the cinema right now.
5 When I was at school, we learned poems _____ and repeated them to the class.

f 💬 What is something you … ?
• know by heart   • do by hand   • often do by mistake

🔄 REVIEW YOUR PROGRESS

How well did you do in this unit? Write 3, 2 or 1 for each objective.
3 = very well   2 = well   1 = not so well

I CAN …	
talk about art, music and literature	☐
talk about sports and leisure activities	☐
apologise and make and accept excuses	☐
write a book review.	☐

CAN DO OBJECTIVES

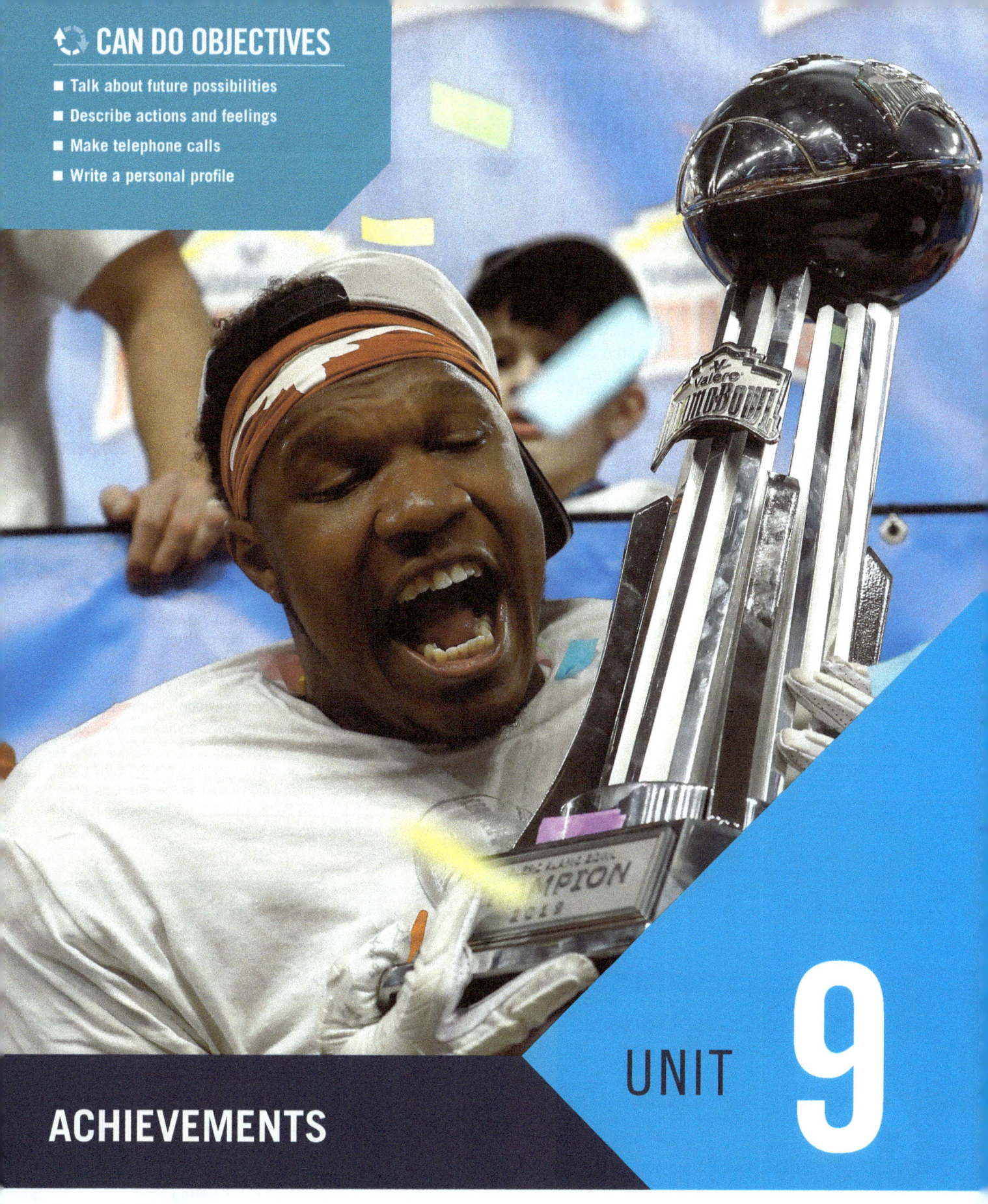

- Talk about future possibilities
- Describe actions and feelings
- Make telephone calls
- Write a personal profile

UNIT 9

ACHIEVEMENTS

GETTING STARTED

a Look at the picture and answer the questions.
1 Why is the man celebrating?
2 How does he feel now? How do you think he felt before the game?
3 How do you think he will remember this achievement when he is older? Why?

b Ask and answer the questions.
1 Think of an achievement in your life. It could be in sport, education, work or your personal life. Tell your partner about it. How did you feel?
2 What is something you would like to achieve in the next five years? Ten years?

9A IF I DON'T PASS THIS EXAM, I WON'T BE VERY HAPPY

Learn to talk about future possibilities
- **G** First conditional
- **V** Degree subjects; Education collocations

1 VOCABULARY Degree subjects

a Ask and answer the questions.
1. Do most people in your country go to university? What are three popular degree subjects?
2. Is it important to go to university? Why / Why not?

b 09.01 Look at the pictures. Match the university degree subjects with the pictures. Listen and check.

- [ ] law
- [ ] drama
- [ ] medicine
- [ ] art
- [ ] psychology
- [ ] engineering
- [ ] education
- [ ] business management

c Are the subjects in 1b common degrees in your country? Why do you think people study each subject?

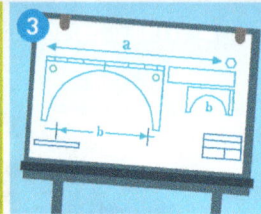

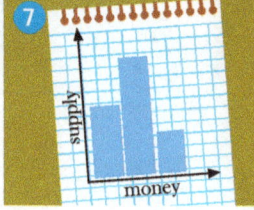

2 READING AND SPEAKING

a Read the introduction and look at the names of the degrees in the article. Which degrees have you heard of before? What exactly do you think students learn in each of the degrees?

b Read the article and check your ideas in 2a. Underline the words which tell you what the students study.

c Discuss the meaning of any new words you underlined in the article with a partner.

d Work in pairs. Ask and answer the questions.
1. Which jobs do you think people can do with the degrees in the article? What kind of companies could they work for? Could they be self-employed?
2. Which degree in the article do you think would be the most useful in your country? Which would be the least useful?
3. Which degree would be the most fun or interesting for you? Which would you do well at?

UNUSUAL DEGREES

Are you thinking about going to university? Do you think mathematics, physics and history sound boring? Well, there are a lot of unusual degrees that you might not know about. Here are some of our favourites.

Football Studies
Students learn about football and business, society and the media. They also study sports injuries and coaching. You don't need to play football to apply – there won't be any footballs in the exam room.

Citrus Studies
Yes, you can do a degree in oranges, lemons and limes! Students learn how to grow citrus fruits, which includes a lot of chemistry and biology. You'll get really healthy from all that fresh fruit!

Toy Design
Not ready to grow up yet? Then maybe you'd like to learn how to design toys for children. But don't think it will be easy just because you see the word 'toy'. Students on this course study child psychology, 3D design and mechanical engineering.

Bakery Science
Eating cake or biscuits is probably something you do for fun. But for students on this course, it's part of studying. Students learn about chemistry and how to manage production. There is a bakery at the university, so students can practise what they're learning.

UNIT 9

3 VOCABULARY
Education collocations

a Look at the words and phrases. Tick (✓) the expressions that refer to positive study habits or their results.

- ☐ pass your exams
- ☐ get low marks
- ☐ revise
- ☐ fail your exams
- ☐ take notes
- ☐ hand an essay in late

b ≫ Now go to Vocabulary Focus 9A on p. 140.

4 LISTENING

a ▶09.03 Listen to five students talking about their studies. Which speakers have good study habits? Which have bad study habits?

good habits _____   bad habits _____

b ▶09.03 Listen again. Which speaker … ? Write the letters of the speakers, A–E.

1 ☐ has just finished all their exams
2 ☐ is worried about an exam
3 ☐ has to make an important decision
4 ☐ is finding it difficult to complete a piece of work
5 ☐ knows what subject they want to study at university

c Which students in 4a are the most similar to you when you study?

Popular Music
You might think that students who do this degree just listen to pop music all day. But that's not true. Pop music involves the science of sound, production, and engineering. Students get lectures from some really important people in the music industry.

Ceramics
If you like using your hands, then a degree in ceramics might be for you. Students learn how to produce all kinds of ceramics – from fine art to dinner plates. They don't write any essays – all their marks are for exhibitions of their work.

5 GRAMMAR First conditional

a ▶09.04 Listen to the sentences and complete the missing words.

1 If I _____ , I'm going to have a big party!
2 If I _____ _____ soon, I'll miss the deadline.
3 I might fail the year if she _____ _____ me more time.
4 If the questions _____ too hard, I might be OK.
5 I'm sure I'll get the marks I need if I _____ hard.

b Look at the sentences in 5a. Answer the questions and complete the rules.

1 Are the students talking about the present or the future?
2 Are the events possible or certain to happen?
3 What tense are the verbs in the *if* clause? Complete the rule.

> We use *if* + subject + _____ to talk about a possible future situation. We use a future form to talk about the result of this situation.

c ≫ Now go to Grammar Focus 9A on p. 160.

d ▶09.06 Pronunciation Listen to the sentences. Notice the pause (//) between the two parts of the sentences.

1 If it rains this weekend, // I'll stay at home.
2 If I don't study hard, // I might not pass the exam.
3 If I see you after class, // I'll give you the book.
4 If I wake up at 10 am tomorrow, // I'll be in trouble at work.
5 If I have enough money next year, // I'm going to buy a new car.

e ▶09.06 Listen again and repeat.

f Look at the sentences in 5d again. Change the second half of the sentences so they are true for you.

g Work in pairs. Student A: Read a sentence from 5d. Student B: Ask an *if* question. How many exchanges can you make?

> If it rains this weekend, I'm going to watch TV at home.

> What if there aren't any good programmes?

> If there aren't any good programmes, I'll probably …

6 SPEAKING

a Think about your own future. Write down four important plans that you have. Think about:
- jobs
- relationships
- hobbies
- travel

b Work in small groups. Tell the group your plans. Listen to the other students' plans and ask *if* questions.

> Next week, I'm going to have a job interview in Madrid.

> Will you move to Madrid if you get the job?

89

9B I MANAGED TO STOP FEELING SHY

Learn to describe actions and feelings
- **G** Verb patterns
- **V** Verbs followed by *to* + infinitive / verb + *-ing*

1 SPEAKING AND LISTENING

a Which of these situations do you find easy? Which do you feel shy in?

1 speaking to people you don't know at a party
2 speaking to a stranger on a train or bus 
3 talking in front of a big group of people 
4 asking a stranger for directions 

b Read the sentences about shy people. Do you think they are true (*T*) or false (*F*)?
1 More people are shy now than in the past.
2 Shy people are not interested in talking to other people.
3 Technology like the Internet can help shy people.
4 Shy people often have negative ideas about the future.

c ▶09.07 Listen to an interview about shyness with Dr Lamb on a news programme. Check your answers to 1b.

d ▶09.07 Listen again. What does Dr Lamb say about … ?
1 when shyness becomes a problem
2 why technology may cause shyness
3 the worries shy people have
4 how she helps shy people

e What do you think of Dr Lamb's advice? What do you do if you feel shy or nervous?

2 READING

a Is it easy being a celebrity? Why / Why not? What kinds of problems do celebrities have?

b Work in pairs. Student A: Read about the three celebrities on this page. Student B: Read about the three celebrities on p. 91. Which problems from the list below did they have?
- family disagreements
- shyness with strangers
- language problems
- bullying
- shyness with women
- being away from home

c Tell your partner about the three celebrities you read about.

THE NOT-SO-EASY LIVES OF CELEBRITIES

JENNIFER LAWRENCE
The actress Jennifer Lawrence seems like a strong woman, and growing up, she needed to be. When she was a child, she was often bullied. During elementary school, for instance, she changed schools a lot. Every time she did, there were students who were unkind to her. Other children also bullied her because she dressed differently. Lawrence thinks this experience has made her stronger and because of it she has managed to survive in the film business. Her advice is to pay no attention to bullies 'because you come across people like that throughout your life.'

ASHLEIGH BARTY
At the age of 15, Ashleigh Barty toured the world playing tennis. But she didn't like touring at all and she missed being with her family. She decided to give up playing tennis and live at home in Australia, where she started playing cricket. She really enjoyed playing a team sport with her friends. She says that she began to feel like a normal teenager, but she also reached a high level in the sport and played in national events. In 2017, she started playing tennis again and has now become a world champion player.

SALMA HAYEK
When Mexican actress Salma Hayek moved to America, she couldn't speak English. She also has dyslexia, so she found reading and writing difficult. But Salma refused to give up. She learnt to speak English quickly, and in less than a year, she was in her first English-language film. She says, 'Some people read really fast, but you'll ask them questions about the script and they'll forget. I take a long time to read a script, but I read it only once.'

UNIT 9

d Cover the article. Can you remember who these sentences are about?
1 This person became famous at a very young age.
2 This person went to university to do a degree in business.
3 This person left home at an early age.
4 This person had a hard time whenever they changed schools.
5 This person learned to speak English quickly.
6 This person avoids meeting other artists.
Read the text again and check.

e Answer the questions in pairs.
1 Who does Lady Gaga feel shy around?
2 Does Salma Hayek think it's better to read a script quickly?
3 How did bullying help Jennifer Lawrence's career?
4 Why did Ashleigh Barty feel good when she took a break from tennis?
5 How did Ed Sheeran first become well-known?
6 What did Benicio Del Toro's father want him to do?

f Who do you think had the most difficult problem to deal with? Do you admire any of the celebrities? Why / Why not?

You might think that the rich and famous have easy lives. But many had serious problems before they became successful.

ED SHEERAN
English singer Ed Sheeran is popular all over the world, but he worked hard to get where he is today. He always knew he **wanted to be** a musician, and at 14 he packed a few clothes and his guitar, left home and went to London. At first, he had no money and slept in parks, but he didn't **stop playing**. He released songs on YouTube videos and gradually reached a wider and wider audience. Although he is so well-known, he's still a very shy person, and says he doesn't enjoy having conversations at parties, especially with women.

LADY GAGA
Lady Gaga is famous for her unusual clothes and amazing performances. But she says she's actually very shy, and she **avoids meeting** other artists. She says, 'I might not be shy with people that I know, but with people that I don't know, I am very shy.'

BENICIO DEL TORO
Oscar winner Benicio Del Toro came from a family of lawyers. His father wanted him to become a lawyer, too. He went to university to do a degree in business, but before he finished, he **decided to leave** to study acting. But Del Toro doesn't regret not finishing university. His dad thought he should go to law school part-time and work on his acting the rest of the time. 'I couldn't do that. I had made up my mind to become an actor.'

3 GRAMMAR Verb patterns

a Look at the sentences below. What verb form follows the underlined verbs?
1 He decided to leave to study acting.
2 He didn't stop playing.

b Look at the table and the highlighted words in the article. Complete the table with the verbs.

Verbs followed by *to* + infinitive	Verbs followed by verb + *-ing*
decide	stop

c Now go to Grammar Focus 9B on p. 160.

4 VOCABULARY Verbs followed by *to* + infinitive / verb + *-ing*

a Find five more verbs in the article that are followed by verb + *-ing*. Add them to the table in 3b.

b Work in pairs. What do the verbs in 4a mean?

c Now go to Vocabulary Focus 9B on p. 141.

5 SPEAKING

a Choose five topics from the list below. Think of an idea for each one. Write key words in each of the boxes, for example:
• something you've **arranged to do** soon

    visit parents

• something you **regret doing** when you were younger
• something you **promised to do** but didn't
• something difficult you **managed to do** recently
• something you're **avoiding doing** at the moment
• something you **forgot to do** that was very important
• a place you would **recommend visiting** in your town or city
• something you **enjoy doing** when you have some free time
• something that you **miss doing**
• something you have **given up doing**
• something you **don't enjoy doing**

b Work in pairs. Try to guess your partner's ideas from their key words. Use the words in **bold** in 5a to ask questions.

Are you avoiding visiting your parents?

Did you forget to visit your parents?

No. Of course I'm not avoiding visiting my parents. I love visiting them.

Yes, I did. We had plans, but I forgot.

91

9C EVERYDAY ENGLISH
Who's calling, please?

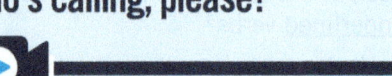

Learn to make telephone calls
- **P** Main stress: contrastive
- **S** Dealing with problems on the phone

1 LISTENING

a Ask and answer the questions.
1. How often do you use the phone to talk to friends and family? How long are your calls?
2. When do you speak to people you don't know on the phone?
3. Have you ever spoken English on the phone? Who did you speak to? Did you have any problems?
4. Do you ever find speaking on the phone difficult? When?

b 09.10 Watch or listen to Part 1. Who is Annie trying to call? Is she going to call again later?

c 09.10 Watch or listen again. Answer the questions.
1. Why can't Annie speak to Mark?
2. What does Annie ask Mark's colleague to do?
3. What does Mark's colleague offer to do?
4. What two pieces of information does Mark's colleague ask for?

2 USEFUL LANGUAGE
Phoning people you don't know

a 09.11 Complete the sentences with the words in the box. Then listen and check.

available   back   calling   got   there
possible   put   speaking   take

1. Is it _____ to speak to Mark Riley?
2. I'll just _____ you through.
3. Is Mark _____?
4. I'm afraid he's not _____.
5. Can I _____ a message?
6. Who's _____, please?
7. This is Annie Morton _____.
8. Shall I ask him to call you _____?
9. Has he _____ your number?

b Which sentences in 2a do you use if … ?
1. you are calling
2. you have received a call

c Which sentence in 2a do you use … ?
1. to say that you will connect the call
2. to say that someone else is busy
3. to ask for the caller's name
4. to suggest a future call

d Work in groups of three. You are a caller, a receptionist and a colleague. Use the expressions in 2a to have a conversation like the one in Part 1.

3 LISTENING

a 09.12 Watch or listen to Part 2. When do Annie and Mark arrange to meet?

b 09.12 Watch or listen again. Answer the questions.
1. How is Annie feeling about her work situation?
2. What has Annie done about her work problems since she talked to Rachel?
3. Why does Mark suggest Annie comes to the office?
4. Why does Rachel want to speak to Mark?

4 USEFUL LANGUAGE
Phoning people you know

a 09.13 Listen and complete the sentences.
1. Hi, _____ _____ Annie?
2. Hi, _____ Mark here.
3. Is now a _____ _____?
4. Sorry, can I _____ _____ back?
5. I've _____ _____ go.
6. Speak _____ _____ soon. Bye.

b 09.14 Correct five mistakes in the conversation. Listen and check.

A Oh hi, are you Bernice?
B Yes?
A It's Andrea here.
B Oh, hi.
A Is now a free time?
B Well, I'm a bit busy. Can I call you?
A Sure. Call me back when you're free. Is everything OK?
B Yeah, fine. But I've to go. Speak you soon.
A OK, bye.

c Practise the conversation in 4b with a partner. Use your own names.

UNIT 9

6 PRONUNCIATION Main stress: contrastive

a ▶09.16 Listen to the exchange. Which of the underlined words is emphasised most strongly?

Mark Sorry, was that three thirty tomorrow?
Annie No, two thirty.

b Why does Annie say the time differently? Choose the best answer.

1 because she doesn't understand what Mark said
2 because she is correcting what Mark said

c Work in pairs. Complete the questions about your partner. If you don't know, guess.

1 Were you born in _____? (place)
2 Is your birthday in _____? (month)
3 Do you live in _____? (place)
4 Do you come to class by _____? (transport)
5 Do you have a _____ phone? (make of mobile phone, e.g., *Samsung*)
6 Do you prefer to listen to _____? (type of music)

d 💬 Ask and answer the questions in 6c. Correct any mistakes your partner makes about you.

> Were you born in Madrid?

> No, I was born in Valencia.

7 SPEAKING

a 💬 Work in pairs. Choose one of the situations and have a telephone conversation.

Caller
1 Call reception and ask for Mr Taylor.
2 Call your friend to arrange a trip to the cinema.
3 Call your friend about the trip next week.
4 Call Mr Colson's office. Ask him to call you back.

Person receiving the call
1 Mr Taylor isn't in. Take a message.
2 You'd prefer to go to a restaurant. There's someone at the door.
3 You're very busy and you can't hear very well.
4 Answer your colleague Mr Colson's phone. Take a message.

> Hello. Is it possible to speak to Mr Taylor?

> I'm afraid he's not in …

b 💬 Swap roles and have a conversation for a different situation in 7a.

5 CONVERSATION SKILLS
Dealing with problems on the phone

a ▶09.15 Listen and complete the exchanges.

Mark Rachel explained you're looking for a new job.
Annie Sorry, Mark, ¹_____.

Annie How about two thirty tomorrow?
Mark Sorry, ²_____ three thirty tomorrow?
Annie No, two thirty.

b Look at the completed exchanges in 5a. Which phrase do you use … ?

☐ to say that you didn't hear what someone said
☐ to check that you heard what someone said correctly

✓ **UNIT PROGRESS TEST**

→ **CHECK YOUR PROGRESS**

You can now do the Unit Progress Test.

9D SKILLS FOR WRITING
Online learning is new to me

Learn to write a personal profile
W Avoiding repetition

1 LISTENING AND SPEAKING

a 💬 Look at the different ways of learning and answer the questions.

- reading about a topic
- listening to someone explain
- group work
- online or with an app
- in a classroom with a teacher
- one-to-one with a teacher
- studying on your own

1 What different ways have you experienced?
2 Are there any other ways you can think of?
3 Which ways do you prefer?

b ▶09.17 Listen to Claudia and Roberta talking about online learning. Who is worried about online learning? Why?

c ▶09.17 Listen again. Are the sentences true (T) or false (F)? Correct the false sentences.

1 Claudia's going to do an online course next year.
2 Roberta prefers learning in a classroom.
3 Roberta likes to choose when she studies.
4 Roberta couldn't meet her teachers during her online course.
5 Roberta liked reading the students' online profiles.
6 Claudia needs to have excellent IT skills for the course.
7 Claudia must do the introduction course very soon.

d 💬 Make a list of good and bad points for studying in class with a teacher and studying online.

in class with a teacher — good points / bad points
online — good points / bad points

e 💬 Work in small groups. Talk about your ideas. Decide which kind of studying you prefer and tell the group.

2 READING

a Claudia decided to do the online learning introduction course. Read her profile and the profile of another student, Gonzalo. What do Claudia and Gonzalo have in common?

b Read the profiles again. Make notes and complete the table.

	Claudia	Gonzalo
degree subjects		
languages		
reason for doing the online course		
work / free time		

Welcome Visitor

Home   Teach   Learn   Community

Claudia Mancini

Tell us about yourself ...

Hello, everyone. My name's Claudia and I'm doing a psychology degree here in Birmingham. ¹It's a great course, and I'm really enjoying it, although it's hard work. I've just finished my second year, so I've got ²one left – the hardest one!

I was born in Italy, but I came to live in England when I was about eight years old. I speak English and Italian, but I'm better at writing in English than in Italian.

How do you feel about this course?

I'm really looking forward to learning about online courses. ³They're completely new to me. I don't think my IT skills are very good, so this course might be a good way to improve ⁴them.

What do you do when you're not studying?

I have a part-time job in a restaurant. I work there one night a week and all day on Saturday. ⁵This means I don't have a lot of time for myself, but that's OK. It's not forever.

UNIT 9

3 WRITING SKILLS Avoiding repetition

a Look at the sentences. How is the second sentence different from the sentence in Claudia's profile? Underline the different words.

> My name's Claudia and I'm doing a psychology degree here in Birmingham. My psychology course is a great course, and I'm really enjoying the course, although the course is hard work.

Why didn't Claudia use the second sentence above?

b We use different pronouns to avoid repeating information. Notice the highlighted words in the profiles. Find and underline the information the pronouns replace.

c Look at these sentences from Gonzalo's profile. What is the difference between the pronouns *it* and *one*?

> I work as the manager of a gym, and that's why I want to get a degree in business management. Someday I'd like to own it, or one that is similar.

d Read Muneera's profile and change the highlighted words to pronouns.

Muneera Farzath

Tell us about yourself ...

Hello, everyone. My name's Muneera. [1]Muneera's an Arabic name, and [2]Muneera means 'brilliant.' I have a degree in international studies, which I did in English. Arabic is my first language, but I can speak and write English well.
I live in Kuwait with my family – my father, my mother and my two brothers. [3]My family all work in my father's electronics store.

How do you feel about this course?

I'm looking forward to this course, and I hope [4]this course will help me to study online more easily. [5]Studying online is something I find very difficult.

What do you do when you're not studying?

In my free time, I like seeing my friends. I often go to the cinema with [6]my friends. One of [7]my friends, Aaminah, is also taking this course, so you'll meet [8]Aaminah here, too!

4 WRITING

a Write a student profile about yourself for an online English language course. Use the same headings as the students on this page. Make notes.
- Tell us about yourself …
- How do you feel about this course?
- What do you do when you're not studying?

b Write your student profile. Make sure you use pronouns to avoid repeating information.

c Work in pairs. Exchange profiles. Check that your partner has used pronouns to avoid repetition.

Gonzalo Lopez

Tell us about yourself ...

Hi, everyone. I'm Gonzalo and I come from Mexico. Next year, I really want to start working on a business degree. I've already got one in sports science. I did it here in Mexico City, but [6]it was in English, not in Spanish. I'm sure you've already guessed that I can speak Spanish as well as English – [7]it's my first language, after all.

How do you feel about this course?

If I pass this online introduction course and an English test, then I'll get a place at the business school. I'm excited about being in Mexico while studying with people in the UK. [8]It's really cool.

What do you do when you're not studying?

I work as the manager of a gym, and that's why I want to get a degree in business management. Someday I'd like to own it, or [9]one that is similar. In my free time, I watch sports. I'll watch any sport and I'll try anything, but my favourite sport is football. I also have a girlfriend, Janina. Luckily, she likes football, too, so I can watch matches with [10]her!

95

UNIT 9
Review and extension

1 GRAMMAR

a Choose the correct answers.
1 If I *study / will study* hard, I think I'll pass my exams.
2 I *go / 'm going to go* on holiday later in the year if my boss lets me.
3 If I *don't / won't* go to the lesson, I might miss something.
4 I might get a pay rise if I *work / 'll work* hard this year.
5 I *might buy / buy* tickets for the concert next week if I have enough money.
6 If I *won't / can't* find a job in my country, I'll move abroad.

b Complete the conversation between a careers adviser and a student with the best answers.
A So have you thought about what to do after your course?
B I've decided ¹*to leave / leaving* education and find a job.
A OK, and what kind of job do you want ²*to do / doing*?
B I'm not sure, but I need to start ³*to think / thinking* about it!
A Well, let's think about the work environment. Imagine ⁴*to work / working* in an office – does that sound good?
B Not really. I really love ⁵*to be / being* outside. And I don't like ⁶*to use / using* computers.
A OK, I'd like you to go away and make a list of outdoor jobs you could do. Then we can arrange ⁷*to talk / talking* again.
B All right, I'll come back next week.
A Great. And don't forget ⁸*to bring / bringing* the list!

c 💬 Practise the conversation in 1b.

2 VOCABULARY

a Write the names of the degree subjects.
1 I'm learning to become an actor. d _ _ _ a
2 When I finish, I'm going to work as a teacher.
   e _ _ _ _ _ _ _ _ n
3 I'm going to study this so I can become a doctor.
   m _ _ _ _ _ _ e
4 I want to be a manager at a big company one day.
   b _ _ _ _ _ _ s m _ _ _ _ _ _ _ _ _ t
5 I'm learning to design roads and bridges.
   e _ _ _ _ _ _ _ _ _ _ g
6 I study how the brain works. p _ _ _ _ _ _ _ _ y

b Complete the sentences with the verbs in the box.

fail   get (x2)   hand in   revise   take

1 If you _____ into a good university, you'll find a good job.
2 It's important to _____ notes when you're in the lesson.
3 It's embarrassing to _____ an exam.
4 It's difficult to _____ good marks without studying.
5 It's a bad idea not to _____ until the evening before you have an exam.
6 If you _____ work late, the teacher should give you zero.

c 💬 Do you disagree with any of the sentences in 2b?

3 WORDPOWER Multi-word verbs with *put*

a Match sentences 1–6 with the replies a–f.
1 ☐ Where are your chemistry notes?
2 ☐ Have you seen my glasses?
3 ☐ Don't you have a meeting with your teacher today?
4 ☐ Come on – the exam starts in 20 minutes.
5 ☐ Can I borrow your dictionary?
6 ☐ Are you still on the phone?

a I think you **put** them **down** there, next to your books.
b I **put** them **away** in my notebook after I finished studying.
c OK – but **put** it **back** in my bag once you're finished.
d Yes. I'm waiting for them to **put** me **through** to the right person.
e I just want to **put on** my coat. It's always cold in that big room.
f No, she **put** it **off** until next week – she's too busy at the moment.

b Match the multi-word verbs with *put* in 3a with the meanings.
1 ☐ decide to do something later than you planned
2 ☐ start to wear
3 ☐ put something in the place where you usually keep it
4 ☐ put an object on the floor or on top of something
5 ☐ connect someone on the telephone to the person they want to speak to
6 ☐ return something to the place it was before

c Complete the sentences with expressions with *put*.
1 My mum <u>puts</u> her things <u>down</u> and then can't find them!
2 After I do the washing, I _____ my clean clothes _____ in the wardrobe.
3 I _____ my work _____ until I really need to do it.
4 Most receptionists _____ you _____ to the right person when you call.
5 I _____ _____ my favourite clothes at weekends.
6 I _____ things _____ when I've finished using them.

d 💬 Work in pairs. Which of the sentences in 3c are true for you?

🔄 REVIEW YOUR PROGRESS

How well did you do in this unit? Write 3, 2 or 1 for each objective.
3 = very well   2 = well   1 = not so well

I CAN ...	
talk about future possibilities	☐
describe actions and feelings	☐
make telephone calls	☐
write a personal profile.	☐

96

CAN DO OBJECTIVES

- Talk about moral dilemmas
- Describe problems with goods and services
- Return goods and make complaints
- Write an apology email

UNIT 10

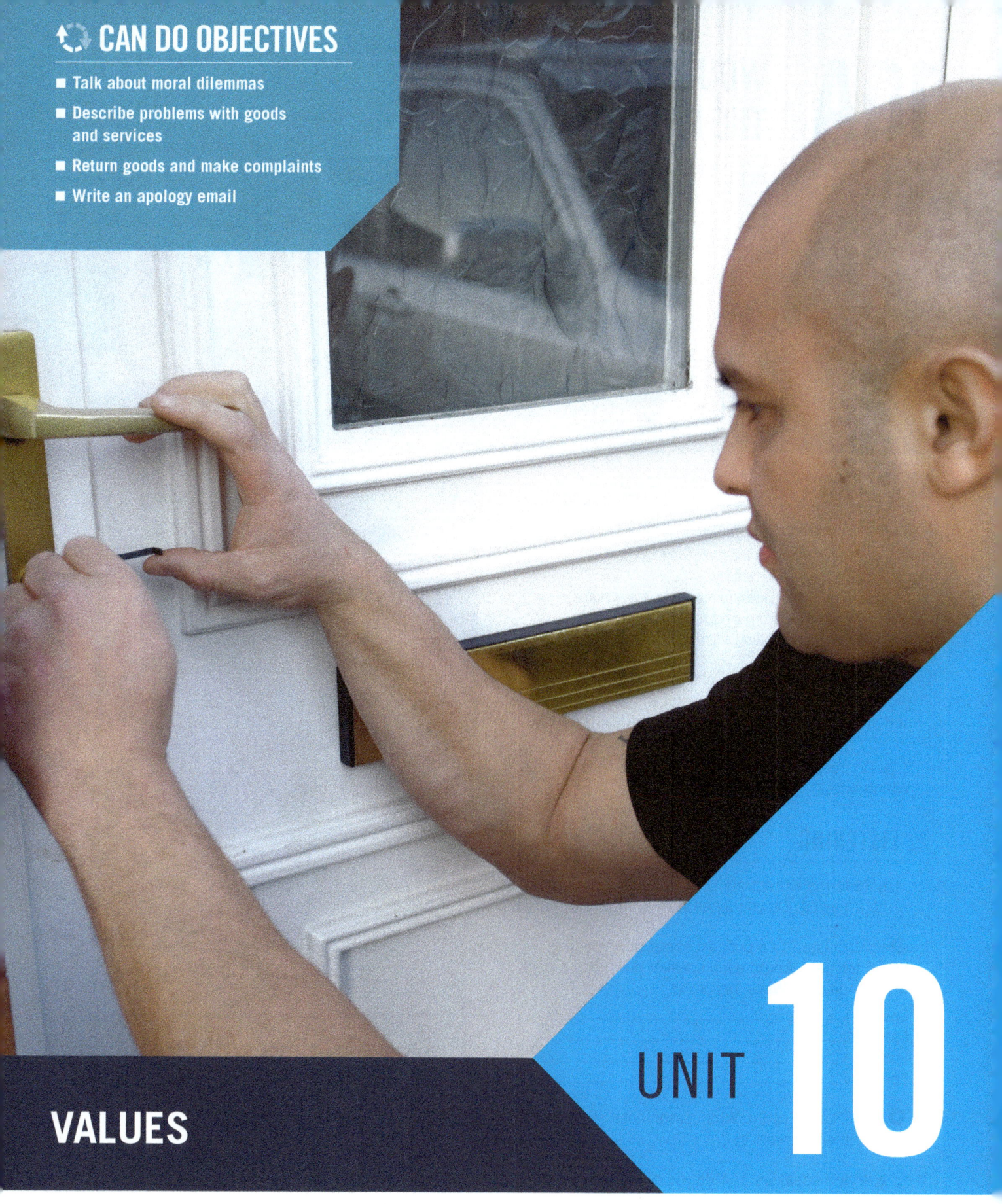

VALUES

GETTING STARTED

a 💬 Describe what is happening in the picture. Do you think the man is breaking the law? Why / Why not?

b 💬 What do you think happens next? Think of three ideas.

c 💬 Ask and answer the questions.
1 Imagine you looked out of your window and saw this happening. What would you do?
2 Would your answer be the same if … ?
- it was at night
- you were abroad
- you knew the man
- you were out with friends

Explain your answers.

97

10A WOULD YOU DO THE RIGHT THING?

Learn to talk about moral dilemmas
- G Second conditional
- V Multi-word verbs

1 SPEAKING

a Match the activities to pictures 1–5.
- a ☐ driving too fast on the motorway
- b ☐ parking your car illegally
- c ☐ taking printer paper from work to use at home
- d ☐ taking a towel from a hotel
- e ☐ illegally downloading a film from the Internet

b Work in pairs. Which of the things in the pictures do you think is the worst thing to do? Put the activities in order from 1 (worst) to 5 (least bad).

c Do people in your country often do these things? Which ones?

2 LISTENING

a Read the extract about downloading books without paying. Do you agree with Philip Pullman?

b ▶ 10.01 Listen to a podcast about downloading books for free. Would each speaker download a book without paying? Write *Yes* or *No*.

Speaker 1 _____
Speaker 2 _____
Speaker 3 _____
Speaker 4 _____

c ▶ 10.01 Listen again. What reason does each speaker give for their answers in 2b?

d Which speakers 1–4 do you disagree with? Which speakers do you feel similar to?

Downloading without paying is wrong, says author Philip Pullman

Philip Pullman, the author of the famous *His Dark Materials* book series, says that downloading books illegally is 'the very opposite of freedom of speech' because it makes it harder for writers to earn money from their work. He says this harms both writers and readers, because if writers can't make money from writing, then the number of books available will go down.

3 GRAMMAR Second conditional

a ▶10.02 Complete the sentences from the listening with a verb. Listen and check.
1 I'd try to download it for free if I really _____ to read it.
2 If it _____ in the library, you could get it for free anyway.
3 If I _____ it for my studies, I'd look for a site where I could download it.
4 I'd download it without paying if I _____.
5 If I _____ in a bookshop and I _____ a book I liked, I wouldn't steal it.
6 Well, if it _____ available and I really _____ to read it, I might download it as an ebook.

b Look at the sentences in 3a. Choose the correct option, a or b, to complete the sentences.
1 We use the second conditional to talk about … .
   a a real future situation
   b an imagined present or future situation
2 The verb form that follows *if* is … .
   a a present tense
   b a past tense
3 The highlighted verbs in 3a are … .
   a *would* + infinitive
   b *had* + infinitive

c ▶▶▶ Now go to Grammar Focus 10A on p. 162.

d ▶10.04 Pronunciation Listen to the sentences. Notice how the vowel sounds in **bold** are pronounced.
1 W**ou**ld you download it without paying?
2 Yes, I w**ou**ld.
3 No, I w**ou**ldn't.
4 I w**ou**ldn't steal it.
5 Why w**ou**ld you pay?

e ▶10.04 Listen again and answer the questions about the sentences in 3d.
1 Do you hear the /l/ or is it silent?
2 When is *would* (or *wouldn't*) unstressed? Tick (✓) one.
   ☐ questions   ☐ negatives   ☐ short answers
3 When *would* is unstressed, is it pronounced … ?
   ☐ /wʊd/   ☐ /wəd/

f Think of two different ideas to complete each sentence.
1 If it wasn't against the rules, … I'd listen to music at work.
2 If it wasn't so expensive, …
3 … if I practised.

g 💬 Compare your sentences with your partner's.

If it wasn't against the rules, I'd play my music at work.   *Why?*   *It helps me concentrate!*

4 VOCABULARY Multi-word verbs

a 💬 What's happening in each picture below? Choose the best thing to do next in each situation.

- **carry on** driving
- **stop** and look at the damage

- **look after** a lost cat
- **not do** anything

- **hand in** lost money to the police station
- **look for** the person who dropped it

- **put off** your plans
- **say no**

Can you finish this tonight?

Dinner - Georgie 7:00pm

b Look at the multi-word verbs in **bold**. Match them with the dictionary definitions.
1 _____ protect something or someone, and provide the things they need
2 _____ decide or arrange to do something at a later time
3 _____ continue doing something
4 _____ give something to someone in a position of authority

c ▶▶▶ Now go to Vocabulary Focus 10A on p. 142.

5 SPEAKING

a 💬 Ask and answer the questions.
1 Do you always tell the truth? Why / Why not?
2 Who is the most honest person you know? Why did you choose that person?

b ▶▶▶ Communication 10A How honest is your partner? Do the quiz to find out. Student A: Go to p. 131. Student B: Go to p. 132.

10B I'M TOO EMBARRASSED TO COMPLAIN

Learn to describe problems with goods and services

G Quantifiers; *too / not enough*
V Noun formation

1 READING AND SPEAKING

a In your country, is it OK to complain in a shop? What do people complain about?

b What are these people complaining about? Match the complaints 1–4 with the words in the box.

service   quality   price   delivery

1 The pizza is much cheaper in the other restaurant.
2 I bought this watch last week, and it's already broken.
3 I ordered the rug two weeks ago, but it hasn't arrived yet.
4 I've been in this queue for 20 minutes now – they're so slow.

c Have you had any similar problems to those in 1b recently?

d Read the first sentence of the article below. Does the information surprise you?

e Read the text quickly and underline:
1 the top four nations of complainers in Europe
2 the survey questions
3 what British people complain about most
4 the maximum time British people are happy to queue
5 the most common reason not to complain.

f Read the text again. Are there any things that people in your country wouldn't complain about but British people do? Why / Why not?

2 GRAMMAR Quantifiers; *too / not enough*

a Look at the complaints and answer the questions.

The service is <u>not</u> good <u>enough</u>.
Thirty-one percent are <u>too</u> embarrassed to complain.
There are<u>n't enough</u> shop assistants.
The queue is<u>n't</u> moving quickly <u>enough</u>.
There are <u>too many</u> people in the pool.
There's <u>too much</u> salt on my food.

1 Which of the underlined words say something is ... ?
   a   more than the right amount
   b   less than the right amount
2 Do we put *enough* before or after ... ?
   a   adjectives   b   adverbs   c   nouns
3 Which word do we use after *too* with ... ?
   a   countable nouns
   b   uncountable nouns

b Now go to Grammar Focus 10B on p. 162.

c Choose the correct options to complete the complaints.
1 The water was *too much / too* cold.
2 There were *too much / too many* children running around.
3 The room wasn't *warm enough / enough warm*.
4 There was *too / too much* noise, so we couldn't hear everything.
5 There weren't *enough seats / seats enough* for everyone.
6 We didn't stop for *long enough / enough long* in each place.

d What do you think the situation was for each complaint in 2c?

The BIGGEST COMPLAINERS in EUROPE

A recent survey has found that British people complain more than the people of any other European nation. Ninety-six percent of British people said that they would complain if they received poor service in a shop. The top four complaining nations also included Germany, Italy and Sweden.

In the survey, shoppers across Europe were asked how often, why and when they complain. Shoppers who don't complain were asked why not.

What do the British complain about?

The most common reason British shoppers give for a complaint is that the service is not good enough. If there aren't enough shop assistants or the queue isn't moving quickly enough, the British get angry. The British love a well-organised queue. When asked how long they queue before they get annoyed, they said more than five minutes was too long. Poor-quality products, rude staff and delivery problems are also common reasons. Seventy-six percent of British shoppers feel, 'If customers don't complain, companies can't improve.'

Why do some choose not to complain?

For the few British people who don't complain, 42% don't have time, 37% feel it doesn't help and 31% feel too embarrassed.

COMPLAINTS around the WORLD

A recent survey has revealed the countries where people like to complain the most. The survey asked 30,000 people in 30 different countries the question, 'Have you made a complaint in the last 12 months?'

At the top of the list was the UK, with Sweden second and Australia third. At the bottom of the list were Saudi Arabia, China and Poland.

TOP TEN	BOTTOM TEN
1 UK	30 Saudi Arabia
2 Sweden	29 China
3 Australia	28 Poland
4 Canada	27 Russia
5 USA	26 Turkey
6 Brazil	25 Spain
7 Argentina	24 Egypt
8 South Africa	23 Thailand
9 France	22 Indonesia
10 Venezuela	21 Japan

3 LISTENING

a Look at the results of an international survey above. Where is your country on the list? If it's not there, where on the list do you think it would be?

b 10.07 Listen to a radio programme about the survey. Answer the questions.
1 What two countries are the guests from?
2 Are the guests surprised by the survey results?

c 10.07 Listen again. Answer the questions.
1 What two reasons does the first guest give for why people in her country complain more these days?
2 What does the second guest say are two advantages of buying things online in his country?

d Is your country similar to the guests' countries?

e Work in pairs. Complete the sentences to make seven good pieces of advice.
1 Don't wait to complain. Do it _____ the problem happens.
2 Be polite: Choose your words carefully, and don't _____.
3 Be clear: Give a good _____ of the problem.
4 Give the company a time limit. Say you want a _____ within ten days.
5 Don't be afraid to go to the top: Speak to the _____, or write to the _____ of the company.
6 Email is usually the best way to complain: You can _____ the problem in detail and avoid getting too _____.
7 Tell them how you _____. Say how the problem spoiled your _____.

f 10.08 Now listen to an interview with an expert on complaining. Is his advice the same as yours?

g Ask and answer the questions.
1 Which advice from the listening would work in your country? Which advice wouldn't? Why?
2 Is there any different advice you would give to a visitor to your country if they wanted to complain about something?

4 VOCABULARY Noun formation

a Complete the table with words from this lesson.

Verb	Noun
_____	choice
complain	_____
deliver	_____
_____	explanation
decide	_____
describe	_____
enjoy	_____
_____	queue

b 10.09 Pronunciation Listen to the words in 4a. Underline the stressed syllable in each word.

c 10.09 Listen again. Notice when the vowel sound changes, for example, ch**oo**se /uː/ ch**oi**ce /ɔɪ/. Then listen again and repeat.

d Complete the sentences with words from 4a.
1 Do you have a good c_____ of shops where you live?
2 When was the last time you made a c_____ in a shop?
3 Why did the product break? What was the company's e_____?
4 Have you ever bought something online that was different from the d_____ when it arrived?
5 Have you ever had a problem with the d_____ of something you bought?
6 What's the worst d_____ you've ever made when buying something?

e Ask and answer the questions in 4d.

5 SPEAKING

Ask and answer the questions. Who is the biggest complainer?

1 Would you complain if … ?
   • your bill at a restaurant was a bit too high
   • you booked a hotel room with one large bed, but you got a room with two single beds
   • you ordered a pizza, but they delivered the wrong one
   • you ordered something online and it arrived a week late
   • you couldn't hear a film in the cinema because other people were too noisy
2 How would you complain in each situation? What would you say?

10C EVERYDAY ENGLISH
Can I exchange it for something else?

Learn to return goods and make complaints

P Sentence stress
S Sounding polite

1 LISTENING

a What reasons can you think of for returning each of these things to a shop?
- a pair of jeans
- a fitness tracker
- a sandwich
- a present you've received

b Look at the notice in a shop. Match the highlighted words with the definitions.

> **For customers who wish to return goods to this shop**
>
> We will give a refund or exchange your goods for products of equal value if:
> i) you bought the goods less than 14 days ago
> ii) you have a receipt.
>
> Thank you for shopping with us.

1 _____ a piece of paper that shows how much you paid for something
2 _____ to change a product you bought for a different one
3 _____ money given to you when you return something to a shop
4 _____ _____ things that are sold in a shop

c Are the rules in 1b the same as shops in your country? Do all shops in your country have the same rules? Explain any differences.

d 10.10 Watch or listen to Part 1. What does Leo want to return? Why? Why isn't it possible?

2 USEFUL LANGUAGE
Returning goods and making complaints

a 10.10 Look at the phrases. Which of the phrases did you hear in Part 1? Watch or listen again and check. Tick (✓) the phrases.

Returning something to a shop
☐ Could you help me, please?
☐ I'd like to return this clock, please.
☐ It doesn't fit.
☐ I've changed my mind.
☐ It was a present, but [I've already got one].
☐ I'd like a refund.
☐ Can I exchange it for something else?

Complaining
☐ Could I speak to the manager, please?
☐ I'd like to make a complaint.
☐ I've been here for [a very long time].
☐ Your sales assistant hasn't been very helpful.
☐ This isn't what I ordered.
☐ It doesn't work.

b Look at the phrases you didn't tick in 2a. What shopping situations could you use them in?

c 10.11 Now look at the phrases that shop assistants use. Complete them with the missing words. Listen and check.

| refund | receipt | replace | sorry | right away | exchange |

1 Would you like to _____ it for something?
2 Do you have a _____?
3 I'm terribly _____ …
4 I'll ask someone to look at that for you _____.
5 I'll _____ it immediately.
6 I'll give you a full _____.

d Complete the conversations with words from 2a and 2c. Where are the people in each conversation?

1 **A** I'd like to make ¹_____ _____.
   B What's the problem?
   A This phone doesn't ²_____. It's completely dead.
   B I'm ³_____ sorry. I'll ask someone to ⁴_____ _____ that for you right away.

2 **A** I'd like to exchange these jeans please. They don't ⁵_____ – they're too small.
   B OK. Do you have a ⁶_____?
   A Yes, here you are.

3 **A** Excuse me?
   B Yes, sir?
   A We've been ⁷_____ for an hour, but we haven't ordered yet.
   B I'm terribly sorry, sir, but we're extremely busy. We'll be with you as soon as we can.
   A Right. Could I speak to the ⁸_____, please?

e Work in pairs. Practise the conversations in 2d.

102

UNIT 10

3 LISTENING

a 🎥 ▶ 10.12 Leo is going to speak to the manager about his clock. Do you think he will get a refund? Why / Why not? Watch or listen to Part 2 and check.

b 🎥 ▶ 10.12 Watch or listen again. Answer the questions.
1 What three questions does the manager ask Leo?
   • What _____?
   • Is there anything _____?
   • Why do you _____?
2 What reasons does Leo give for returning the clock?
3 Why does the manager agree to let Leo return the clock?
4 What does Leo decide to do in the end?
5 What reason does he give for his decision?

c 💬 What was the last thing you returned to a shop? Why did you return it?

4 PRONUNCIATION Sentence stress

a ▶ 10.13 Listen to the questions. Which of the highlighted words are stressed?
1 Do you have a receipt?
2 Could you help me, please?
3 Could I speak to the manager, please?
4 Why do you want a refund?
5 What would you like to exchange it for?
6 How can I help?

b Look at your answers in 4a. Which kinds of word are not normally stressed in questions?
☐ question words (e.g., why, what)
☐ auxiliary verbs (e.g., do, be, can, could)
☐ pronouns (e.g., I, you)
☐ main verbs (e.g., help, speak)

c ▶ 10.13 Listen again and repeat the questions in 4a.

5 CONVERSATION SKILLS
Sounding polite

a Look at the pairs of sentences. Which sentence in each pair is more polite? Which did Leo use?
1 a It's a bit ugly.   2 a It's not very adult.
   b It's ugly.   b It's childish.

b Choose the correct words to complete the rules.

> To describe a problem more politely, we use:
> • not very / a bit + negative adjective
> • not very / a bit + opposite positive adjective

c Write two ways to say each adjective more politely.
1 *dirty*: a bit _____, not very _____
2 *slow*: not very _____, a bit _____
3 *rude*: not very _____, a bit _____
4 *cold*: a bit _____, not very _____

d 💬 Work in pairs. Think of things you could complain about using the phrases in 5c. Make sentences.

> This seat isn't very clean.

> The waiter was a bit rude.

6 SPEAKING

a 💬 Work in pairs.
Student A: you are a customer. Choose something to complain about. Use ideas from this lesson or your own ideas. Think about:
• where you are
• what the problem is
• what you want
Student B: deal with Student A's complaint.

b 💬 Swap roles. Choose a different thing to complain about and deal with the complaint.

> Could you help me, please?

> Of course. What seems to be the problem?

> This food isn't very hot ...

✓ UNIT PROGRESS TEST

➡ CHECK YOUR PROGRESS

You can now do the Unit Progress Test.

10D SKILLS FOR WRITING
We're really sorry we missed it

Learn to write an apology email
W Formal and informal language

1 LISTENING AND SPEAKING

a What would you do in these situations? Read and make notes.
1. You invite a lot of people to a party and ask them to reply to your invitation. However, some people don't reply.
2. You go into a shop, and the two shop assistants continue having a private conversation and don't offer you any help.

b Compare your ideas in 1a with a partner.

c ▶ 10.14 Listen to Tim, Vicki and Rebecca. Match each person with a situation in 1a. Who talks about a different situation? What is it?

d ▶ 10.14 Listen again and answer the questions.
1. What did Tim want to ask the shop assistants?
2. What did he do when the shop assistants didn't help him?
3. What would Vicki do if she was the manager of a company?
4. What does she say she won't do in the future?
5. Why did Rebecca want people to reply to her invitation?
6. Why did she feel embarrassed at her party?

e Think of an experience you had where you felt someone's behaviour was rude. Make notes. Use the questions to help.
- When?
- Who?
- Where?
- What happened?
- What was the result?

f Tell a partner about your experience.

2 READING

a Read the three apology emails. Which email is about … ?
1. ☐ customer service
2. ☐ work
3. ☐ a social situation

b Read the emails and answer the questions.
1. What is each person apologising for?
2. What offer or suggestion does each person make?

c What are the relationships between the writer of each email and the person they are writing to? Which relationship is the most formal?

a

Hi Jack and Brenda,

A quick message to say we're really sorry we had to leave early last Saturday. The dinner was terrific and we had a great time. It's a shame the woman looking after the kids felt unwell and we had to go home. You must come over to our house for dinner.

We'll be in touch soon.

All the best,

Don

104

3 WRITING SKILLS Formal and informal language

a   Look at the phrases from the emails in 2a. Match 1–4 with a–d below.

	Informal language	Semi-formal	More formal
1	Hi Jack and Brenda,	Dear Celia,	Dear Mrs Palmer,
2	A quick message to say …	I'm writing to let you know …	We are writing to …
3	We're really sorry …	I'm very sorry to …	We are writing to apologise …
4	All the best, Don	Best wishes, Katie	Yours sincerely, Keith Hughes

a ☐ reason for writing   b ☐ sign off   c ☐ greeting   d ☐ apology

b   Look at the examples in the table. Which type of email does not use contractions? Why?

c   Make this email between two close friends more informal. Use the examples in 3a to help you.

Dear Mark,

I hope you are well. I am writing you a quick message to say we got the invitation to your party. We apologise, but we cannot come. We are going to a wedding that day. We will be in touch soon.

Yours sincerely,

Paul

---

d   Look at the first paragraph of each apology email in 2a. How do the writers organise their ideas?

1   apologise, then explain
2   explain, then apologise

Do they apologise and explain in the same sentence or in two separate sentences?

4 WRITING

a   You are going to write an informal email of apology. Write to Rebecca in 1a or use your own idea. Make notes using these ideas.
   • Think about how you can say you're sorry.
   • Think of an explanation for what you did.
   • Make an offer or a suggestion to make things better.

b   Write the email. Use informal language.

c   Read other students' emails. Is the correct kind of language used? Would you feel better if you received this apology?

---

b

Dear Mrs Palmer,

Thank you for your email of 22 May about the delivery problem you had. We are writing to apologise about the long delivery time you experienced. Recently, we have had a few problems and we are working hard to reduce these times for our customers.

We hope you will shop with us again, so we are offering you a 10% discount on the next book you buy from us. This is our way of saying sorry about the problems you have had.

Yours sincerely,

Keith Hughes

Customer Service Manager

---

c

Dear Celia,

I'm writing to let you know that we need to rearrange tomorrow's meeting. I'm very sorry about that.

Unfortunately, Garry has just asked me to prepare a report on the staff we have here in our London office – he says it's urgent. Could we meet next Monday afternoon instead? I'm very sorry to put our meeting off, but I have to finish this report by the end of the day tomorrow. Let me know if next Monday afternoon is possible for you.

Best wishes,

Katie

UNIT 10
Review and extension

1 GRAMMAR

a Complete the conversation with the correct forms of the verbs in brackets.

A There was an interesting story in the newspaper yesterday. A man found £10,000 in a bag on the train and he gave it to the police.
B He sounds very honest. What ¹_____ you _____ (do) if you ²_____ (be) in the same situation?
A Well, I think if it ³_____ (be) a lot of money, I ⁴_____ (keep) it!
B But if someone ⁵_____ (see) you take it, you ⁶_____ (get) into trouble. And if you ⁷_____ (hand) it in, I think the owner ⁸_____ (give) you some money to thank you.
A Maybe, but the newspaper said the owner of the bag wanted to take the man out for dinner.
B Only dinner? I ⁹_____ (expect) more than that if I ¹⁰_____ (give back) a bag full of money!

b 💬 Practise the conversation in 1a.

c Choose the correct answers.
1 I can't work here. There's too *much / many* noise.
2 It's not *warm enough / enough warm* to sit outside.
3 We had *a few / a bit of* time before our flight to look round the duty-free shop.
4 It was a great concert – there were *too many / a lot of* fans in the crowd.
5 We don't have *money enough / enough money* to buy it.
6 They don't have *many / much* kinds of bread in this shop.

2 VOCABULARY

a Choose the correct answers.
1 There isn't much *choice / choose* in the shops in my town.
2 I never *complain / complaint* in shops.
3 I'm not very good at making a quick *decide / decision*.
4 I don't believe the *descriptions / describes* of products.
5 I really *enjoy / enjoyment* going shopping.

b 💬 Which of the sentences in 2a are true for you?

c Complete the sentences with the correct forms of the verbs in the box.

| break | carry | come | feel | look | pass | join | turn |

1 Can you _____ after my bag while I get some coffee?
2 I was sorry to hear that Sara and Michael have _____ up.
3 I don't really _____ like going out this evening.
4 He got offered a great job, but he _____ it down.
5 Mrs Robson isn't here at the moment, but I can _____ on a message.
6 This is fun. Why don't you _____ in?
7 I asked him to be quiet, but he _____ on talking.
8 _____ round for coffee tomorrow if you've got time.

3 WORDPOWER Multi-word verbs with *on*

a Read the sentences. Which of the expressions in **bold** are about … ?
• continuing to do something
• wearing something

1 He was really tired, but he **carried on** jogging.
2 Louise really needs to **get on with** her essay tonight.
3 It was sunny, so he **put on** his sunglasses.
4 I don't know if I can **go on** living in this flat.
5 I **tried on** the trousers, but they weren't very comfortable.
6 It was cold inside, so he **kept** his coat **on**.

b Read the definitions of the 'continuing' expressions. Complete the sentences with the best verbs.

> carry on, go on: continue to do
> keep on: continue to do, often something annoying
> get on with: continue work or activities you need to do

1 My phone _____ on switching off. It's really annoying.
2 I'm going home now. I have to _____ on with my revision.
3 My father _____ on working until he was 80.

c Match the 'wearing' expressions 1–3 with the meanings a–c.
1 ☐ try on clothes
2 ☐ put on clothes
3 ☐ keep clothes on

a you do this in the morning or when you feel cold
b this is when you continue to wear clothes longer than normal
c you usually do this in a clothes shop

d Match the sentence halves.
1 ☐ I always try on
2 ☐ I want to carry on
3 ☐ I have to get on with
4 ☐ I usually keep my shoes on
5 ☐ In winter, I usually put on

a studying English next year.
b when I go to someone's house.
c clothes before I buy them.
d a hat and scarf when I go out.
e some really important work tomorrow.

e 💬 Which of the sentences in 3d are true for you?

🔄 REVIEW YOUR PROGRESS

How well did you do in this unit? Write 3, 2 or 1 for each objective.
3 = very well   2 = well   1 = not so well

I CAN …	
talk about moral dilemmas	☐
describe problems with goods and services	☐
return goods and make complaints	☐
write an apology email.	☐

CAN DO OBJECTIVES

- Explain what technology does
- Talk about discoveries
- Ask for and give directions in a building
- Write a post expressing an opinion

UNIT 11
DISCOVERY AND INVENTION

GETTING STARTED

a Look at the picture and answer the questions.
1. What is on these people's heads? What do you think they are for?
2. Which kinds of people might use this technology? Why?
3. Would you like to try this technology? Why / Why not?

b Ask and answer the questions.
1. What is the most interesting or unusual piece of technology you have seen or used? What did it do? How useful was it?
2. What modern problem would you like technology to be able to solve? How might this technology work?

107

11A IT'S A ROBOT THAT LOOKS LIKE A HUMAN

Learn to explain what technology does
- **G** Defining relative clauses
- **V** Compound nouns

1 VOCABULARY Compound nouns

a Ask and answer the questions.
1. Do you prefer watching TV, going to the cinema or reading books? Why?
2. What kinds of TV programmes, films or books do you like? Why do you like them?
3. Think of a book you know that has been made into a film. Do you think it's better to read the book first or watch the film first? Explain your answer.

b All of the words below can go together with the word *fiction*. Which two items form a compound noun (noun + noun)?
1 science   2 romantic   3 crime   4 historical   5 literary

c Match the words 1–5 with the words a–e to make compound nouns.
1. book _____
2. TV _____
3. film _____
4. sound _____
5. action _____

a film
b shop
c track
d poster
e series

d Look at the first word in each compound noun. Is it singular or plural?

e ▶▶ Now go to Vocabulary Focus 11A on p. 142.

2 READING AND LISTENING

a Read the summaries of three science-fiction stories. For each one, complete the information in the table.

	Robur the Conqueror	*Star Trek*	*Blade Runner 2049*
Created		1966	
Main character	Robur		
Time setting			2049

b Read the summaries again. Which sentence matches each summary? Write *Robur the Conqueror* (*R*), *Star Trek* (*S*) or *Blade Runner 2049* (*B*).
1. ☐ People want to discover new worlds.
2. ☐ The main character is a kind of policeman.
3. ☐ The main character wants to show he has the best machine.
4. ☐ A character has to find people that are like him.
5. ☐ A character takes some people on a trip around the world.
6. ☐ The characters are often in danger.

c Some of the imaginary inventions in these stories are things we have now. Which four of these inventions were predicted in the stories?
1. 3D printers
2. mobile phones
3. jet planes
4. contactless payment
5. helicopters
6. wireless headphones
7. drone adverts
8. driverless cars

SCIENCE FICTION through the YEARS

Robur the Conqueror by Jules Verne

Written in 1886 and set at the end of the 19th century, this novel is not as well known as Verne's other books, such as *Around the World in Eighty Days*. The title character, Robur, is an inventor who has built a new kind of heavier-than-air flying machine with propellers. His invention, the *Albatross*, is more powerful than traditional lighter-than-air airships and can move quickly through the sky. Angry that people doubt him, Robur kidnaps three members of a flying club and takes them on a trip around the world in the *Albatross* to show them what a great machine it is. However, the club members set fire to the *Albatross* and escape. They think that Robur is dead and his invention has been destroyed. When they return home, they build their own airship. On its first flight, it flies too high and drops out of the sky. Robur arrives in his rebuilt *Albatross* and saves the crew. Everyone agrees that he is the master of the air.

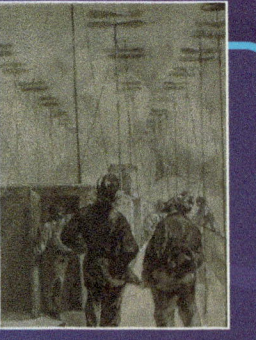

Star Trek

Star Trek started as a TV series in 1966 and lasted for three years. The series is set in the 23rd century. It tells the story of Captain James T. Kirk and his crew on the starship *USS Enterprise* as they explore space and travel to different planets. Together, they face danger and have many strange adventures. The starship *Enterprise* had a lot of futuristic inventions that seemed amazing in the 1960s. For example, there was a machine called a 'replicator', which could make food and small objects very quickly, and another called a 'communicator', which let the crew talk to each other directly when they were away from the starship. Since the 1960s, many different *Star Trek* TV series and films have been made.

108

UNIT 11

d ▶ 11.02 Listen to the podcast *From Fiction to Fact*. Which of these inventions do the people talk about? Did you have the same answers?

e ▶ 11.02 Listen again. Are the sentences true (*T*) or false (*F*)? Correct the false sentences.
1 Robur's *Albatross* moves easily in a similar way to a helicopter.
2 Igor Sikorsky designed the first helicopter in Russia.
3 After the first *Star Trek* TV series, they only made *Star Trek* films.
4 Many *Star Trek* fans prefer the first TV series to the films.
5 The *Blade Runner* films are set in the future, but they make us think about our lives today.
6 The *Blade Runner* films show a future world that is tidy and well organised.

f Work in pairs. Ask and answer the questions.
1 Which of the four inventions do you think is the most useful? Which do you think is the most enjoyable?
2 What other kinds of inventions have you seen in science-fiction books or films? Have they become real yet? If not, do you think they will become real in the future?

3 GRAMMAR Defining relative clauses

a Complete the examples with the words in the box. Notice the underlined words.

person   machines   world   stories   inventor

1 _____ which have excited readers for more than a hundred years
2 _____ that would go on to become reality
3 a(n) _____ who has built a new kind of heavier-than-air flying machine
4 a(n) _____ that looks like a human being, but is part robot
5 a future _____ where everything is clean and perfect

Blade Runner 2049

This was the second *Blade Runner* film – the first came out in 1982. Both films are based on a short story written by Philip K. Dick in 1968. The main character in *Blade Runner 2049* is K, played by Ryan Gosling. K is a 'replicant' – a person that looks like a human being, but is part robot. K works for the Los Angeles Police Department as a 'blade runner' – a replicant whose job is to track down other replicants that are out of control. In the film, K discovers an important secret that is a danger to society, and he has to find a replicant child to hide the secret. The films show what Los Angeles might look like in the future, with a crowded, high-tech environment, flying cars and images of products shown in the sky. It also questions whether human memory is more important than digital memory.

b Look at the underlined words in 3a. Complete the rules.

In defining relative clauses, use:
• _____ or _____ to describe people
• _____ or _____ to describe things
• _____ to describe places.

c Complete the sentences with *who*, *which*, *that* or *where*.
1 Robots are machines _____ do human jobs.
2 Detectives are police officers _____ solve difficult crimes.
3 Earth is the planet _____ we all live.
4 Flying taxis will be small planes _____ are like driverless cars.
5 Cyborgs are people _____ have some robot body parts.

d ▶ Now go to Grammar Focus 11A on p. 164.

e Look at the sentences. What are A and B describing?

A It's a person who gives you medicine when you're not feeling well.

B It's a thing that is very comfortable. You sleep on it.

_____   _____

f ▶ **Communication 11A** Work in pairs. Student A: Go to p. 131. Student B: Go to p. 133.

4 SPEAKING

a Have you started using any new technology recently? What is it? Why did you get it?

b Look at the inventions in the pictures. What do you think they are for? Compare your ideas with a partner.

c Check with your teacher. How many did you get right?

109

11B I THINK THEY DISCOVERED IT BY CHANCE

Learn to talk about discoveries
- G Articles
- V Adverbials: luck and chance

1 READING

a Look at the pictures and match headlines 1–3 to the stories. Which story are you most interested in reading? Why?

1. 5,000-year-old body found in the Alps
2. Farmers uncover ancient army in the fields
3. Scientist discovers how to cook food in seconds

b Now read the stories and answer the questions for each story.
1. Who made the discovery?
2. What were they doing when they made the discovery?
3. What exactly was the invention/discovery?

c Read the stories again and answer the questions.
1. How did Percy LeBaron Spencer test his machine?
2. Why weren't the police careful with Ötzi's body? What damage did they do?
3. Why don't archaeologists know exactly how many terracotta soldiers there are?

d Ask and answer the questions.
1. Which discovery do you think was the luckiest?
2. How important do you think each of the discoveries was? Put them in order from 1 to 3, where 1 is the most important. Give reasons.
3. What important discoveries can you think of from your lifetime?

LUCKY DISCOVERIES

Some of our most important discoveries happen when we aren't expecting them at all …

In 1991, two German tourists, Helmut and Erika Simon, were hiking in the mountains in Italy, near the border with Austria. They were coming back down the mountain when one of them saw something in the ice. As they got closer, they realised that they were looking at a man's body. They reported the body and carried on hiking.

When the police arrived the next day, they tried to get the body out of the ice. Everyone thought that it was the body of an unlucky mountain climber, and they weren't very careful. They accidentally tore the clothes and also broke one arm. But when scientists studied the body, they were shocked. Amazingly, the body was 5,000 years old. He was quickly given the name *Ötzi the Iceman*. Ötzi is one of the oldest, most complete human bodies ever found.

Percy LeBaron Spencer, an engineer, was working on radar for the army. One day, he was walking past a machine when the chocolate bar in his pocket melted. He was curious, so he did a test. He put a small bowl of popcorn in front of the machine. As expected, a minute later the popcorn started popping and jumping out of the bowl.

Spencer realised the microwaves from the radar were heating the food. Next, he made a metal box and sent microwaves into it through a hole. When he put some food in the box, it cooked. This was the first microwave oven – invented totally by chance.

In 1974, local farmers were digging in Xi'an, a city in China. They were looking for water, but instead they found a life-size soldier made out of terracotta. Fortunately, the farmers stopped digging before they damaged anything, and soon archaeologists arrived to look at the area. Surprisingly, there was not just one but thousands of clay soldiers. They were made around 2,200 years ago, and they were buried on purpose – together with the body of the first emperor of China.

Archaeologists now believe that there are around 6,000 soldiers and their horses in the terracotta army, but most of them are still buried underground. All of the soldiers look different. Some are tall, some are short, and they all have different clothes and faces. Archaeologists think 700,000 people helped to make them.

2 GRAMMAR Articles

a Read the sentences and the rules for articles. Match the rules with examples 1–8.

He put ¹**a small bowl of popcorn** in front of the machine... a minute later, ²**the popcorn** started popping and jumping out of ³**the bowl**.

In 1974, some local farmers were digging in ⁴**Xi'an**, a city in ⁵**China** ... Fortunately, ⁶**the farmers** stopped digging ...

⁷**Archaeologists** think 700,000 people helped to make ⁸**the terracotta army**.

a ☐ Use no article before plural nouns to talk generally.
b ☐☐ Use no article before most countries and place names.
c ☐ Use *a/an* the first time you talk about something.
d ☐☐☐ Use *the* if you have already mentioned something.
e ☐ Use *the* when there is only one of something in the world.

b ⟫ Now go to Grammar Focus 11B on p. 164.

c Complete the text with *a/an*, *the* or Ø (no article).

New Species of Lizard Discovered on Menu

In 2010, Ngo Van Tri, of ¹____ Vietnam Academy of Science and Technology, was at ²____ small village restaurant. While he was eating, he saw ³____ box of lizards on ⁴____ cooking bench. He thought they looked unusual, so he sent some pictures to ⁵____ biologist in America, L. Lee Grismer.

When Grismer saw ⁶____ pictures, he was sure ⁷____ lizards were special. He wanted to be ⁸____ scientist to make ⁹____ discovery, so he got on ¹⁰____ plane to ¹¹____ Vietnam. Then he rode on ¹²____ motorbike for eight hours to get from ¹³____ airport to ¹⁴____ restaurant. But, unfortunately, while he was travelling, ¹⁵____ restaurant owner cooked ¹⁶____ lizards and served them to his customers. When Grismer arrived, they were all gone. Luckily, ¹⁷____ nearby restaurant also had the same kind of lizard on their menu. The species of lizard was new to scientists – but not to the Vietnamese villagers!

d ▶11.05 Listen and check.

e Work in pairs. Answer the questions about the story in 2c.
1 Who discovered the lizards?
2 Why did he take pictures of the lizards?
3 How did Grismer travel to Vietnam?
4 What happened while Grismer was travelling?
5 Where did Grismer find the lizards in the end?

f 💬 Cover the story and try to tell it with a partner. Use the prompts to help you.
- small village restaurant
- box of lizards
- biologist
- plane
- motorcycle
- restaurant owner
- luckily
- new species

3 VOCABULARY
Adverbials: luck and chance

a Work in pairs. Look at the highlighted words and phrases in the four stories on these pages. What do they mean?

b Add the opposite words and phrases from the stories to the table.

1 _____	unfortunately
2 _____	
3 _____	on purpose
4 _____	
5 _____	as expected
6 _____	

c ▶11.06 Listen to the words and phrases. Underline the stressed syllables.

luckily   fortunately   accidentally   by chance
unfortunately   surprisingly   amazingly
on purpose   as expected

d Write about three occasions when something unexpected happened to you. Use three of the new words and phrases.
I lost my house keys last week. Luckily, my neighbour had an extra key.

e 💬 Compare your sentences with other students in the class. Whose are the most interesting?

4 SPEAKING

⟫ **Communication 11B** Student A: Go to p. 131. Student B: Go to p. 133.

11C EVERYDAY ENGLISH
It's straight ahead

Learn to ask for and give directions in a building

- **P** Sound and spelling: /ɜː/ and /ɔː/
- **S** Checking information

1 LISTENING

a Ask and answer the questions.
1. Have you ever got lost? When was the last time it happened?
2. Do you like to ask for directions or do you prefer to use maps?
3. Have you ever got lost in a building?

b 11.07 Annie goes to visit Mark at his office. Why does she get lost? Watch or listen to Part 1 and find out.

c 11.07 Watch or listen to Part 1 again. Complete the directions the receptionist gives to Annie.
It's on the ¹_____ floor. Go ²_____ the stairs and turn ³_____. Go through the ⁴_____ and turn ⁵_____. Then go ⁶_____ the corridor and it's the ⁷_____ door on the ⁸_____.

2 USEFUL LANGUAGE Asking for and giving directions in a building

a 11.08 What phrase does Annie use to ask for directions? Complete the question with the words in the box. Then listen and check.

is tell you can me

Excuse me, _____ _____ _____ _____ where the reception _____?

b 11.09 Match the phrases with the pictures. Listen and check. Repeat the phrases.

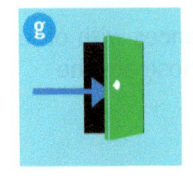

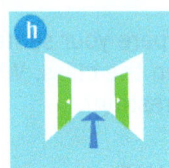

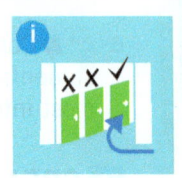

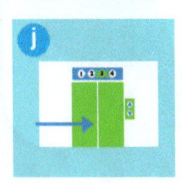

1. ☐ It's over there, by the trees.
2. ☐ It's on the second floor.
3. ☐ It's straight ahead.
4. ☐ Go through the door.
5. ☐ Go down the corridor.
6. ☐ Turn left.
7. ☐ Go down the stairs.
8. ☐ It's the third door on the left.
9. ☐ Take the lift to the third floor.
10. ☐ Go round the corner.

c Cover the phrases and try to remember the directions for each picture.

3 CONVERSATION SKILLS
Checking information

a 11.10 What does Annie do to make sure she's understood the directions? Watch or listen to Part 2 and check your ideas.

b 11.11 Read and listen to the three exchanges. Look at the underlined phrases 1–4. Which phrases do we use … ?
- to check information by repeating it
- to show we understand

R First, go up the stairs to the first floor and turn left.
A ¹So go up the stairs to the first floor and turn left.

A ² Sorry, the fourth office?
R No, the first.
A ³ Right, I think I've got that.

A ⁴So can I just check? Go up the stairs and turn right …
R No, turn left.

c Work in pairs. Student A: Write three directions for the building you are in and read each one to your partner.
Student B: Listen and repeat the information to check it's correct. Use the phrases in 3b. Then swap roles.

> Go through that door. Then go up the stairs to the second floor.

> So I go through that door, then I go up the stairs to the second floor?

> That's right.

d 11.12 Watch or listen to Part 3. What does Mark think about Annie getting a job at his company?

e Would you give Annie a job at your company? Why / Why not?

UNIT 11

4 PRONUNCIATION
Sound and spelling: /ɜː/ and /ɔː/

a ▶ 11.13 Listen to the vowel sounds in **bold**. Then listen and repeat.

/ɜː/ the f**ir**st office
/ɔː/ the f**ou**rth office

b Look at sentences 1–5. Which of the words in *italics* have the /ɜː/ sound?
1 The *third / fourth* floor.
2 On *Tuesday / Thursday* evening.
3 It's office number *thirty / forty*.
4 It's hard to *walk / work* there.
5 There's a *board / bird* in the meeting room.

c ▶ 11.14 Listen to the sentences in 4b. Circle the words you hear. Listen again and repeat.

5 SPEAKING

Look at the building. Take turns to ask for directions to different places. Give your directions from the entrance. Follow your partner's directions. Are they correct?

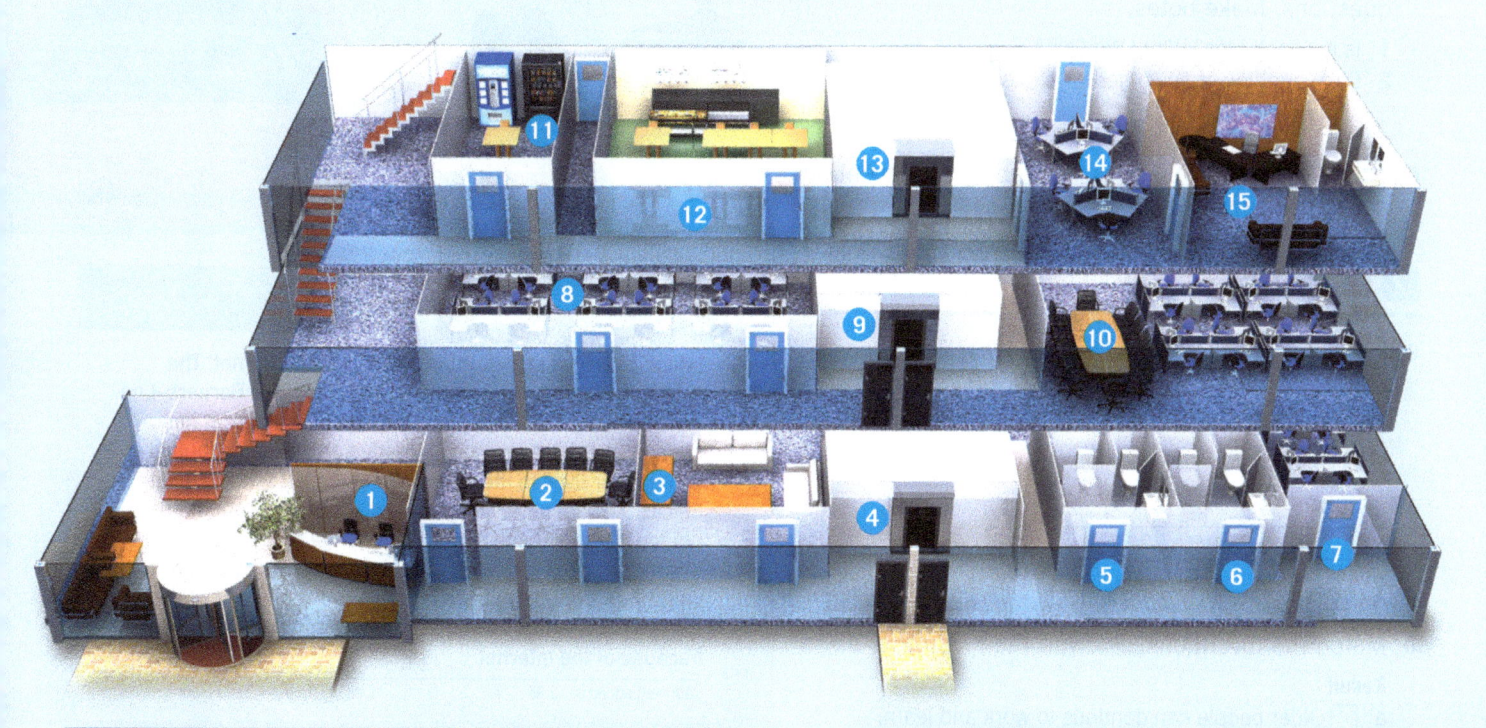

1 Reception
2 Meeting room 1
3 Staff lounge
4 Lift – Ground Floor
5 Gents toilets
6 Ladies toilets
7 HR / Finance
8 IT
9 Lift – First Floor
10 Meeting room 2 / Sales and Marketing
11 Snacks and drinks machine
12 Buildings and maintenance
13 Lift – Second Floor
14 Administration
15 Director's suite

✓ UNIT PROGRESS TEST

→ CHECK YOUR PROGRESS

You can now do the Unit Progress Test.

11D SKILLS FOR WRITING
In my opinion, it's because of the Internet

Learn to write a post giving an opinion

W Giving opinions; Expressing results and reasons

1 LISTENING AND SPEAKING

a 💬 Look at the pictures of ideas for inventions. What do you think the inventions are?

b ▶ 11.15 Listen to people talking about the inventions. Complete the first row of the table.

c ▶ 11.15 Listen again and complete the table.

	Amir	Uta	Pierre
What's the invention?			
Why is it important / useful?			
Do they think it will happen?			

d Think about each invention and answer the questions. Make notes.
  1 Is it a good idea? Why / Why not?
  2 Can you think of any other ways to solve the same problems?

e 💬 Work in small groups. Talk about the inventions and compare your answers.

2 READING

a People were asked the question, *What is the most important invention of the last 2,000 years?* Read the posts and write the names of the inventions.

Invention
  1 _____
  2 _____
  3 _____
  4 _____

b Match the inventions 1–4 with their results a–d.
  Result
  a ☐ Older people can continue to work and learn.
  b ☐ All the different sciences could develop.
  c ☐ Everyday life will change completely.
  d ☐ People could record and send information.

c Read the posts again and answer the questions.
  1 Which of the four inventions was the earliest? Which was the latest?
  2 In what way might schools, offices, etc., change as a result of the Internet?
  3 How did the invention of paper change communication?
  4 How would the world be different without numbers?
  5 How do reading glasses make a difference to the writer of the fourth post?

---

① Mark Turner

I think the most important invention is the Internet. The 'World Wide Web' was invented in 1989 by Tim Berners-Lee and now we all use it in our daily lives. The Internet has changed our lives so much already and it will continue to change our lives in the future. We still have schools, post offices, newspapers, cinemas and shopping centres, but not for long. All these things will change as a result of the Internet. For example, we may stop using shops or offices as we will do everything from home. Choose any part of the way we live today and it will be completely different in the future – because of the Internet.

Comment added at 12:35   Like | Reply | Send Mark a message

② Eva Sorensen

Around 100 CE, the Chinese invented paper, and by 600 CE paper was used all over Asia. As a result of this, people were able to write down information, keep it and send it over long distances. Paper completely changed the way people communicated, as previously people wrote on clay or stone, which was heavy and broke easily. Later there were printed books and then, in our time, the Internet, but it all started with the invention of paper. So it seems to me that paper is a really important invention, perhaps one of the most important ever.

Comment added at 11:16   Like | Reply | Send Eva a message

114

UNIT 11

3 WRITING SKILLS
Giving opinions; Expressing results and reasons

a Look at the example and underline the phrase which shows the writer is giving an opinion. Then underline four more phrases for giving opinions in posts 2–4.

I think the most important invention is the Internet.

b Look at the sentences. Correct the phrases for giving opinions.
1 From my view, the most important invention is the wheel.
2 According to my opinion, the steam engine changed the world the most.
3 I belief the car is a very important invention.
4 It seems like me that the jet engine has made the biggest difference.

c Each example 1–4 below describes a change. What is the cause or reason for each change? What is the result?
1 **Because of** the invention of numbers, science could develop.
2 Around 100 CE, the Chinese invented paper. **As a result of** this, people could send messages over long distances.
3 We may stop using shops and offices, **as** we can now do everything online at home.
4 **Because** they had reading glasses, people could stay active in old age.

d Look at the words and phrases in **bold** in 3c. Which … ?
- are followed by a noun / noun phrase / pronoun and a comma
- connect two clauses in the same sentence

| Home | Forum | Useful links | Contact us |

3 **Tomas Valnek**

I believe the most important invention is the Hindu-Arabic number system, which was invented around the sixth century in India. It spread throughout the Middle East and was finally brought to Europe in the 13th century. People could add numbers together easily for the first time. Because of this system, science could develop. Numbers are essential to almost all aspects of life, and without this invention, there might be no science, engineering or computers.

Comment added at 10:55   Like | Reply | Send Tomas a message

4 **Haruki Okuzawa**

In my opinion, the most important invention has been reading glasses. Reading glasses were invented in Italy around 1280 and they changed the world. Because they had reading glasses, people could read, stay active and work, even in old age. In my view, that's really important, especially as I'm over 60 myself. I can still do a lot of things because of my reading glasses. I don't know where I would be without them.

Comment added at 10:47   Like | Reply | Send Haruki a message

---

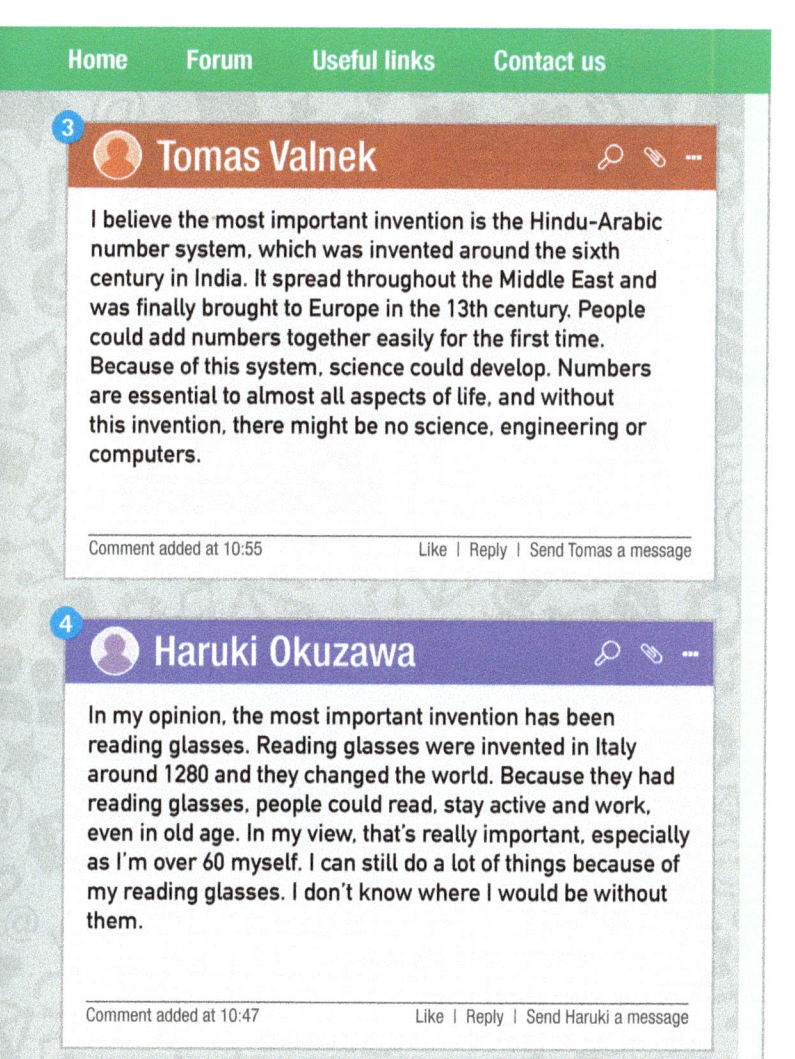

e Which two words or phrases from examples 1–4 in 3c can complete each sentence?
1 _____ they can use email, most people have stopped sending letters by post.
2 _____ cheap air travel, people are able to visit countries anywhere in the world.
3 Most people now have mobile phones. _____ this, they can now keep in touch wherever they are.

f Look at these notes about the invention of the telephone. Make sentences using:
- a phrase for giving your opinion
- words/phrases from 3c to connect a cause with a result.

> The telephone:
> most important invention /
>   19th century
>   talk to people in other places
>   we can communicate more quickly

g Write one more sentence about the telephone using your own ideas.

4 WRITING

a 💬 Choose one of these inventions to write about or use your own idea.
- cars
- planes
- glass
- photography
- boats
- TV

Think about the questions below and make notes. Walk around the class and collect ideas from other students.
- Why is the invention important?
- What good or bad results has it had?
- How was life different before?
- What other things have changed because of it?

b Write a post for the website. Remember to explain results and reasons using *as*, *because*, *because of* and *as a result of*.

c Read another student's post and respond to it. You can:
- agree or disagree and say why
- add another idea.

d Look at the response you received. Have they … ?
- agreed or disagreed with your comment
- used phrases to give opinions
- used the correct language to connect reasons and results

115

UNIT 11
Review and extension

1 GRAMMAR

a Write sentences with relative clauses. Add *be* and a relative pronoun.

1. He / the man / invented the colour TV.
2. These / the mobile phones / work under water.
3. That / the machine / makes the screens for the computers.
4. This / the place / they found the statue.
5. These / the people / discovered the ancient city.
6. This / the shop / they sell that delicious bread.

b Complete the conversation with *a/an* or *the*.

A I saw ¹_____ brilliant film last week.
B Oh, yeah? Why was ²_____ film so good?
A It was ³_____ great story. I think it's probably ⁴_____ best crime film I've ever seen. It's about ⁵_____ group of criminals in ⁶_____ USA. They want to steal ⁷_____ painting from ⁸_____ gallery.
B It sounds good. I saw ⁹_____ good film last week, too. ¹⁰_____ story's simple, but ¹¹_____ actors are great. And it's got ¹²_____ amazing ending.

c Practise the conversation in 1b.

2 VOCABULARY

a Choose two words in the box to make a compound noun for each definition 1–8.

bag   bottle   cash   kitchen   knife
lights   machine   office   road   rock
shopping   signs   star   street   ticket   top

1. You get money from this when the banks are closed.
2. This is a famous musician.
3. People go here to pay for a journey on a train or a concert.
4. These tell you what to do when you're driving your car.
5. These help you see when you're driving in the dark.
6. You put the things you buy in a supermarket into this.
7. You use this to cut things when you're making food.
8. Please put this back on when you've finished drinking.

b Choose the correct answers.

1. I *accidentally / luckily* broke your mug – I'm really sorry.
2. We thought our product was probably too expensive, and *as expected / on purpose*, it wasn't successful.
3. The money was found *by chance / unfortunately* by an old man while he was looking for a book.
4. They wanted to build a house there, but *amazingly / luckily* someone told them about the plan to build an airport.
5. A You did that *on purpose / as expected*!
   B No, it was just an accident!
6. They thought it was a modern painting. *Surprisingly / By chance*, after some tests, they found that it was much older.

3 WORDPOWER Preposition + noun

a Match the phrases 1–7 with their meanings a–g.

1. ☐ People who go abroad **on business** are lucky.
2. ☐ Buses and trains where I live usually arrive **on time**.
3. ☐ There are a lot of houses **for sale** on my street.
4. ☐ I once met an old friend **by chance** when I was abroad.
5. ☐ You should book a hotel **in advance** if you visit my city.
6. ☐ I sometimes broke things **on purpose** when I was a child.
7. ☐ You can always tell if two people are **in love**.

a available to buy
b having strong romantic feelings
c not by chance, because it was planned
d at the expected time
e without planning it
f working, but in a different place
g before something happens

b Which of the sentences in 3a are true for you?

c We sometimes use a preposition without an article before a place name. This means 'in a particular place for the usual reason'.

He's at home. NOT *He's at the home.*

Match the sentences 1–4 with the pictures a–d.

1. ☐ Mara's at work. She's an accountant.
2. ☐ My brother's at university. He studies science.
3. ☐ My daughter's not at school today. She's on a class trip.
4. ☐ The police found the stolen painting in his house. Now he's in prison.

d Underline the preposition + noun combinations in sentences 1–4 in 3c. Write a sentence about somebody you know (of) who is in each place.

⟳ REVIEW YOUR PROGRESS

How well did you do in this unit? Write 3, 2 or 1 for each objective.

3 = very well   2 = well   1 = not so well

I CAN ...	
explain what technology does	☐
talk about discoveries	☐
ask for and give directions in a building	☐
write a post expressing an opinion.	☐

116

CAN DO OBJECTIVES
- Tell a story
- Talk about family relationships
- Agree and disagree in discussions
- Write a short story

UNIT 12

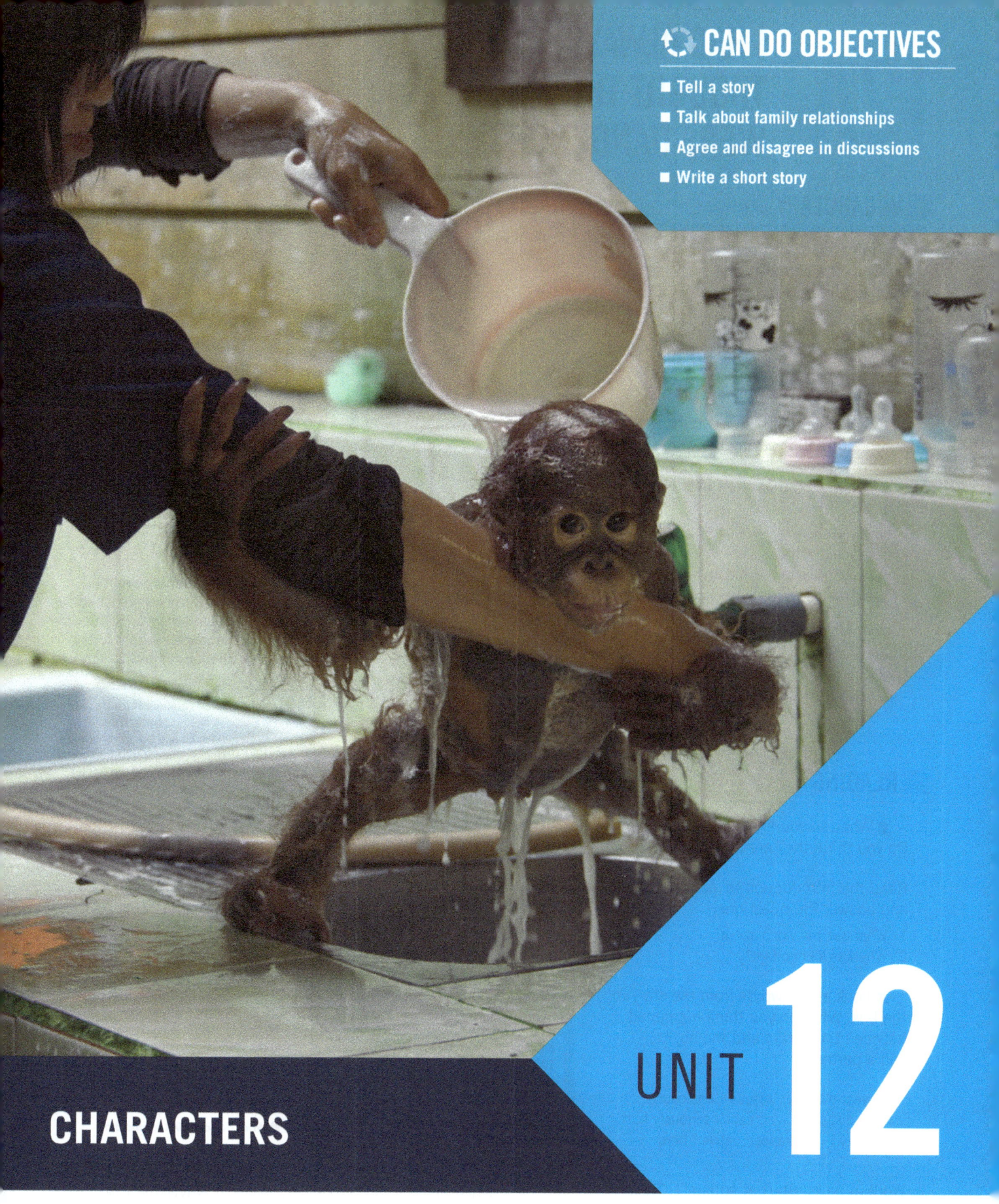

CHARACTERS

GETTING STARTED

a Look at the picture and answer the questions.
1. What kind of animal is this? What kind of place is it in?
2. What is the woman's job? Do you think she enjoys it? Why?
3. Would you enjoy this job? Why / Why not?

b Ask and answer the questions.
1. Do you think some animals have personalities? Explain your answer.
2. How can people help animals? How can animals help people?

117

12A I HAD ALWAYS THOUGHT THEY WERE DANGEROUS

Learn to tell a story
- G Past perfect
- V Animals

1 VOCABULARY Animals

a In pairs, match pictures 1–8 with the names of the animals below.

☐ whale ☐ mosquito
☐ spider ☐ gorilla
☐ tiger ☐ parrot
☐ camel ☐ bee

b ▶12.01 Listen and check your answers. Practise saying the words in 1a.

c Which of the animals in the pictures … ?
1 have you seen
2 have you touched
3 would you like to see and why
4 would you be scared to be close to and why

> I saw a whale when I was in Sri Lanka.

> I'm not frightened of most spiders, but this one probably bites.

2 READING

a What do you know about gorillas? Do you think they are dangerous?

b Read the introduction to *Jambo's Story* and answer the questions.
1 What was the video about?
2 Why was it important?

c Look at the words from the story in the box. What do you think happened between the gorilla and the boy? Tell a partner.

five-year-old boy   rescue   enclosure
wall   disappear   scream   seriously hurt
stroke (v.)   zookeeper   alive   hero

d Work in pairs. Start at square 1. Read each section and answer the questions together. Follow the instructions.

e Ask and answer the questions.
1 Why do you think Jambo protected the boy?
2 Have you changed your opinion of gorillas after reading the story?
3 Would you like to watch the video of what happened?

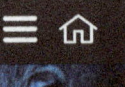

JAMBO'S STORY

In 1986, a video of a frightening event involving a gorilla and a boy was watched by millions of people around the world. The video, which is still popular on the Internet today, changed people's opinions of gorillas forever.

1 On 31 August, 1986, a couple took their two young sons to Jersey Zoo. When the family arrived, they went to see the gorillas straight away. The father noticed that the children were too small to see the animals, so he picked up his five-year-old son, Levan, and put him on top of the enclosure wall. Then he turned round to pick up his other son.

What do you think happened next?
Go to 3 to find out.

2 Jambo! People had always thought that gorillas were dangerous animals, but the video changed their minds. Journalists named Jambo 'the Gentle Giant', and soon letters, cards and even boxes of bananas arrived for him at the zoo. Jambo died in 1992, but a statue at the zoo reminds the world of this wonderful animal.

Go to 2e and answer the questions.

3 When the father turned back, Levan had disappeared. The boy had fallen off the wall, into the gorilla area. The shocked parents looked down and saw that their son was lying on the ground, about four metres below them. He wasn't moving.

What do you think the father did next?
Go to 5 to find out.

4 Jambo moved carefully around Levan. He softly stroked his back. Then he sat down between Levan and the other gorillas. When he saw that a young gorilla had come too close, Jambo stood up and did not let him pass. His message to the other gorillas was clear: 'Don't touch him!' Jambo pulled gently at Levan's clothes and after a while Levan opened his eyes and started to cry.

What do you think Jambo did when Levan started to cry?
Go to 6 to find out.

5 Levan's father tried to climb down into the enclosure to rescue the boy, but he was stopped by the other zoo visitors. Slowly, the gorillas came closer to Levan. A large crowd of people had come to see what was happening. Everyone was screaming and shouting. They were scared that the gorillas might seriously hurt the boy.

Jambo, a 200 kg male gorilla, got to Levan first.

What do you think Jambo did?
Go to 4 to find out.

6 Jambo ran away and his gorilla family followed him. Some time later, zookeepers rescued Levan from the enclosure. He had broken several bones in the fall and had seriously hurt his head, but he was alive. A man had filmed everything, and millions of people around the world watched the video on the news. The zookeepers became heroes and so did …

Who else do you think became a hero?
Go to 2 to find out.

118

UNIT 12

g 💬 What kinds of animals do you think caused problems 1–5?
  1 When I woke up, I had a red and itchy spot on my skin …
  2 This morning I found a dead mouse on the kitchen floor …
  3 I suddenly felt a pain in my arm …
  4 There was hair all over my new coat …
  5 Suddenly, she screamed …

h Complete sentences 1–5 in 3g using *because* + past perfect.

i 💬 Have you ever had any bad experiences with animals? What happened?

3 GRAMMAR Past perfect

a Look at the verbs in **bold** in the sentences. Which action happened first? Write *1* (first) or *2* (second) after each of the verbs.
  1 When the father **turned back** (__), Levan **had disappeared** (__).
  2 Zookeepers **rescued** (__) Levan from the enclosure. He **had broken** (__) several bones.

b Look at the sentences in 3a again. Complete the rule with the words in the box.

  simple   perfect   participle

  > We use the past _____ to make it clear that something happened **before** a past _____ action.
  > We form the past perfect with *had* + past _____ .

c Read *Jambo's Story* again and underline more examples of the past perfect.

d ⟫ Now go to Grammar Focus 12A on p. 166.

e ▶12.03 **Pronunciation** Look at the vowels in **bold** in the past participles in the box. Put the words in the correct column in the table. Then listen and check.

  br**ou**ght   ch**o**sen   dr**u**nk   bec**o**me   b**ou**ght   c**au**ght
  fl**ow**n   th**ou**ght   sw**u**m   st**o**len   thr**ow**n   w**o**n

/ʌ/	/ɔː/	/əʊ/
drunk	brought	chosen

f ▶12.04 Practise saying the sentences with the correct vowel sounds. Then listen and check.
  1 He'd never **thought** of getting a pet.
  2 Had you ever **swum** with whales before?
  3 The camel had **thrown** him off before it started to run.
  4 A mosquito had **flown** into the room in the night!
  5 I went to the zoo because I'd **won** a free ticket.
  6 After three hours, I still hadn't **caught** a fish.

4 SPEAKING AND LISTENING

a 💬 Work in pairs. Look at the pictures. Put them in order to make a story.

b ▶12.05 Listen to the story. Check your answers to 4a.

c 💬 Tell the story of Willie the parrot. Use the pictures to help you.

d 💬 Do you know any stories about … ?
  • animals helping or saving humans
  • humans helping or saving animals

119

12B HE SAID I WAS SELFISH!

Learn to talk about family relationships
G Reported speech
V Personality adjectives

1 LISTENING

a When you were a child, did you get on well with other children? What about with your brothers and sisters?

b Look at the pictures below. What do you think is happening in each picture?

c ▶12.06 Listen and match stories 1–3 to the pictures. Were you right about what was happening?

d ▶12.06 Listen again. Are the sentences true (*T*) or false (*F*)? Correct the false sentences.

Claire
1 Claire told her sister that the cows were horses.
2 Claire found it funny when her sister jumped on the cow.
3 Claire's sister went back home on her own.
4 Claire told her mum the truth about what had happened.

Jeremy
1 Jeremy wanted to do something nice for his brother.
2 Jeremy's brother thought the soup looked good.
3 Jeremy drank some of the soup first.
4 Jeremy's brother was ill after eating the soup.

Tanya
1 Tanya couldn't read as well as her sister.
2 Tanya hated her father saying nice things about her sister.
3 Tanya's father asked her to read aloud to the visitors.
4 Tanya knew the stories in the books.

e Answer the questions in small groups.
1 Which story did you like best? Why?
2 Did you do anything like this when you were a child?

2 GRAMMAR Reported speech

a Look at these examples of reported speech from the stories. What did the people actually say? Match 1–7 with a–g.
1 I said that she could ride one of the horses.
2 I told my mum that my sister had tried to ride a cow and I had saved her.
3 My brother said that he wasn't feeling very well.
4 I told my brother that I was going to make grass soup.
5 I told him that I had drunk some.
6 My dad told them that he was very proud of my sister.
7 I said that I had just finished reading the books.

a ☐ 'I'm not feeling very well.'
b ☐ 'I'm very proud of your sister.'
c ☐ 'I'm going to make grass soup.'
d ☐ 'You can ride one of the horses.'
e ☐ 'She tried to ride a cow and I saved her.'
f ☐ 'I've just finished reading these books.'
g ☐ 'I've drunk some.'

b Look at the highlighted verbs in 2a. How do the verbs change when we report what someone said in the past? Complete the rules.

present simple	➤ past simple
present continuous	➤ _____
present perfect	➤ _____
past simple	➤ _____
am/is/are going to	➤ _____
can	➤ _____

c Look at the reported speech in 2a again. Complete the sentences with *said* or *told*.
1 I _____ him that I had drunk some.
2 I _____ that I had drunk some.

d ≫ Now go to Grammar Focus 12B on p. 166.

e ▶12.08 **Pronunciation** Listen to how *that* is pronounced in the following two exchanges. What difference do you notice? Do you think they both have the same meaning?

A Hi, Chris. Jane wants to know where her diary is.
B I haven't got it. I told her [1]*that* yesterday.

A Hi, Chris. Jane wants to know where her diary is.
B Yeah, I've just seen her. I told her [2]*that* I hadn't got it.

f ▶12.09 Report the sentences 1–6. Then listen and check your answers.
1 'You can't read my diary.' *I told her …*
2 'I'm going to tell Dad.' *She said …*
3 'I'm not talking to you.' *I told him …*
4 'I don't want to play with you.' *She said …*
5 'It's not fair!' *He told me …*
6 'You broke my toy!' *I said that he …*

g Practise saying the reported sentences in 2f.

h Do you remember anyone saying any of the things in 2f to you?

> My sister always said it wasn't fair when I won games.

i Can you remember any other things people have said to you? Make notes on:
- something a teacher said to you
- something someone told you to frighten you
- something that made you feel good
- something that wasn't true.

j Tell a partner about your answers in 2i.

3 VOCABULARY Personality adjectives

a Write down the names of four family members. What kind of people are they? Tell your partner one thing about each person.

b Now go to Vocabulary Focus 12B on p. 143.

4 READING AND SPEAKING

a Ask and answer the questions.
1 Which people in your family are you closest to? Why?
2 Does anyone in your family have a strong personality? What are they like?

> I'm very close to my younger sister. We tell each other everything.

> My father is very easygoing, and he has a very loud laugh.

b Work in pairs. Complete *Brothers and Sisters: The Facts* with words in the box. There are different possible answers.

> are more sociable   play together   live to over 100 years old
> get on with women   fight   do activities   ~~possessions~~
> earns a higher salary   do better at school   talk

c Communication 12B Go to p. 132.

BROTHERS and SISTERS
THE FACTS

1. **80%** of fights between brothers and sisters are about <u>possessions</u>.

2. Children who are of a similar age _____ less.

3. Children who are more than three years apart in age _____ less.

4. When sisters are together, they prefer to _____ rather than do anything else.

5. When brothers, or brothers and sisters, are together, they prefer to _____.

6. Children with no brothers and sisters _____ and get better jobs.

7. The oldest child in a family is normally more intelligent and usually _____ than younger brothers and sisters.

8. Younger brothers and sisters _____ when they become adults.

9. Boys with older sisters find it easier to _____ when they are adults.

10. Older brothers and sisters have more allergies, but more of them _____.

12C EVERYDAY ENGLISH
I'm pretty sure it's Japanese

Learn to agree and disagree in discussions

P Main stress: contrastive

1 LISTENING

a Ask and answer the questions.
1. What kind of things do you normally talk about with your friends?
2. Do you ever argue? What do you argue about?
3. Do you like quizzes? Do you ever argue about general knowledge and facts?

b With a partner, discuss the quiz questions below. Do you agree on the answers?

1. Look at these car companies. What country is each one from?

		a		b	
1	Geely is …	a	☐ German	b	☐ Chinese
2	Honda is …	a	☐ Korean	b	☐ Japanese
3	Hyundai is …	a	☐ Chinese	b	☐ Korean
4	Kia is …	a	☐ French	b	☐ Korean
5	Mazda is …	a	☐ German	b	☐ Japanese
6	Mitsubishi is …	a	☐ American	b	☐ Japanese
7	Nissan is …	a	☐ Japanese	b	☐ Korean
8	Saic is …	a	☐ Chinese	b	☐ German
9	Suzuki is …	a	☐ Korean	b	☐ Japanese
10	Toyota is …	a	☐ Chinese	b	☐ Japanese

2. Check your answers at the bottom of page 122.

c 12.11 Watch or listen to Part 1. Which companies from b do Leo and Mark talk about? Do they agree on the answers? What do they start arguing about?

d 12.11 Watch or listen again. Who agrees with the statements below, only Mark (M) or both Leo and Mark (B)?
1. ☐ Nissan cars are made in South Korea.
2. ☐ Toyota is the biggest car company in Japan.
3. ☐ Mazda is a larger company than Suzuki.

e 12.12 Watch or listen to Part 2. What does Mark do to end the argument? Do you know who is right?

2 USEFUL LANGUAGE
Agreeing and disagreeing

a 12.11 Look at these phrases. Which of the phrases do Mark and Leo use? Watch or listen again to Part 1 and tick (✓) phrases you hear.

☐ That's true.   ☐ You're absolutely right.
☐ I'm afraid …   ☐ Definitely.
☐ Exactly.   ☐ That's right.
☐ I don't think so.   ☐ Oh, please.
☐ I'm sorry, but …   ☐ I'm not sure about that.

b Look at all the phrases in 2a and answer the questions.
1. Which phrases show we agree?
2. Which phrases show we disagree?
3. Which phrases show we very strongly agree?
4. Which phrase shows we very strongly disagree?

c 12.13 Listen and repeat the phrases from 2a. There are sometimes some extra words.

d 12.14 Complete these conversations with the expressions from 2a. Then listen and check.

1
A Rock music is the best kind of music.
B I'm not _____ _____ that. Classical music is more relaxing.

2
A Basketball is the most interesting sport.
B _____ true. It's so fast and exciting.

3
A Beach holidays are boring.
B You're _____ right. I prefer to stay in big cities.

4
A English food is boring.
B Oh, _____. It's much more interesting than it used to be!

5
A It's a bad idea to listen to music when you study.
B I'm _____, but I think it helps you concentrate.

e Complete the sentences with your own ideas.
1. _____ is the best artist ever.
2. _____ is really boring.
3. _____ is an amazing singer.
4. _____ is a great film.
5. _____ is a really relaxing place.
6. _____ is a very funny person.

f Compare your sentences with your partner. Use phrases from 2a to agree or disagree.

Answers to Exercise 1b (quiz)
1b 2b 3b 4b 5b 6b 7a 8a 9b 10b

UNIT 12

3 PRONUNCIATION
Main stress: contrastive

a ▶ 12.15 Listen to Leo and Mark talking about Nissan. Notice how the underlined words have extra stress.

Leo Nissan's a Japanese company.
Mark Er, it's actually a Korean company.
Leo No, it's Japanese.

b Complete the rule.

> To show that we disagree with someone, we put **extra** / **less** stress on the information we think is different.

c 💬 Practise the exchange in 3a using these ideas.
1 Coffee's really bad for you. (good for you)
2 Business management is an easy subject. (difficult)
3 The best way to travel is by plane. (by train)
4 Tennis is a really boring sport. (exciting)
5 The shops in this area are excellent. (terrible)

> Coffee's really bad for you.

> Er, it's actually good for you.

> No, it's bad for you.

d 💬 What's your real opinion about each idea in 3c? Tell your partner. Do you agree?

4 SPEAKING

a Think about these opinions. Which do you agree with? Think of reasons why you agree or disagree. Make notes.

- Money makes people happy.
- Celebrity magazines are fun to read.
- Italian food is the best in the world.
- There should be no speed limits on motorways.
- Children should stay at school until 5 pm.
- Video calls are better than normal phone calls.

b 💬 Work in pairs. Compare your ideas. How many opinions do you agree about?

> I think celebrity magazines are fun to read.

> Oh please. They're silly. I don't care about celebrities.

> I'm sorry, but I think they're fun. It's interesting to read about other people's lives.

✓ **UNIT PROGRESS TEST**

→ **CHECK YOUR PROGRESS**

You can now do the Unit Progress Test.

123

12D SKILLS FOR WRITING
A few hours later, they started baking again

Learn to write a short story
W Linkers: past time

1 SPEAKING AND LISTENING

a Work in groups. Discuss the questions.
1 What kinds of bad or dangerous weather do you know? Make a list. What is the worst or most dangerous weather you have experienced?
2 Look at the photos of a hurricane. Which countries have problems with hurricanes?
3 Why are hurricanes dangerous? Make a list of ideas. Use the photos and the words below to help you.

wind   rain   floods   damage   buildings
electricity   trees   cars   rescue

b Read the Fact File about Hurricane Harvey, a big storm that caused a lot of damage. Which of your ideas from 1a does it mention?

FACT FILE: HURRICANE HARVEY

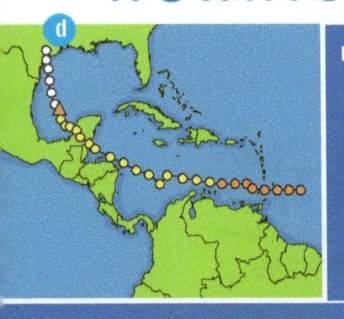

- Hurricane Harvey passed over the Caribbean and the Yucatán peninsula in Mexico as a strong storm. Then it moved north and became a Category 4 hurricane. It crossed the coast of Texas in the USA in August 2017.

- In the area around Houston, Texas, the winds reached 200 km an hour, and there was heavy rain for four days. Around 60 cm of rain fell in the first 24 hours.

- Thirty-nine thousand people had to leave their homes, and 204,000 homes were damaged. One million cars were destroyed. In total, the damage cost around $125 billion.

c ▶ 12.16 Listen to two news reports about Hurricane Harvey. Which pictures a–d does each report go with?

d ▶ 12.16 Listen again and answer the questions.

Report 1
1 What is Stevie's job?
2 Where is she?
3 Why can't she rescue people?

Report 2
4 Where is Jennifer? Why?
5 Are they able to rescue people?
6 What was the street like this morning? What's it like now?

2 READING

a Look at the pictures and the heading of the article on p. 125. What do you think the news story will be about?

b Read the story quickly. Were your ideas correct?

c Read the story again and make notes about what happened at these times: Saturday morning, Saturday evening, Saturday night, Sunday, Sunday night, Monday morning.

UNIT 12

Houston's Storm Bakers:
A True Story of Bravery and Baking

Everyone knew the storm was coming. 'Hurricane Harvey', the reporters called it. For the people of Houston, Texas, it was a busy day and an anxious one. They all remembered what had happened when Hurricane Katrina had hit New Orleans 12 years earlier. Nowhere was it busier than at *El Bolillo*, a popular city-centre Mexican bakery. On that Saturday morning, everyone wanted to stock up on bread, and by midday they had sold out. The bakers closed up shop and went home, thinking their day's work was done.

A few hours later, though, four of the bakers decided to go back and start baking again. Later that night, when they tried to go home, they found they were trapped because the streets were flooded. The next day, the flood waters were even higher, so they still couldn't leave the bakery.

The four trapped bakers had nothing to do except watch as the rain and the flood waters got higher. After a while, they decided that the best way to pass the time was just to keep on working. They knew that after the storm, people would be hungry, so they decided that if they couldn't help their own families, at least they could help the neighbourhood by getting plenty of bread ready.

And so they worked all day and all night, taking turns to sleep on sacks of flour between the ovens. The water rose almost to the door of the bakery, but it never came inside, so the electricity didn't stop working.

On Sunday, the owner of the bakery tried to rescue the workers, but the police turned him back – they said it was still too dangerous. When he finally reached the bakery the following morning, he could hardly believe his eyes. The shelves were piled high with fresh Mexican bread of all kinds – *bolillos*, *kolaches* and *pan dulce*, a kind of sweet bread, and one of their most popular products. Altogether, they produced an incredible 4,000 loaves of bread, and used about 2,000 kilos of flour.

As the bakers knew that people were short of food in the city, especially bread, they decided to load up their cars and deliver it all free of charge to grateful volunteers and flood victims.

3 WRITING SKILLS Linkers: past time

a Add the correct words to complete the time linkers in the sentences from the story. Then check your answers in the story.

| a while | later | midday | morning | next day | that night |

1 Everyone wanted to stock up on bread, and **by** _____ they had sold everything.
2 **A few hours** _____, though, four of the bakers decided to go back and start baking again.
3 **Later** _____, when they tried to go home, they found they were trapped.
4 **The** _____, the flood waters were even higher, so they still couldn't leave the bakery.
5 **After** _____, they decided that the best way to pass the time was just to keep on working.
6 When he finally reached the bakery **the following** _____, he could hardly believe his eyes.

b Look at the linkers again. Which word has the same meaning as *next*?

c We can use time expressions in two ways:
1 to show **when** something happened
   • the following day
   • later that night
2 to show the **length of time** between two events
   • a few hours later
   • after a while

Which words and phrases below could you use instead of the highlighted words? Write *1* or *2*.

☐ 2 five minutes   ☐ many years   ☐ week
☐ evening   ☐ about a month   ☐ a few days
☐ a short time   ☐ morning   ☐ a week

d Correct the mistakes with the linkers in the sentences.
1 She left university. About two years after, she got a job.
2 I sent an email applying for the job. Week later, I had an interview.
3 He bought a new car. Later morning, he crashed it.
4 I went to bed early. Following the morning, I went for a walk.
5 I started watching a film, but after the while I fell asleep.

4 WRITING

a Think of a story about something that happened to you or people you know. It could be a time when you or they:
• were in a dangerous situation
• experienced very bad weather
• had a lucky escape
• were worried about something that turned out to be OK.

Think about the questions below and make notes.
• What happened?
• How did you/they feel?
• What did you/they do?
• What happened in the end?

b Using your notes, write your story.

c Look through your story. See if you can add time linkers, like those in 3a, to connect the events in your story.

d Work in groups. Read your story to the other students and answer any questions.

e Choose one story from your group. Tell it to the whole class.

125

UNIT 12
Review and extension

1 GRAMMAR

a Which action in the sentences happened first? Write *1* or *2*.
1. ☐ I arrived late for my flight because ☐ I'd written the wrong time in my diary.
2. ☐ The man had run away by the time ☐ the police got there.
3. ☐ When I saw the questions in the exam, I realised ☐ I'd revised the wrong things.
4. ☐ It had snowed during the night and ☐ some of the roads were closed.
5. ☐ I was tired because ☐ I'd worked so hard the day before.

b Choose the correct answers.
A ¹*Did you read / Had you read* the story about the man who was almost attacked by a shark yesterday?
B No, what ²*happened / had happened*?
A He was swimming and he ³*saw / had seen* a dolphin next to him. Then suddenly, the dolphin ⁴*hit / had hit* a shark. The swimmer ⁵*didn't see / hadn't seen* the shark before the dolphin hit it!
B That's incredible. Well, I ⁶*read / had read* another nice animal story. There was a goat that ⁷*took care of / had taken care of* a farmer for five days. The farmer ⁸*fell / had fallen* over and he couldn't walk or get help.

c Report the statements.
1. 'We can't leave the party.' He said …
2. 'Marc has moved to a new flat.' She told me …
3. 'I'm seeing Sarah later.' He said …
4. 'I'll help you with the shopping.' She said …
5. 'Michele has got a great new job.' He told me …
6. 'I'm going to get a new car.' He said …
7. 'I don't like the hotel.' She told me …

2 VOCABULARY

a Complete the animal words.
1. w _ _ le
2. sp _ _ _ _ r
3. g _ r _ _ _ _ a
4. t _ g _ r
5. m _ _ q _ _ _ _ o
6. p _ r _ _ t

b Choose an adjective in the box to describe each person in 1–8.

anxious   careless   funny   generous
honest   reliable   selfish   sensible

1. Jo really makes me laugh. _____
2. Manfred only thinks about himself. _____
3. Jill always tells the truth. _____
4. Shin Li always gets worried about little things. _____
5. If Ben says he'll do something, he always does it. _____
6. Steve often loses or breaks things. _____
7. Jack always gets me great presents. _____
8. Daniela never makes stupid decisions. _____

3 WORDPOWER *age*

a Look at the sentences. Which is about … ?
☐ children who are almost the same age
☐ children who are different ages
1. Children who are more than **three years apart in age** play together less.
2. Children who are **about the same age** fight less.

b Match the expressions 1–4 with the definitions a–d.
1. ☐ **At your age**, I was studying a lot, not going out all the time.
2. ☐ I learned to swim **at an early age**. I was only about three years old.
3. ☐ She's **about my age**, I think, because we were at university at the same time.
4. ☐ It isn't always easy to learn new things in **old age**.

a a similar age to me
b younger than expected, during childhood
c when someone is over 70
d the age you are now

c Complete the sentences with the phrases in the box.

about my age   apart in age   at an early age
at your age   early twenties   middle-aged
about the same age   old age

1. John looks much older than Martin, but surprisingly they're _____.
2. Mozart started to write music _____ – he was only five years old.
3. _____, I never used a computer for homework. I wrote everything by hand.
4. I had a lot of fun when I was 21 – it's great to be in your _____.
5. My brother and I are only two years _____, so we played together all the time when we were little.
6. My grandparents are still really active – I think that's important in _____.
7. The person I spoke to was _____, maybe a year younger or older than me.
8. Don't say to her that she's _____ – she thinks 45 is still very young.

d 💬 Work in pairs. Use each of the phrases in 3c to describe someone you know.

⟳ REVIEW YOUR PROGRESS

How well did you do in this unit? Write 3, 2 or 1 for each objective.
3 = very well   2 = well   1 = not so well

I CAN …	
tell a story	☐
talk about family relationships	☐
agree and disagree in discussions	☐
write a short story.	☐

COMMUNICATION PLUS

3C STUDENT C

a You are a shop assistant. Look at the photos of your products and read the descriptions.

Large rubber duck £8.99
– Fun gift: children
– Floats in the bath
– Makes a noise when you press it

Modern spice rack £25.99
– Perfect gift: cooks, food lovers
– 10 jars, quality herbs and spices
– Fixes to wall or free-standing

Coloured pencils £4.99
– Great gift: artists
– 36 bright colours
– Colour in books or draw your own pictures

Scented candles £9.99
– Colourful gift for the home
– Three scents: vanilla, rose, pine
– Creates a perfect atmosphere

Classic clock £49.99
– Stylish gift: married couple
– Traditional design
– Batteries included

Animal slippers £19.99 one pair
SALE £29.99 for two pairs
– Fun gift: men, women, children
– Various designs

b Students A and B are customers in your shop. Listen to their questions and describe some of your products. Ask your customers to pay for the product when they have chosen.

c ⟫ Now swap roles. Go to p. 129.

2B STUDENT A

a Read *Did You Mean Capri?* and answer the questions.
1 Where were they going?
2 How were they travelling?
3 What was the problem?
4 Who helped solve the problem? How?
5 What happened in the end?

DID YOU MEAN CAPRI?

SWEDISH TOURISTS MISS THEIR DESTINATION BY 600 KM

Two Swedish tourists on holiday in Italy got a surprise after a spelling mistake on their GPS took them 600 kilometres from their destination.

The Swedish couple were travelling around Italy and wanted to go to Capri. Capri is an island in the south of the country, famous for its beautiful coastline and a popular tourist destination. The couple put their destination into their car's GPS, but they made a spelling mistake. They accidentally typed CARPI instead of CAPRI. There is a real place named Carpi in Italy, but it is a small town in the north of the country.

The couple followed the GPS directions. Although they were travelling to an island, it didn't worry them that they didn't cross a bridge, take a boat, or see the water. When they arrived in Carpi, they went to the tourist office. They asked for directions to the Blue Grotto, a famous sea cave in Capri. But, of course, the tourist official didn't understand. He thought they wanted to go to a restaurant called the Blue Grotto.

When the official realised that the couple thought they were in Capri, he explained their mistake. The couple got back into their car and started driving south. The official said, 'They were surprised but not angry.'

b ⟫ Now go back to p. 21.

127

4B STUDENT A

a Read the sentences to Student B. Listen to their reply.
1. My flight arrives at 5 pm.
2. I'd like to buy some clothes.
3. I don't understand the menu.
4. I don't like crowds.
5. I'd love to see some art.

b Listen to Student B's sentences. Choose the correct reply.
- I'll take you to the airport soon.
- Shall we visit the castle?
- Shall I come and pick you up?
- I'll take you to a nice park.
- I'll find a good place to eat nearby.

c Now go back to p. 40.

2C STUDENT B

a Read card 1. Think about what Student A will ask you.

1 You are a platform attendant at a UK train station.
- first train to Manchester at 7:10 am
- trains every hour
- prices: adult £45, student £32
- passengers can only use tickets on the train booked
- no lockers in UK train stations
- waiting room is near the station entrance

b Start the conversation with Student A. Say, 'How can I help you?'

c Now look at card 2. Listen to Student A and reply. Find out the information you need.

2 You want to visit Warwick Castle.
- where / castle?
- open?
- cost / adult and child tickets?
- where / buy tickets?
- how often / tours?
- bring a picnic?

2B STUDENT B

a Read *Coach Passengers Asked to Get Out and Push* and answer the questions.
1. Where were they going?
2. How were they travelling?
3. What was the problem?
4. Who helped solve the problem? How?
5. What happened in the end?

COACH PASSENGERS ASKED TO GET OUT AND PUSH

A group of coach passengers got some unexpected exercise when their coach broke down and the driver asked them to get out and push. The driver asked his 25 passengers for help after the 11:15 am coach from Heathrow Airport to Norwich broke down while it was turning a corner.

A 77-year-old passenger, who was travelling back from a holiday in Italy with his wife, said, 'We heard an awful noise … and the driver could not get the coach to move.' The coach was stopping other cars from using the road, so ten passengers got out and tried to push the coach, which weighed 14 tonnes.* The passenger said, 'It was an amazing sight … Luckily, there were lots of strong young men and women on board.'

A car stopped to help and pulled the coach along with a rope while the people pushed it 200 metres to the coach station. The passengers then waited over an hour with their luggage for another coach to arrive so they could complete their journey.

The coach company says the coach driver was wrong to ask his passengers to help, and that they will give him training immediately.

* 14 tonnes = 14,000 kg

b Now go back to p. 21.

5B IF YOUR PARTNER *DOESN'T* HAVE A JOB …

a Ask your partner about the job they would like to have in the future.

Do you think … ?
- it'll be easy to find work
- you'll earn a good salary when you start
- you'll need to speak English at work
- there'll be a lot of other people who want this job
- you'll work for a company or be self-employed
- you'll move to another place for work
- you'll use your education

b Then swap roles and answer your partner's questions. Give more information if you can.

c Now go back to p. 50.

128

Communication Plus

3C STUDENTS A AND B

a You want to buy a present for a friend. Choose someone you both know.

b Student C is a shop assistant. Ask about the products in the shop. Choose the best product for your friend and buy it.

c Now swap roles. Student B: You are the shop assistant – go to p. 127. Student A: Stay on this page.

3A RESULTS

Mostly a: You are a big spender. You spend a lot of money without thinking. Maybe you need to start to plan your spending a bit better.

Mostly b: You are a smart spender. You spend money, but you do it carefully. You find all the sales. But you don't buy things that you don't need!

Mostly c: You are a non-spender. You don't like spending, and you only do it when you really have to.

>>> Now go back to p. 28.

5B IF YOUR PARTNER *HAS* A JOB …

a Ask your partner about their future in their job.
   Do you think … ?
   - you'll work longer hours
   - you'll earn more money
   - you'll need new skills
   - you'll go to more meetings
   - you'll travel abroad for work
   - you'll need to speak English at work
   - you'll become a boss

b Then swap roles and answer your partner's questions. Give more information if you can.

c >>> Now go back to p. 50.

6A STUDENT A

a Read the advice for people who are always late.

No one wants to be the person who always arrives last. Here's some advice to help you get there on time, whatever the occasion.

Imagine the worst. Don't think that everything will go perfectly and you will arrive at a place in the shortest time possible. Leave earlier than you need to. Then, when you can't find a parking place or there's a long queue, it won't make you late.

I'm always late.

Tell people how much time you have. When someone starts talking to you and you don't have much time, say, 'I only have five minutes.' Then, after five minutes, make sure you leave. Say, 'I'm sorry, but I have to go.' Nobody will think you are rude.

Find things to do while you wait. Some people are always late because they hate waiting for other people. If this is you, take something to do while you are waiting. Don't try to do 'just one more thing' before you leave for an appointment.

b Cover the article. Tell Student B about the advice.

c Listen to Student B's advice for the same problem.

d Answer the questions with Student B.
   1 Which piece of advice is the most useful?
   2 Do you know anyone who needs this advice?

e >>> Now go back to p. 59.

129

4C STUDENT B

a Student A is going to invite you to dinner. Complete your diary with plans for three evenings.

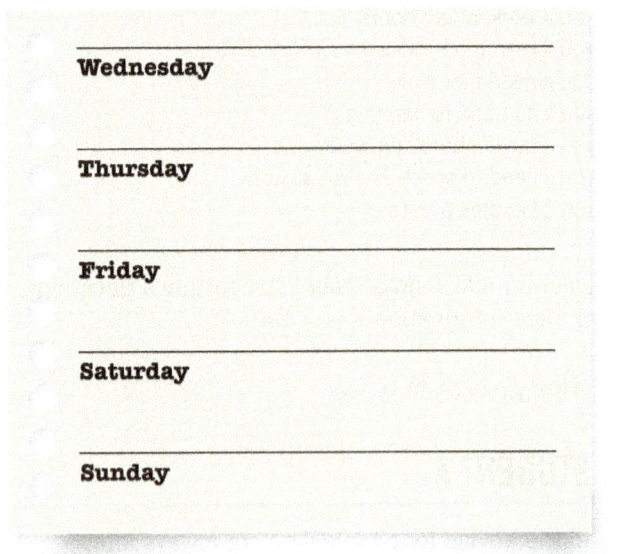

```
Wednesday
_____

Thursday
_____

Friday
_____

Saturday
_____

Sunday
_____
```

b Answer Student A's call. Plan an evening for dinner. Offer to bring something.

1C STUDENT B

a Read card 1. Think about what you want to say.

b Listen to Student A and reply. Use your own name.

> **1** You are walking down the street and you see your friend.
> - Say hello.
> - Listen to your friend's news and respond.
> - Give your news:
>   - You moved to a new flat last week.
>   - *your own idea*
> - Say goodbye.

c Now look at card 2. Start the conversation with Student A. Use your own name.

> **2** You meet a new colleague for the first time.
> - Say who you are.
> - Listen to what they say and respond.
> - Give some information:
>   - You work in IT.
>   - *your own idea*
> - Say goodbye.

d ⟫ Now go back to p. 13.

4B STUDENT B

a Listen to Student A's sentences. Choose the correct reply.
- Shall I read it for you in English?
- Shall we go to a gallery?
- OK – so we won't go to the market.
- I'll meet you at the airport.
- Shall we go to a shopping centre?

b Read the sentences to Student A. Listen to their reply.
1 My hotel doesn't have a restaurant.
2 I'd like to go for a walk.
3 My flight leaves in three hours.
4 I'm interested in history.
5 There's a long queue for taxis.

c ⟫ Now go back to p. 40.

6A STUDENT B

a Read the advice for people who are always late.

> No one wants to be the person who always arrives last. Here's some advice to help you get there on time, whatever the occasion.
>
> **Make a list of everything you need to do** the day before an important event. Do you need to wear smart clothes? Buy a gift? Find out train times? Then do all the jobs on your list so you'll be ready to go the next day.
>
> **Do only the things you need to do.** Use your time carefully before an appointment. Don't try to be perfect. Think about each action. Do you really need to print that document? If it's not necessary, don't do it.
>
> **Think about how other people feel.** Being late tells other people, 'My time is more important than yours.' People who are often late don't usually understand how rude it is. Remember this and you will have another reason to arrive on time.

I'm always late.

b Listen to Student A's advice about the same problem.

c Cover the article. Tell Student A about the advice.

d Answer the questions with Student A.
1 Which piece of advice is the most useful?
2 Do you know anyone who needs this advice?

e ⟫ Now go back to p. 59.

Communication Plus

11B STUDENT A

a Read the stories about three accidental discoveries. Answer the questions.

1 Who made each discovery?
2 What exactly was the discovery?
3 How did they make the discovery?

> 1 Car keys were invented by an American businessman, Louis Spencer, in 1912. Until then, cars didn't have keys because there weren't many of them and cars couldn't travel very far. But one day, Spencer had some important papers that he wanted to leave in his car. He had the idea for the car key.
>
> 2 Matches were invented by John Walker, a pharmacist in England, in 1826. He was trying to find a way to start fires quickly. He didn't make much money from his idea – he wanted to share it with everyone because he already had enough money.
>
> 3 Saccharin was invented by accident in 1878 by Constantin Fahlberg, a pharmacist in the United States. He was eating some bread at home, but it tasted sweeter than normal. He realised that he had some chemicals on his hands from his day at work. The chemicals were making the bread taste sweet. At work the next day, he started working on saccharin.

b Use your dictionary to check new words. You may have to explain words to your partner.

c One of the three stories is not true. Tell them to your partner, then talk about them and decide which one is not true.

d When you have decided which story in each set is not true, check your answers at the bottom of p. 132.

11A STUDENT A

Look at the list. Take turns describing the words to Student B, but do not say the words. How many words can you describe in two minutes?

| scientist | album | laptop | novel | pilot | visa |
| hotel | bank account | Greece | Chris Hemsworth |

It's a thing that …
It's a place where …
It's a person who …

>>> Now go back to p. 109.

10A STUDENT A

a Take turns asking and answering questions with Student B. Underline their answers below. If you answer *maybe*, you must explain your answer.

> If a shop assistant gave you a £20 note instead of £10, would you tell them?

> Maybe. I'd tell them if they were young.

1 If a shop assistant gave you a £20 note instead of a £10 note, would you tell them?
Yes 0, Maybe 3, No 4

2 If someone had food in their teeth, would you tell them?
Yes 0, Maybe 1, No 3

3 If you found a wallet with £1,000 and an ID card in it, would you hand it in at a police station?
Yes 0, Maybe 1, No 4

4 If you got a present you didn't like, would you wrap it up and give it to someone else?
Yes 2, Maybe 1, No 0

5 If you dropped your friend's sandwich on the kitchen floor and they didn't see, would you throw it away and make a new one?
Yes 0, Maybe 2, No 3

6 If someone lent you something you really liked and then forgot about it, would you give it back anyway?
Yes 0, Maybe 1, No 3

7 If your friend was upset and wanted to come round, but you were really tired, would you tell them you were busy?
Yes 3, Maybe 2, No 0

8 Would you tell a friend if you didn't like their new hairstyle?
Yes 0, Maybe 1, No 2

b Add up Student B's score and check the results on p. 133. Does your partner agree with their result?

12B ANSWERS

a Read the facts. Did you complete them correctly?

BROTHERS and SISTERS
THE FACTS

1. **80%** of fights between brothers and sisters are about possessions.
2. Children who are about the same age fight less.
3. Children who are more than three years apart in age play together less.
4. When sisters are together, they prefer to talk rather than do anything else.
5. When brothers, or brothers and sisters, are together, they prefer to do activities.
6. Children with no brothers and sisters do better at school and get better jobs.
7. The oldest child in a family is normally more intelligent and usually earns a higher salary than younger brothers and sisters.
8. Younger brothers and sisters are more sociable when they become adults.
9. Boys with older sisters find it easier to get on with women when they are adults.
10. Older brothers and sisters have more allergies, but more of them live to over 100 years old!

b Work in pairs. Talk about the facts. Do you think they are true? Use examples from your own family or other people you know.

c As a class, vote on each fact. How many of the facts does your class agree with?

11B ANSWERS

Student A: Story 1 is not true.
Student B: Story 3 is not true.

10A STUDENT B

a Take turns asking and answering questions with Student A. <u>Underline</u> their answers below. If you answer *maybe*, you must explain your answer.

> If a friend cooked dinner for you and you didn't like it, would you eat it?

> Maybe. I'd eat it if it were something really expensive.

1 If a friend cooked dinner for you and you didn't like it, would you eat it?
   Yes 2, Maybe 1, No 0

2 If you were at a cash machine and the person in front of you forgot to take their cash, would you run after them?
   Yes 0, Maybe 2, No 4

3 If you wanted to see a film that didn't come out at the cinema in your country for three months, would you download it?
   Yes 3, Maybe 2, No 0

4 If you were looking after a friend's pet fish and it died, would you replace it before they came back?
   Yes 2, Maybe 1, No 0

5 If you hit a parked car and no one saw you, would you keep on driving?
   Yes 4, Maybe 3, No 0

6 If you saw a job advertisement that was perfect for your friend, but you also wanted to apply, would you pass on the information?
   Yes 0, Maybe 1, No 3

7 If you spilt some water on someone's mobile phone, would you tell them?
   Yes 0, Maybe 1, No 3

8 If your friend offered you a free ticket to a concert, but you were working that day, would you tell your boss you were ill and go along?
   Yes 4, Maybe 2, No 0

b Add up Student A's score and check the results on p. 133. Does your partner agree with the result?

Communication Plus

7B HEALTH QUIZ

a Do the quiz. Choose the answers that are true for you. Add up your score.

Are you healthier than you used to be?

1 I used to do more sport and exercise in the past.
   a Agree (–1)   b Not sure (0)   c Disagree (+1)

2 I used to have a healthier diet.
   a Agree (–1)   b Not sure (0)   c Disagree (+1)

3 I eat less red meat today than I used to.
   a Agree (+1)   b Not sure (0)   c Disagree (–1)

4 I go to the doctor more than I used to.
   a Agree (+1)   b Not sure (0)   c Disagree (–1)

5 I used to sleep more than I do now.
   a Agree (–1)   b Not sure (0)   c Disagree (+1)

6 I used to get ill more often than I do these days.
   a Agree (+1)   b Not sure (0)   c Disagree (–1)

Scores

Below 0: You used to be healthier in the past than you are now.

0: You are just as healthy today as you were in the past.

More than 0: You are healthier today than you used to be.

b Compare your results with your partner. Whose health has changed the most? What are the most important differences in your health between now and the past?

10A RESULTS

0–5 points: You tell the truth to people even if they don't want to hear it. You may be the most honest person around, but you're not always the most popular.

6–13 points: You care about other people, and you don't want to upset them with the truth. Sometimes life is easier for people who aren't 100% honest. You're not hurting anyone else – that's the important thing.

14–25 points: You don't always do what other people think is the right thing. Watch out – you might cause problems for yourself one day!

11B STUDENT B

a Read the stories about three accidental discoveries. Answer the questions.
   1 Who made each discovery?
   2 What exactly was the discovery?
   3 How did they make the discovery?

1 Coca-Cola was invented by John Pemberton, a pharmacist in the USA. He was trying to make a medicine for headaches. For the first eight years, the drink was only sold in chemists' as a medicine, not in normal shops as a soft drink.

2 Velcro was invented by George De Mestral, a Swiss engineer, in 1941. One day, after a day's walk in the Alps with his dog, he noticed that there were lots of seeds in his dog's fur. The seeds were difficult to remove, and he looked at them using a microscope to see what was happening. From this, he had the idea for Velcro.

3 Exercise bikes were invented by the Austrian cyclist Hans Weger in 1854. He was trying to fix a problem with his bike, so he put the back wheel between two piles of books to look at what was happening. Then he realised that a bike like this would be perfect for exercise at home. The exercise bike was invented.

b Use your dictionary to check new words. You may have to explain words to your partner.

c One of the three stories is not true. Tell them to your partner, then talk about them and decide which one is not true.

d When you have decided which story in each set is not true, check your answers at the bottom of p. 132.

11A STUDENT B

Look at the list. Take turns describing the words to Student A, but do not say the words. How many words can you describe in two minutes?

| dentist | airport | freezer | mobile phone | plumber |
| luggage | fiction | Japan | *To Kill a Mockingbird* | tourist |

It's a thing that …
It's a place where …
It's a person who …

⟫ Now go back to p. 109.

133

VOCABULARY FOCUS

1A Common adjectives

a ▶ 01.03 Listen to the conversations and look at the pictures. Underline the adjectives.

b Look at these adjectives and answer the questions. Use the conversations in **a** to help you.

delicious /dɪlɪʃəs/	ugly /ʌgli/	serious /sɪərɪəs/
rude /ruːd/	all right /ɔːlraɪt/	silly /sɪli/
boring /bɔːrɪŋ/	strange /streɪndʒ/	

Which adjectives mean … ?
1 OK _____
2 not normal _____
3 not beautiful _____
4 not polite _____
5 the food is good _____
6 not serious _____
7 bad (for a problem) _____
8 not interesting _____

c Now look at these adjectives.

gorgeous /gɔːdʒəs/	horrible /hɒrɪbəl/
lovely /lʌvli/	amazing /əmeɪzɪŋ/
awful /ɔːfəl/	perfect /pɜːfekt/

Which adjectives mean … ?
- very nice/good _____ _____ _____ _____
- very bad _____ _____

d ▶ 01.04 Listen to the adjectives in **b** and **c**. How many syllables are there in each word? Underline the stressed syllable in each word.

e Practise the conversations with a partner.

f ≫ Now go back to p. 8.

Speech bubbles:
1. What a silly game! / Don't be boring! Join in.
2. Perhaps he had a serious problem. / It's very rude to arrive so late.
3. The food here is delicious. / Yes. The fruit salad is gorgeous!
4. The weather's awful today. / Yes, it's horrible outside.
5. The weather's lovely today! / It's a perfect day for a BBQ.
6. Yes, but the music's all right. / It's a strange band to have at a wedding.
7. The room looks amazing. / I think the carpet's a bit ugly.

2A Tourism

a ▶ 02.07 Match the holiday items with the pictures. Listen and check. Repeat the words.
- ☐ backpack
- ☐ foreign currency
- ☐ guidebook
- ☐ map
- ☐ passport
- ☐ suitcase
- ☐ sunglasses
- ☐ suntan lotion

b 💬 Which of the items in **a** do you always take on holiday?

c ▶ 02.08 Complete the travel phrases with the words in the box. Listen and check.

~~holiday~~ sightseeing visa campsite souvenirs money accommodation hotel hostel adventure luggage

1 We **went away on** _holiday_ for three weeks.
2 We needed to **get** a _____ from the embassy before we travelled.
3 We also **exchanged** some _____ at the bank.
4 We **booked** all of our _____ online.
5 When we arrived, we **checked into** our luxury _____ and **unpacked** our _____.
6 We **did** some _____. The castles and gardens were gorgeous!
7 We **bought** _____ for our friends and family.
8 The second week, we **checked out of** our hotel and **stayed in** a _____. It was cheap and friendly.
9 The third week, we **stayed on** a _____ by the beach.
10 We **had** a great _____ and we didn't want to come home.

d 💬 Work in pairs. Think of your last holiday. Which of the things in **c** did you do? Tell your partner.

e ≫ Now go back to p. 19.

Vocabulary Focus

2B Travel collocations

a ▶ 02.09 Listen to sentences 1–8 and look at the journey on the map. Match the words in **bold** with their definitions (a–h).
1. ☐ We **travelled around** Europe last year.
2. ☐ We **set off** in June.
3. ☐ We **took off** late but …
4. ☐ … we **landed** on time in Berlin.
5. ☐ We **hitchhiked** across Germany.
6. ☐ A kind man **gave us a lift** to Frankfurt.
7. ☐ We **boarded** a train to Paris.
8. ☐ We **changed** at Strasbourg.
9. ☐ We **got to** Paris at seven-thirty.

a get on a bus/train/plane
b get off one bus/train/plane and get on a different bus/train/plane
c drive another person to their destination
d leave an airport by plane
e stand by the road and ask for free rides
f arrive at a place
g arrive at an airport by plane
h visit many different places in a large area
i start a journey

b 💬 Cover the sentences in **a** and use the map to retell the story.

c Match the travel problems with the pictures.
1. ☐ They **missed** their train.
2. ☐ My car **broke down** on the motorway.
3. ☐ There was a lot of **turbulence** /ˈtɜːbjʊləns/ during the flight.
4. ☐ I **had an accident** on the drive to work.
5. ☐ The **traffic jam** went on for miles down the road.
6. ☐ There was **something wrong with** the plane.
7. ☐ There was a **strike**, so there were no buses.
8. ☐ We **got lost** in the city centre.
9. ☐ There was a **long queue** /kjuː/ at the ticket office.
10. ☐ There was a **delay** at the station.

d ▶ 02.10 Listen and check. Then listen and repeat.

e 💬 Cover the sentences in **c** and try to remember them. Use the pictures to help you.

f 💬 Ask and answer the questions.
1. Which of the problems in the pictures have you had on journeys this year?
2. Is there a country you'd like to travel around?
3. When was the last time a friend or family member gave you a lift?
4. How do you feel when a plane takes off and lands?
5. What is your least favourite way to travel? Why?

g ≫ Now go back to p. 20.

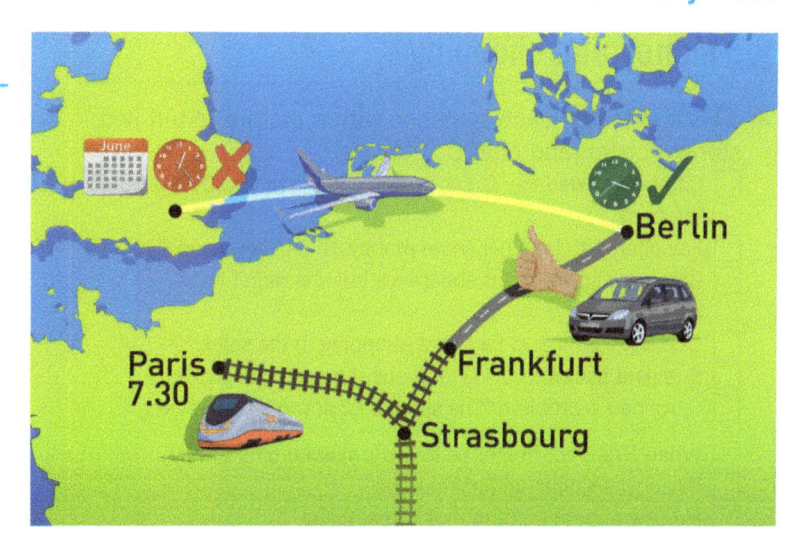

135

3A Money and shopping

a ▶03.01 Match each sentence with a picture to tell two stories. Listen and check.

- ☐ Carol now **owed** Fay £700, so she **got a loan** for £1,000 from the bank.
- ☐ Fay offered to **lend** her some money, so she **borrowed** £100.
- ☐ Carol saw some shoes she loved, but she didn't have any **cash**.
- ☐ One day, Carol and Fay went shopping in **the sales**.
- ☐ She **paid back** the £700 (and spent the rest on shoes).
- ☐ Carol had a problem. She **spent** a lot of money on shoes.

- ☐ When Brian got home, he found a **special offer** online.
- ☐ Brian was **saving up for** a camera.
- ☐ He saw a great camera, but it **cost** £499.
- ☐ He asked the shop assistant for a **discount**, but she said no.
- ☐ So he got the camera for £399! He was very happy!
- ☐ Brian **couldn't afford** it. He only had £400 in his **bank account**.

b 💬 Cover the sentences and use the words in the box to tell the stories.

| **Carol** spend money on   the sales   cash   lend |
| borrow /ˈbɒrəʊ/   owe /əʊ/   get a loan /ləʊn/   pay back |

| **Brian** save up for   cost   afford /əˈfɔːd/ |
| bank account /əˈkaʊnt/   discount /ˈdɪskaʊnt/ |
| special offer |

c ⫸ Now go back to p. 28.

4A Clothes and appearance

a 💬 Read the lists of words. Which words do you already know?

| **Underclothes:** socks, underwear /ˈʌndəweə/, tights /taɪts/ | **Accessories:** necklace, sunglasses, belt, scarf, handbag, bracelet /ˈbreɪslət/, earrings /ˈɪərɪŋz/, tie /taɪ/, gloves /glʌvz/ |
| **Footwear:** trainers, boots, flat shoes, high heels, sandals /ˈsændəlz/ | **Clothing:** jumper, suit, raincoat, top, tracksuit /ˈtræksuːt/, sweatshirt /ˈswetʃɜːt/, shorts |

b Write the correct word from **a** next to each picture.

c ▶04.01 Listen and check your answers in **b**. Repeat the words.

d Cover the words. Can you remember the names of all the things in the pictures?

e Match the sentence halves.
1 ☐ I need a haircut, so I'm **going**
2 ☐ I'm going to go shopping and **get**
3 ☐ I want to **look**
4 ☐ He should **have**
5 ☐ It's an expensive restaurant, so please **wear**
6 ☐ She has very long nails, so she often **goes**

a **a new outfit** for the party.
b **something nice**.
c **to the hairdresser's** this afternoon.
d **a shave** before he goes to his job interview.
e **my best** because all my family are coming.
f **to the beautician's**.

f ▶04.02 Listen and check your answers to **e**.

g 💬 Work in pairs. Ask and answer the questions.
- When was the last time you wanted to look your best?
- What did you wear? Did you get a new outfit?
- Did you have a shave / go to the hairdresser's / go to the beautician's?

h ⫸ Now go back to p. 38.

Vocabulary Focus

5A Work

a ▶05.01 Match the jobs with the pictures. Listen and check.
1. ☐ gardener /ˈgɑːdnə/
2. ☐ hairdresser /ˈheədresə/
3. ☐ plumber /ˈplʌmə/
4. ☐ scientist /ˈsaɪəntɪst/
5. ☐ lawyer /ˈlɔɪə/
6. ☐ accountant /əˈkaʊntənt/
7. ☐ electrician /ɪlekˈtrɪʃən/
8. ☐ banker /ˈbæŋkə/
9. ☐ IT worker (We usually say *I work in IT*, not *I'm an IT worker*.)

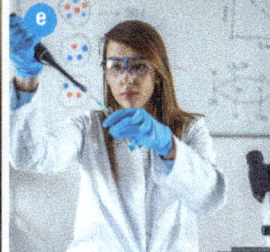

b ▶05.01 Listen to the words in **a**. Which syllables are stressed? Add 2–8 to the chart.

X x	X x x	x X x	x x X x
	gardener		

c ▶05.02 Choose the correct verbs to complete the sentences. Then listen and check. Repeat the sentences.

am   deal with   earn   ~~have~~   make   need   work

1. They __have__ — a nice working environment. /ɪnˈvaɪrənmənt/ / a lot of skills.
2. I _____ — long hours. / weekends. / in a team.
3. You _____ — several years of training. / good qualifications. /kwɒlɪfɪˈkeɪʃənz/ / a university degree. /juːnɪˈvɜːsɪti dɪˌgriː/
4. I _____ — serious problems. / people every day.
5. I _____ a good salary. /ˈsæləri/
6. I _____ self-employed. /ɪmˈplɔɪd/
7. I _____ important decisions. /dɪˈsɪʒənz/

d 💬 Name one job for each description in **c**.

Plumbers have a lot of skills.

e ⟫ Now go back to p. 48.

5B Jobs

a Match the jobs with the pictures.
1. ☐ shop assistant /ˈʃɒp əsɪstənt/
2. ☐ taxi driver /ˈtæksi ˌdraɪvə/
3. ☐ computer programmer /kəmˌpjuːtə ˈprəʊgræmə/
4. ☐ actor /ˈæktə/
5. ☐ musician /mjuːˈzɪʃən/
6. ☐ politician /pɒlɪˈtɪʃən/
7. ☐ builder /ˈbɪldə/
8. ☐ journalist /ˈdʒɜːnəlɪst/
9. ☐ architect /ˈɑːkɪtekt/
10. ☐ designer /dɪˈzaɪnə/
11. ☐ vet /vet/
12. ☐ carer /ˈkeərə/

b ▶05.10 Listen and check. Repeat the words.

c 💬 Which of these jobs are popular in your country? Which would you like to do?

d ⟫ Now go back to p. 51.

137

6B -ed and -ing adjectives

a ▶06.06 Look at the pictures. Complete the sentences with the pairs of words. Listen and check.

annoying / annoyed
1 a Magda was _____ by the music from the neighbour's flat.
   b The music from the neighbour's flat was really _____.

disappointing / disappointed
2 a Will's birthday present was very _____.
   b Will was very _____ by his present.

confusing / confused
3 a Andreas was very _____ by the road signs.
   b The road signs were really _____.

tiring / tired
4 a Sara was _____ after a long day at work.
   b Sara had a really _____ day at work.

frightening / frightened
5 a Mehmet thought the animals were _____.
   b Mehmet was _____ of the animals.

amazing / amazed
6 a The fireworks looked _____.
   b Everyone was _____ by the fireworks.

embarrassing / embarrassed
7 a Liza was _____ by her boyfriend's dancing.
   b Liza's boyfriend's dancing was _____.

surprising / surprised
8 a Anita was _____ to get the news from her sister.
   b Anita got some _____ news from her sister.

shocking / shocked
9 a The price of the meal was _____.
   b They were _____ when they got the bill for the meal.

b ▶06.07 Listen to the -ed adjectives. How many syllables are there? Then listen again and repeat.

amazed /əˈmeɪzd/
excited /ɪkˈsaɪtɪd/
annoyed /əˈnɔɪd/
confused /kənˈfjuːzd/
disappointed /dɪsəˈpɔɪntɪd/
embarrassed /ɪmˈbærəst/
frightened /ˈfraɪtənd/
interested /ˈɪntrəstɪd/
shocked /ʃɒkt/
surprised /səˈpraɪzd/
tired /taɪəd/

c 💬 Talk to a partner. Which word(s) could describe your feelings in these situations?
1 You can't understand the instructions for your new phone.
2 You are walking alone in a forest at night.
3 You hear some very bad news that you can't believe is true.
4 You've just broken a box of eggs in the supermarket.
5 You have an important meeting. Your boss has forgotten to tell you where it is.
6 You've just run 10 km.
7 The weather on holiday was terrible every day.
8 You suddenly get a big pay rise.

d Write a sentence about each situation in **c** using an -ed or an -ing adjective.
My new phone is very confusing.

e 💬 Compare your sentences with a partner. Are they similar?

f ▶ Now go back to p. 60.

Vocabulary Focus

7A *get* collocations

a ▶ 07.05 Complete the sentences with the phrases in the box. Then listen and check.

get better   get a job   get paid
get on well   get ill   get an offer

A I would love to ¹_____ as a designer. But for now I'll take any work.
B You could work as a waiter until you ²_____ from a design company.
A I have a terrible cold at the moment. It's strange – I hardly ever ³_____.
B Oh dear. I hope you ⁴_____ soon.
A How's the new job?
B It's great. I really ⁵_____ with my new colleagues. But I don't ⁶_____ for the first month, so I can't afford to go out for a while.

b 💬 Practise the conversations in a with a partner.

c ▶ 07.06 Complete Ted's story with the phrases in the box. Use the correct form of *get*. Listen and check.

get to know   get engaged   get together
get a place   get divorced   get in touch

Ted studied hard at school and ¹_____ at university. While he was there, he ²_____ Sylvia, another student on his course. They didn't see each other after university, but one day Ted saw Sylvia's photo in a newspaper and decided to ³_____ with her again. They soon ⁴_____ and were a very happy couple. Just six months later, they decided they wanted to spend their lives together, so they ⁵_____. But the story didn't end well. Only a year after the wedding, they ⁶_____.

d Work in pairs. Write your own definitions for these phrases.

get divorced   get together   get on well
get engaged   get in touch   get to know

e Check your definitions in a dictionary or with your teacher. Were you right?

f ≫ Now go back to p. 69.

8B Sports and leisure activities

a Match the sports and activities with the pictures.

1 [b] surfing /sɜːfɪŋ/
2 ☐ snowboarding /snəʊbɔːdɪŋ/
3 ☐ golf /gɒlf/
4 ☐ volleyball /vɒlibɔːl/
5 ☐ skateboarding /skeɪtbɔːdɪŋ/
6 ☐ rock climbing /klaɪmɪŋ/
7 ☐ gymnastics /dʒɪmnæstɪks/
8 ☐ (scuba) diving /(skuːbə) daɪvɪŋ/
9 ☐ yoga /jəʊgə/
10 ☐ jogging /dʒɒgɪŋ/
11 ☐ windsurfing /wɪndsɜːfɪŋ/
12 ☐ athletics /æθletɪks/
13 ☐ ice hockey /aɪs hɒki/
14 ☐ squash /skwɒʃ/
15 ☐ ice skating /aɪs skeɪtɪŋ/

b ▶ 08.06 Listen and check. Underline the stressed syllable of each word in a. Then listen and repeat.

c Read the note below. Which verb do we use with the sports in a: *play*, *do* or *go*?

We usually use the verb *play* with sports that use a ball: *play volleyball / squash*

We usually use *go* with *-ing* forms: *go surfing / skateboarding*

We use *do* with other activities: *do yoga / athletics*

d Write one sport or activity for each adjective. Use the sports and leisure activities in a or your own ideas.

- relaxing
- exciting
- tiring
- boring
- frightening
- fun

e 💬 Work in pairs. Compare your answers to d.

f ≫ Now go back to p. 81.

139

9A Education collocations

a Match phrases 1–7 in **bold** with definitions a–g.

1 ☐ **fail an exam** a get a place at university
2 ☐ **hand in an essay** b study on a three- or four-year course at university
3 ☐ **get into university** c give a finished essay to a teacher
4 ☐ **do a degree in** maths d review class material for an exam
5 ☐ **revise** for an exam e not pass an exam
6 ☐ **take notes** f receive a high mark in an exam or for an essay
7 ☐ **get good marks** g write down main ideas

b Choose the correct words to complete the text.

My brother was always the ambitious one in the family, and he really wanted to ¹*get into / get onto* university. His dream was to ²*make / do* a degree in physics because he wanted to become a scientist. He studied hard at school, and he managed to ³*get / go* a place at a top university – St Andrews!

University was hard, but he enjoyed it. He had to ⁴*take / write* a lot of essays, but he was a good student. He always ⁵*did / took* a lot of notes during his classes, and he only ⁶*handed / put* an essay in late once because he had a broken leg and was in hospital! Because of his hard work, he ⁷*got / made* good marks for all his courses, and he never ⁸*failed / lost* an exam. He was an A+ student. And what about me? Well, that's a different story …

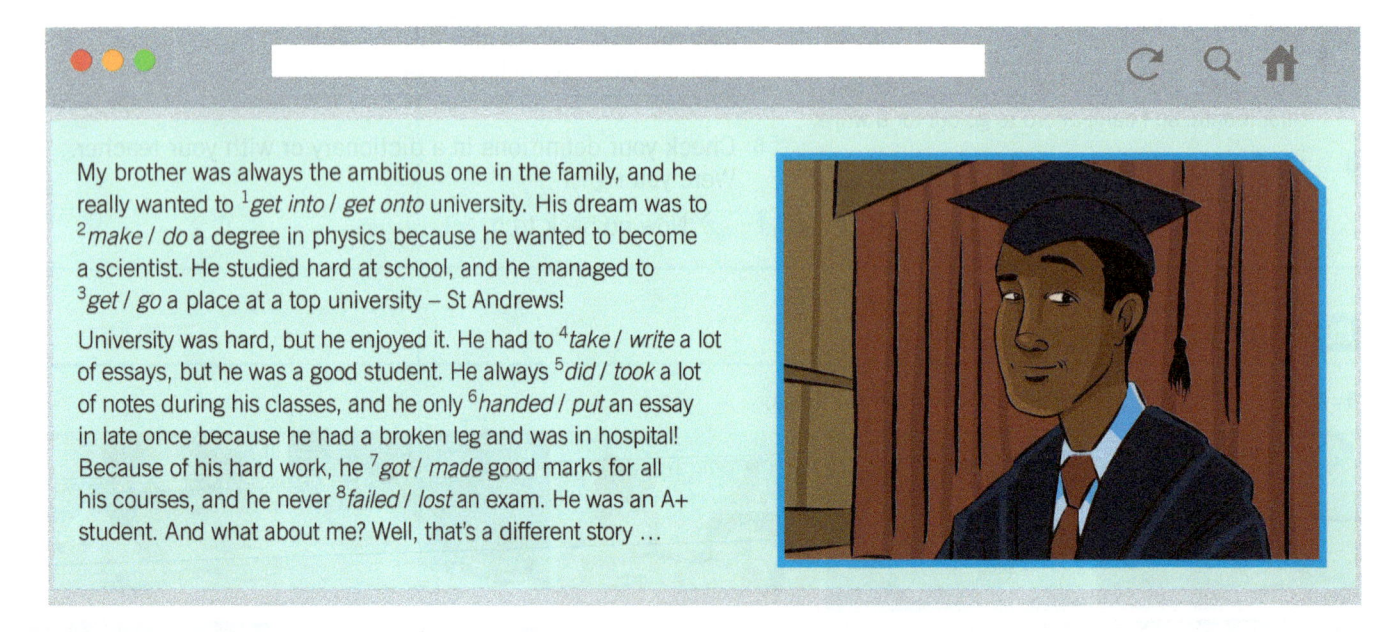

c ▶09.02 Listen and check.

d Complete the sentences with the words below.

| notes | mark | degree | university | essay | place | exam |

1 She's doing a _____ in business management.
2 He handed in his _____ late because he was ill.
3 I need to revise for my _____ next week.
4 She got a very good _____ for her essay: A+.
5 I took a lot of _____ during the lecture. You can read them if you want.
6 She's very intelligent. She got a _____ at Harvard Business School.
7 He got into _____ last year. He's studying history.

e ⟫ Now go back to p. 89.

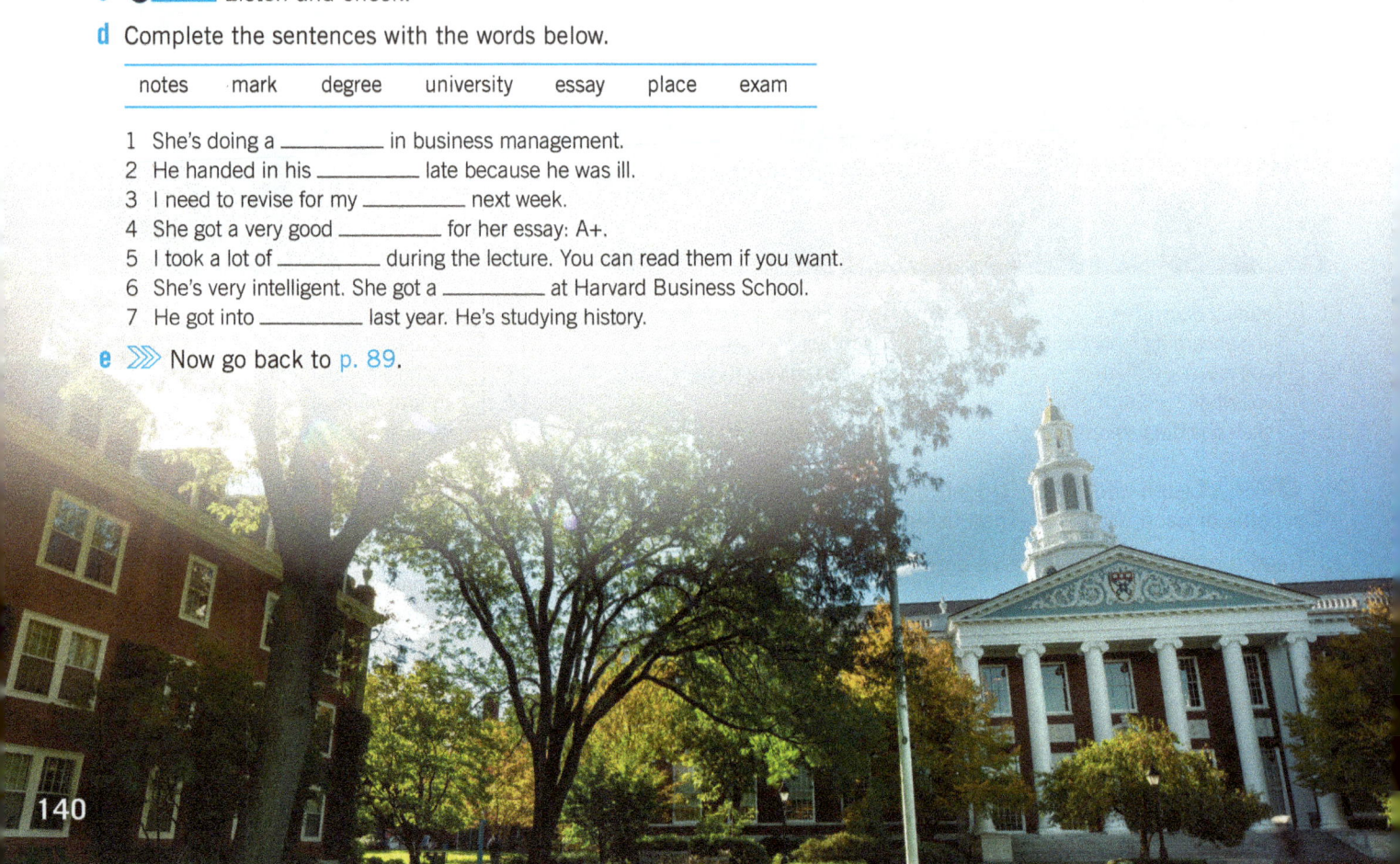

Vocabulary Focus

9B Verbs followed by to + infinitive / verb + -ing

a Match sentences 1–12 with the things the people said.
1 She **refused** to discuss the matter.
2 They **arranged** to meet in the evening.
3 He **forgot** to go to the supermarket.
4 He **recommended** ordering the cake.
5 He **imagined** being somewhere warmer.
6 She **missed** living by the sea.
7 He really **disliked** travelling by train.
8 The shop **seemed** to be closed.
9 They **agreed** to change tables.
10 She **managed** to make the sauce.
11 He **regretted** wearing a suit.
12 She **avoids** eating spicy food.

☐ 'OK, so see you tomorrow evening at 7 pm.'
☐ 'Making the sauce was really difficult, but it tastes all right.'
☐ 'I didn't remember to go to the supermarket. Sorry. I was really busy.'
☐ **'You should try the cake. It's delicious.'**
☐ 'I loved living by the sea. I used to go swimming every morning.'
☐ 'Sorry, I'm not going to talk about this. I've made my decision.'
☐ 'I hate trains. They're so noisy.'
☐ 'I'd love to be on the beach in Greece right now. The sun, the water …'
☐ 'It looks like the shop's closed.'
☐ 'I look so silly in this suit!'
☐ 'OK, let's move to that table over there.'
☐ 'No, thanks. I don't eat curry. It gives me a bad stomach.'

b Complete the table with the verbs in **bold** from **a**.

Verbs followed by *to* + infinitive	Verbs followed by verb + *-ing*
refuse	

c ▶ 09.09 Listen to the sentences in **a** 1–12. <u>Underline</u> the stressed syllable in the words in **bold**. Practice saying the sentences.

d Complete the sentences using the verbs in the table in **b**.
1 *This computer is terrible. Buying it was a big mistake!*
   He _____ buying the computer.
2 *I hate taking exams. I get so nervous!*
   He really _____ taking exams.
3 *Oh, no! It's my mother's birthday. I haven't sent her a card.*
   He _____ to send his mother a birthday card.
4 *It would be wonderful to live in Paris! I could eat great food every day!*
   He _____ living in Paris.
5 *No, I won't pay more money.*
   She _____ to pay more money.
6 *OK, so let's talk tomorrow. I'll call you.*
   They _____ to talk on the phone.
7 *I try not to leave work at 5 pm. The traffic is terrible.*
   She _____ leaving work at 5 pm.
8 *You should read this book on Italy. It's great.*
   He _____ reading a book on Italy.
9 *I want to play with my cat, but he's at my parents' house.*
   She _____ playing with her cat.
10 *Fine with me, I'm happy to share a dessert.*
   They _____ to share one dessert between them.
11 *I finished my essay just in time to hand it in.*
   She _____ to finish her work on time.
12 *You look upset. Are you OK?*
   She _____ to be upset.

e ⟫ Now go back to p. 91.

141

10A Multi-word verbs

a Read the sentences. Which multi-word verbs in the box can replace the words in **bold**?

> passed on   put off   carried on   came round
> looked after   handed in   broke up
> turned down   joined in   felt like

1 I asked him to be quiet, but he just **continued** talking. _____
2 It was a really sunny day, and he **wanted** an ice-cream. _____
3 She **came to my house** to ask for some advice. _____
4 I **cared for** my friend's cat while he was on holiday. _____
5 They used to go out with each other, but they **ended their relationship**. _____
6 He **said no to** the invitation because he had too much work. _____
7 The game looked like fun, so I **did it with them**. _____
8 They **delayed** the meeting because Bob was ill. _____
9 I **took** the keys I found to the receptionist. _____
10 He **told her** the message as soon as he saw her. _____

b Complete the sentences with the correct forms of the multi-word verbs in **a**.

1 My friend _____ for dinner last night. I cooked her spaghetti.
2 She's ill, so we _____ the party until she gets better.
3 Can you _____ my new number to Bob? It's 07806 540 234.
4 Mike and I were together for a year, but we _____ two months ago.
5 Tom started singing a song, and then we all _____. It was quite noisy!
6 Somebody _____ my wallet to the police.
7 She _____ the job offer because the pay was too low.
8 'Do you _____ pizza tonight?' 'Yes, that sounds good.'
9 I'm _____ my niece this evening. She's only seven years old.
10 We were all tired and wanted to stop, but our teacher told us to _____ running.

> 💡 **Tip**
>
> Multi-word verbs have different kinds of grammar. Some transitive multi-word verbs (*hand in*, *pass on*, *put off*) can be separated by an object:
> We **put off** the match. ✓   We **put** the match **off**. ✓
>
> If the object of these multi-word verbs is a pronoun, they must be separated:
> I **handed** it **in**. ✓   ~~I handed in it.~~ ✗
>
> Other multi-word verbs (*feel like*, *look after*) can never be separated:
> He **felt like** an ice-cream. ✓   ~~He felt an ice-cream like.~~ ✗

c ⟫ Now go back to p. 99.

11A Compound nouns

a Write the compound nouns. Use the words in the sentences to help you.
1 A shop that sells shoes is a *shoe shop*.
2 A book with addresses in it is an _____.
3 A shelf you put books on is a _____.
4 An office where you buy tickets is a _____.
5 A ring you put keys on is a _____.
6 A programme on TV is a _____.
7 Lights on a street to help you see when it's dark are _____.
8 A sign by the road is a _____.
9 A machine you can get cash from is a _____.
10 Fiction that describes a new kind of science is _____.

> 💡 **Tip**
>
> • The first word in a compound noun is normally singular:
> a ~~books~~ shop ✗   a bookshop ✓
> This is also true if the compound noun is plural:
> There are three ~~tickets~~ offices in the station. ✗
> There are three ticket offices in the station. ✓
>
> • When a compound noun is used for many years, it sometimes becomes one word, not two. For example, *Cambridge Advanced Learner's Dictionary* says:
> streetlights ✓   NOT ~~street lights~~ ✗
> But not all compounds can be joined together.
> road sign ✓   NOT ~~roadsign~~ ✗
> Check the punctuation in a recent dictionary to be sure.

b 🔊 11.01 Listen to the compound nouns in **a**. Underline the main stressed syllable. Answer the questions.
1 Which word in compound nouns is normally stressed?
2 Which compound noun is stressed differently from the others?

c Practise saying the compound nouns in **a**.

d Make compound nouns with one word from box A followed by one word from box B. How many can you make?

> **A**
> mountain   TV   bread   coffee   shopping   city
> kitchen   video   tea   rock   car   bottle

> **B**
> knife   top   park   door   bag   climbing
> star   screen   cup   centre   game(s)

e Complete the questions using a compound noun from **d**. More than one compound noun may be correct.
1 Do you like playing _____?
2 How long do you spend looking at a _____ every day?
3 Have you ever gone _____?
4 Would you like to be a _____?
5 Who is your favourite _____?
6 What is your favourite _____?

f 💬 Ask and answer the questions in **e**.

g ⟫ Now go back to p. 108.

Vocabulary Focus

12B Personality adjectives

a Read the sentences and match the people who are opposites.

1. ☐ Sara's so **serious** – she doesn't laugh much and she never makes jokes.
2. ☐ Maria always pays for me and helps me with stuff. She's really **generous**.
3. ☐ Andrew is always so **anxious** – he worries about everything.
4. ☐ Mai-Li is very **shy** and doesn't like meeting new people.

a My sister Yasmin hardly ever worries about anything – I'd love to be as **easygoing** as she is.
b Rea is so **selfish** – she only thinks about what she wants, never other people.
c Rosa is a very **sociable** person – she's always out with friends or at parties.
d Jon's a really **fun** person and I always have a good time when I see him.

b Complete the sentences with the words in the box.

generous   sensible   funny   strict
creative   careless   confident   honest
patient   fair   reliable

1 People who make good decisions and don't do silly things are _____.
2 People who know they are good at certain things are _____.
3 People who always keep their promises, arrive on time, etc., are _____.
4 People who make a lot of rules for children are _____.
5 People who make mistakes because they are not careful are _____.
6 People who don't get angry when something takes a long time are _____.
7 People who give a lot to other people are _____.
8 People who treat everyone equally are _____.
9 People who are good at thinking of new ideas are _____.
10 People who always tell the truth are _____.
11 People who make other people laugh are _____.

💡 **Tip**

Fun and *funny* have different meanings.
She's **funny**. = She makes you laugh.
She's **fun**. = She isn't serious or boring.

c ▶12.10 Listen to the adjectives. <u>Underline</u> the stressed syllable in the words with more than one syllable. The first has been done for you. Practice saying the words.

<u>anx</u>ious /ˈæŋkʃəs/   fun /fʌn/   selfish /ˈselfɪʃ/
careless /ˈkeələs/   funny /ˈfʌni/   sensible /ˈsensɪbəl/
confident /ˈkɒnfɪdənt/   generous /ˈdʒenərəs/   shy /ʃaɪ/
creative /kriˈeɪtɪv/   honest /ˈɒnɪst/   sociable /ˈsəʊʃəbəl/
easygoing /ˈiːziɡəʊɪŋ/   patient /ˈpeɪʃənt/   strict /strɪkt/
fair /feə/   reliable /rɪˈlaɪəbəl/

d Which of the adjectives in **c** are negative?

e 💬 Ask and answer the questions.
1 Which of the adjectives do you think describe your personality?
2 Which qualities would you like to have (but don't)?

I think I'm sociable and easygoing.

I'd like to be more patient.

f ⟫ Now go back to p. 121.

143

GRAMMAR FOCUS

1A Question forms

Questions with *be*
In questions with *be*, the verb *be* goes before the subject. We don't add an auxiliary verb.

▶ 01.05

Question word	be	Subject	
How	's	the food?	–
What	was	the party	like yesterday?
–	Are	you	a teacher?
–	Were	they	late?

> 💡 **Tip** When we want to ask for a description or an opinion, we can use:
> **be like**
> A *What **was** the film **like**?*
> B *It was all right.*
> **How …** with the verb **be**
> A *How **was** your holiday?*
> B *Fantastic!*

Questions with other main verbs
In questions with other verbs, we add an auxiliary verb to form questions. The auxiliary verb goes before the subject.

▶ 01.06

Question word	Auxiliary verb	Subject	Main verb	
Where	do	you	live?	–
What time	did	they	arrive	at the party?
–	Does	the film	have	a happy ending?
–	Did	you	make	the food?

In questions with *do* or *did*, the main verb is in the infinitive:
***Does** she **live** here?* NOT *Does she lives here?*
***Did** you **come** by taxi?* NOT *Did you came by taxi?*
Modal verbs like *can* are also auxiliary verbs:
*What **can** you see?*

Wh- questions start with a question word: *Who, What, Where, When, Why, Which, Whose, How, How much, How many, What time, What colour, What kind of car,* etc.

1B Present simple and present continuous

Present simple
We use the present simple to describe:
- routines and habits:
  *I **send** a lot of emails.*
- situations which are generally true or stay the same for a long time:
  *He **doesn't work** very hard.*

We use adverbs of frequency with the present simple:
*I **always / sometimes / rarely / never** write letters.*
*I write letters **once / ten times a week / year**.*

The verb *be* doesn't have the same form as other verbs:
*I **am** a student.   They **are** not here.*
***Is** she always friendly? Yes, she **is**.*

Present continuous
We use the present continuous to describe:
- actions right now, at the moment of speaking:
  *He **isn't cooking** dinner. He's **watching** TV.*
- temporary actions around the present time:
  *They're **travelling** around Asia this year.*

We often use these time expressions with the present continuous:
*I'm working at a supermarket **right now** / **these days** / **at the moment** / **today** / **this summer** etc.*

SPELLING: verb + *-ing*

Most verbs	+ -ing
sleep watch say	sleep**ing** watch**ing** say**ing**
Stressed vowel + one consonant (not w, x, y)	**2× consonant + -ing**
stop run get	stop**ping** run**ning** get**ting**
Consonant + -e	**– -e and + -ing**
live make have	liv**ing** mak**ing** hav**ing**

▶ 01.12

	I / You / We / They	He / She / It
+	We **live** next door.	He **lives** here.
–	I **don't work** here.	She **doesn't work** here.
Y/N?	**Do** your friends **write** emails? Yes, they **do**. / No, they **don't**.	**Does** your sister **write** a blog? Yes, she **does**. / No, she **doesn't**.

> 💡 **Tip** Some verbs, which describe feelings and states, are not usually used in continuous tenses:
> *be   like   love   hate   prefer   know   understand*
> *remember   forget   want   own   need*
> *I **need** a new computer.* NOT *I'm needing a new computer.*
> *He **doesn't understand** you.* NOT *He isn't understanding you.*

▶ 01.13

	I	He / She / It	You / We / They
+	I'm **watching** TV.	She's **helping**.	We're **working** hard.
–	I'm **not feeling** well.	It **isn't raining**.	They **aren't sleeping**.
Y/N?	**Am** I **looking** all right? Yes, I **am**. / No, I'm **not**.	**Is** he **working** late? Yes, he **is**. / No, he **isn't**.	**Are** they **enjoying** the party? Yes, they **are**. / No, they **aren't**.

> 💡 **Tip** *Is not* and *are not* can be contracted two different ways:
> *is not = isn't = 's not*
> *are not = aren't = 're not*

Grammar Focus

1A Question forms

a Underline the main verb in each question.
1 Where do you <u>live</u>?
2 How are you today?
3 Did you see the football match yesterday?
4 Who do you know at this party?
5 What did you do last weekend?
6 What kind of food do you like?
7 What's the food like?
8 Can I sit here?

b Look at the questions in a again. Tick (✓) the questions which have an auxiliary verb.

c Add the word at the end of each line to make correct questions.
1 What kind of books you usually read?   do
   <u>What kind of books do you usually read?</u>
2 You watch the Olympics on TV?   did
   _____
3 What the food like in India?   was
   _____
4 You go to the gym?   do
   _____
5 How much she earn?   does
   _____
6 It cold today?   is
   _____
7 Where they go on holiday?   did
   _____
8 I late?   am
   _____

d Correct the mistake in each question.
1 **A** Why do want you to go home?
   B Because I'm tired.
2 **A** What did you meet at the party?
   B Rashid and Fran.
3 **A** How much your car was?
   B I paid £800.
4 **A** Which did you see film?
   B The new James Bond film.
5 **A** Who key is this?
   B Mine.
6 **A** How many people you did invite?
   B About 20.
7 **A** Was the film like?
   B It was pretty good.
8 **A** What kind music do you like?
   B I like dance music.

e ≫ Now go to back to p. 9.

1B Present simple and present continuous

a Choose the best ending for each sentence from each pair. Write the number in the box.

1 a ☐ I work in a bank, …   1 but I don't enjoy it.
  b ☐ I'm working in a café, …   2 but it's only a summer job.

2 a ☐ She drives to work every day, …   1 so she can't answer the phone.
  b ☐ She's driving right now, …   2 so she spends a lot on petrol.

3 a ☐ I write to my parents …   1 because their phone's broken.
  b ☐ I'm writing to my parents …   2 once a month.

4 a ☐ We aren't eating there …   1 today because it's full.
  b ☐ We don't eat there …   2 because the food is awful.

b Choose the correct answer.
1 *I eat / I'm eating* my lunch now. Can you wait?
2 Look at that man! He *doesn't wear / isn't wearing* any shoes.
3 *She usually goes / She's usually going* to the cinema on Tuesday nights.
4 *I study / I'm studying* hard because I have an exam next week.
5 Some of my friends *look / are looking* at their phones every five minutes.
6 My grandparents *hardly ever visit / are hardly ever visiting* us because they live in Australia.
7 We want to finish the project tonight, so *we work / we're working* late.
8 *Is your brother liking / Does your brother like* video games?

c Complete the conversation with the present simple or present continuous.

A What ¹ <u>are you doing</u> (you / do)?
B ² _____ (I / check) Instagram.
A Really? But you checked it about 20 minutes ago. How often ³ _____ (you / check) your account?
B Well, ⁴ _____ (I / usually check) my account once a day. But today's different. ⁵ _____ (my sister / travel) around Africa at the moment, and I'm worried about her.
⁶ _____ (she / usually send) me a message two or three times a day, but the last time she wrote was a week ago.
A Maybe ⁷ _____ (she / travel) right now, and she can't use the Internet. ⁸ _____ (she / go) on safari?
B No, I don't think so. ⁹ _____ (she / not like) the country. ¹⁰ _____ (she / prefer) cities. Oh … look! Here's a message from her. You were right! ¹¹ _____ (she / drive) through the Masai Mara National Park right now.
A Where's that?
B ¹² _____ (it / be) in Kenya. ¹³ _____ (there / be) a lot of wild animals there.
A Cool … that's amazing. So why ¹⁴ _____ (she / spend) her time on Instagram?

d ≫ Now go to back to p. 11.

145

2A Past simple

We use the past simple to talk about completed actions and situations in the past.
I **went** to Greece last summer. It **was** amazing.
I **didn't want** to leave.
Where **did** you **stay**?

The form of the past simple is the same for all persons.

▶ 02.03 In positive statements, regular verbs have -ed endings:
I **decided** yesterday.
We **played** volleyball on the beach.

However, many common verbs are irregular:
go → I **went** there last year.
have → We **had** a lot of fun.
see → She **saw** the Taj Mahal.

There is a list of irregular verbs on p. 168.

I didn't want to go water skiing, but when I tried it, it was amazing.

To form negative statements and questions, we use the auxiliary verb *did*.

	I / You / We / They / He / She / It
–	I **didn't go** there.
Y/N?	**Did** you **have** fun? Yes, I **did**. / No, I **didn't**.

▶ 02.04 *Be* doesn't have the same form as other verbs:

	I / He / She / It	You / We / They
+	The weather **was** great.	The shops **were** near the beach.
–	I **wasn't** very happy.	We **weren't** tired.
Y/N?	**Was** your tour guide good? Yes, she **was**. / No, she **wasn't**.	**Were** you late for your flight? Yes, we **were**. / No, we **weren't**.

We often use these time expressions with the past simple:
I visited Los Angeles **last** week/year.
　　　　　　　　　　　 two days **ago**.
　　　　　　　　　　　 when I was a child.

They come at the beginning or the end of a sentence:
When I finished school, I went to university.
I went to Greece **two years ago**.

SPELLING: verb + -ed

Most verbs play　watch　show	+ -ed play**ed**　watch**ed**　show**ed**
Ending in -e live　hate　agree　love	+ -d live**d**　hate**d**　agree**d**　love**d**
Stressed vowel + consonant (not w, x, y) stop　plan　prefer	2× consonant and + -ed stop**ped**　plan**ned**　prefer**red**
Consonant -y marry　study　try　worry	– -y, + -ied marr**ied**　stud**ied**　tr**ied**　worr**ied**

2B Past continuous

We use the past continuous to describe something in progress at a particular time in the past.
In 2016, I **was living** in Poland.
At 11 o'clock, he **was waiting** by the fountain.
When they arrived, I **was cooking** dinner.

Use the past continuous with the past simple:

- to describe long and short actions together:
  I **was reading** my book when the plane took off.

- to describe a longer action that stopped suddenly because something else happened:
  When I **was driving** to work, my car broke down.

We can use *when* to connect the two parts of a sentence:
When my car broke down, I was driving to work.
My car broke down **when** I was driving to work.

💡 Tip

We often use the past continuous to describe the situation at the beginning of a story.
In 2015, we **were travelling** across Mexico.
John **was driving** too fast down the motorway.

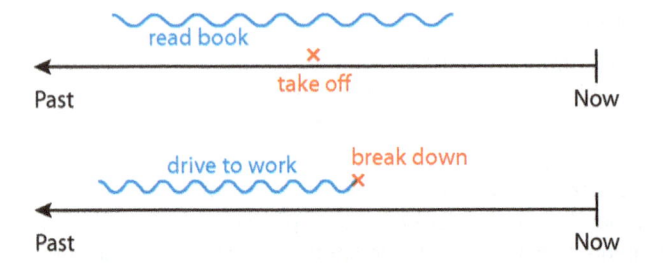

▶ 02.13

	I / He / She / It	You / We / They
+	I **was driving** to work.	You **were standing** on the platform.
–	He **wasn't listening**.	We **weren't watching**.
Y/N?	**Was** she **waiting** for you? Yes, she **was**. / No, she **wasn't**.	**Were** they **travelling** by train? Yes, they **were**. / No, they **weren't**.

Grammar Focus

2A Past simple

a Write the past simple forms of the verbs. Some of them are irregular.

1 ask _____
2 buy _____
3 dance _____
4 enjoy _____
5 find _____
6 forget _____
7 know _____
8 learn _____
9 hurry _____
10 meet _____
11 offer _____
12 prefer _____
13 relax _____
14 say _____
15 wear _____

b Last week, Dan's holiday was very good. Lisa's was very bad. Complete each sentence with the positive or negative form of the verb at the beginning of the line.

DAN — My fantastic holiday

be   1 My plane <u>wasn't</u> late.
arrive 2 My bags _____ at the airport.
be   3 The people at the hotel _____ very nice.
eat   4 I _____ the local food. It was great!
rain   5 It _____.
spend   6 I _____ a lot of money. It was so cheap!
speak   7 I _____ to a lot of people.
have   8 I _____ a good time.

LISA — My terrible holiday

My plane <u>was</u> late.
My bags _____ at the airport.
The people at the hotel _____ very nice.
I _____ the local food. It was awful.
It _____ every day.
I _____ a lot of money. It was so expensive!
I _____ to anybody.
I _____ a good time.

c Dan asked Lisa about her holiday. Write Dan's questions in the past simple.

1 **D** why / your plane / be / late
   <u>Why was your plane late?</u>
   L I think there was a problem with the engine.
2 **D** when / your bags / arrive
   _____?
   L On the last day of my holiday.
3 **D** what / you / wear?
   _____?
   L I bought some new clothes.
4 **D** the people / be / friendly
   _____?
   L No, they were rude.
5 **D** what / weather / be / like
   _____?
   L It rained every day.
6 **D** what / kind of food / you / eat
   _____?
   L Nothing special.
7 **D** you / have / a good time
   _____?
   L No!

d ⟫ Now go back to p. 19.

2B Past continuous

a Complete the sentences with the past continuous forms of the verbs.

1 A year ago, _____ (I / live) with my parents.
2 At nine last night, _____ (we / sleep).
3 **A** What _____ (you / do) at midnight on New Year's Eve?
   B We _____ (watch) the celebrations on TV.
4 _____ (she / not study) when I got home; _____ (she / talk) to her friends online.
5 **A** _____ (Most people / not wear) suits for the job interview.
   B What _____ (they / wear)?

b Choose the best form for each verb. There is one past simple verb and one past continuous verb in each sentence.

1 The doorbell *rang / was ringing* when I *watched / was watching* a film.
2 She *walked / was walking* down the street when she *saw / was seeing* her friend.
3 He *left / was leaving* his job when he *studied / was studying* for his exams.
4 I *did / was doing* some cleaning when I *heard / was hearing* the news on the radio.
5 We *felt / were feeling* tired when we *got / were getting* home.
6 I *didn't visit / wasn't visiting* Cancún when I *worked / was working* in Mexico.
7 I *wasn't looking / didn't look* when I *crashed / was crashing* my bicycle into a tree.

c Use the past continuous and the past simple of the verbs in brackets to complete the sentences about each picture.

1 When I _____ down the street, I _____ ten dollars. (walk, find)

2 It _____ when she _____ the house. (rain, leave)

3 When you _____ me, I _____ dinner. (call, cook)

4 They _____ quietly when the teacher _____ back. (not work, come)

d ⟫ Now go back to p. 21.

147

3A Present perfect or past simple

We use the present perfect to talk about past experiences when we don't specify when they happened. The present perfect refers to the whole past, not a particular time.

Regular past participles end in -ed, e.g., I have **worked** …
Many past participles are irregular, e.g., I have **bought** …

The past simple and the past participle are often different, e.g., I **drove**; I've **driven**.

See p. 168 for a list of irregular verbs.

> **Tip**
>
> **The verb *go* in the present perfect**
> We use *been* instead of *gone* for a past experience:
> I've **been** to China. (= I went there and came back home.)
>
> We use *gone* to say where other people are now:
> She's **gone** to China. (= she's there now.)

▶ 03.04

	I / You / We / They have + past participle	He / She / It has + past participle
+	I've **given** a stranger a lift.	He's **given** a stranger a lift.
−	We **haven't done** any charity work.	He **hasn't done** any charity work.
Y/N?	**Have** you ever helped a stranger? Yes, I **have**. / No, I **haven't**.	**Has** she ever helped a stranger? Yes, she **has**. / No, she **hasn't**.

We often use *ever* and *never* with the present perfect to talk about our whole life experience. *Ever* and *never* come before the past participle in the sentence.

We can also use *once / twice / three times*, etc. at the end of a sentence to say how many times we have had an experience.

A I've **never** visited Thailand. Have you **ever** been there? } Present perfect
B Yes, I have. I've been there **three times**. } for experiences in general

When we ask or talk about specific past times, we use the past simple.

A When was **the last time** you went? } Past simple for
B **Two years ago**, I flew to Phuket. } specific events

3B Present perfect with *already* and *yet*

▶ 03.09 We can use the present perfect with the adverbs *already* and *yet* to show how a recent past event relates to the present.

The present perfect with *already* in positive statements shows that something is complete, often before we expected.
The party was only last week, but Martha has already written all her thank-you notes!

Already usually comes before the past participle.
We also use *already* in present perfect questions to show surprise.
Have you **already done** all your work?
Has Lucas **already cleaned** his room?

Use the present perfect with *yet*:
- in a negative statement to show that something is not complete
  *I **haven't sold** my laptop **yet**.*
- in a question to ask if something is complete.
  ***Have** you **sold** your car **yet**?*

Yet comes at the end of the sentence.
A You **haven't set** the table for dinner **yet**.
B Well, **have** you **cooked** dinner **yet**? I'm hungry!

> **Tip**
>
> Don't use a past time expression (e.g., *five minutes ago, last week*) with the present perfect. Use the past simple to talk about the time when something happened:
> *I've **already seen** this film. I **saw** it **last week**.*
> NOT ~~I've already seen this movie last week.~~

Grammar Focus

3A Present perfect or past simple

a Write the past participles of the verbs.
1. buy — bought
2. do — ___
3. drive — ___
4. give — ___
5. make — ___
6. lend — ___
7. ride — ___
8. save — ___
9. see — ___
10. sell — ___
11. smile — ___
12. spend — ___
13. take — ___
14. want — ___
15. write — ___

b Complete the sentences with the present perfect forms of the verbs in brackets. Use contractions where they are natural.
1. I 've never given (never / give) money to charity.
2. A _____ (you / ever / sell) anything on eBay?
   B Yes, I have. Several times.
3. She _____ (live) in a lot of different countries.
4. I know that restaurant – we _____ (eat) there before. The food's excellent.
5. I _____ (never / sing) in front of a large group of people – and I never want to!
6. A _____ (he / ever / cook) for more than ten people?
   B No, he hasn't. What about you?
7. She _____ (help) me several times – she's very kind.
8. My car _____ (never / break) down, and it's more than ten years old.
9. How many times _____ (the children / see) this film?
10. We _____ (never / try) this, so it'll be a new experience.

c Correct the mistakes in these sentences.
1. Have you ever ~~climb~~ a mountain?
   Have you ever climbed a mountain?
2. I never saw that film.
   _____
3. Did you ever been to Canada?
   _____
4. Where have you been on holiday last year?
   _____
5. She broken her leg two times.
   _____
6. I've worked in a hospital a long time ago.
   _____
7. In your life, how many times did you move to a new home?
   _____
8. When we went to London, we've visited Kew Gardens.
   _____

d ⟫ Now go back to p. 29.

3B Present perfect with *already* and *yet*

a Match the questions and answers.
1. [g] Would you like some food?
2. [ ] Did you like the film?
3. [ ] Has Junko called yet?
4. [ ] Where's Liza?
5. [ ] Would you like to go for a walk?
6. [ ] Can you email Marc about the meeting?
7. [ ] Have you written your essay yet?
8. [ ] What did you think of the report?

a No, I haven't heard from her yet.
b I've already emailed him.
c I don't know. She went out an hour ago, and she hasn't come back yet.
d I'm afraid I haven't read it yet.
e No, thanks. I've already been out.
f We haven't seen it yet.
g No, thanks. I've already had lunch.
h Yes, I've already given it to our teacher!

b Put the words in the correct order to make sentences or questions.
1. they / have / us / yet / paid ?
   Have they paid us yet?
2. already / I've / money / all / spent / my .
   _____
3. arrived / our visitors / have / already .
   _____
4. shops / I / yet / haven't / to / the / been .
   _____
5. raining / yet / started / it / hasn't .
   _____
6. he / yet / any / has / money / saved ?
   _____

c Look at Jeff's list of things to do. Write sentences about what he has already done (✓) and what he hasn't done yet. Use *already* / *yet* and the present perfect.
1. _He hasn't gone shopping yet._
2. _____
3. _____
4. _____
5. _____
6. _____
7. _____
8. _____
9. _____
10. _____

Jeff To Do – Wednesday
1. go shopping
2. pay Mark back
3. buy paper for the printer ✓
4. check my emails ✓
5. ask Dad for some money
6. write to Daniel ✓
7. finish writing my project ✓
8. clean the flat
9. take out rubbish
10. have a haircut ✓

d ⟫ Now go back to p. 31.

149

4A Present continuous and *be going to*

I'm meeting Mary at the library to study tomorrow. After the exams, we're going to celebrate!

Present continuous

The present continuous is more natural to talk about **arrangements** – when you have agreed on something with other people or you have already spent money.

I'm getting married next week. (We have arranged and paid for everything.)
I'm meeting Mary at the library tomorrow. (We have arranged a time and place for the meeting.)

> **Tip**
> When we use the present continuous with a future meaning, we usually mention the time (e.g., *tomorrow*, *next week*). We don't need to mention the time with *be going to*:
> *She's leaving **tomorrow**.* (future arrangement)
> *She's leaving.* (right now)
> *She's going to leave.* (future plan)

(For the form of the present continuous, see Grammar reference 1B.)

be going to

Be going to + infinitive tells people about a **plan** or **intention** – when you have already decided to do something in the future.

We're going to get married next year. (We have decided this, but we haven't booked anything yet.)
After the exams, we're going to celebrate. (But we don't know exactly where or what time.)

▶ 04.04 *be going to* + infinitive

	I	He / She / It	You / We / They
+	I'm going to watch TV.	She's going to help.	We're going to work hard.
−	I'm not going to play.	It's not going to arrive today.	They're not going to sleep.
Y/N?	Am I going to pick him up? Yes, I am. / No, I'm not.	Is he going to work late? Yes, he is. / No, he isn't.	Are they going to bring anything? Yes, they are. / No, they aren't.

We use both the present continuous and *be going to* + infinitive to talk about future plans – things we have decided to do in the future. In most situations, both forms are possible.

I'm taking an English exam next year. ✓
I'm going to take an English exam next year. ✓

4B will / won't / shall

We use *will* to show we are deciding something while we are speaking:
A *Would you like tea or coffee?*
B *Er … I'll have tea, please.*

This is often to make **offers** and **promises**:
A *Oh, no – I've left my money at home!*
B *Don't worry – I'll pay.*
A *Can I tell you a secret?*
B *Of course. I promise I won't tell anyone else.*

We can make a **request** with *will*:
Will you take a photo?
Will you give me a lift to the cinema tomorrow?

We use *shall* in questions to make **offers** and **suggestions**:
Shall I get the bill? (= I'm offering to get it.)
Shall we go to the cinema this weekend? (= I'm suggesting this.)

We can also use *shall* to **ask for a suggestion**:
A *What shall we do this evening?*
We often reply to these questions with *Let's* + infinitive:
B *Let's go to a nice restaurant.*

Will and *shall* are modal auxiliary verbs. They are the same for all persons.

▶ 04.08

	I / You / We / They / He / She / It
+	I'll pay for dinner.
−	We won't be late.
Y/N?	Will you help me? Yes, I will. / No I won't.

Short forms: *will* = 'll, *will not* = won't

▶ 04.09

I / You / We / They / He / She / It
Shall I pay for dinner?
Shall we leave soon?
What shall I wear?

150

Grammar Focus

4A Present continuous and *be going to*

a Complete the sentences with the correct forms of the present continuous, using the verbs in brackets.
1. My parents _are buying_ (buy) me a computer for my birthday.
2. He _____ (study) French next year.
3. _____ (I / not walk) home tonight.
4. '_____ (you / wear) a suit to the interview?' 'No, _____.'
5. 'When _____ (your sister / move) to Italy?' 'In about two weeks.'
6. _____ (we / go) to the cinema after work.
7. _____ (I / not come) into the office on Friday morning because _____ (I / go) to the doctor.

b Look at the sentences in **a** again. What arrangements do you think the people have made for each plan?
1 *The parents have already ordered the computer.*

c Megan and Anna are planning a party. Complete the conversation with the correct form of *be going to*.

A So, how's the party planning going?
M Well, we've made a list of what we need to do. And I ¹'m going to invite (invite) everybody by text today.
A What ²_____ (you / do) about music?
M I ³_____ (not play) my music. We ⁴_____ (ask) Gary to deal with that. He's a DJ, you know! But ⁵_____ (we / write) a list of our favourites for him.
A Great. ⁶_____ (there / be) a lot of food?
M Yes, quite a lot. Rachael loves cooking, so ⁷_____ (she / make) the food the day before the party.
A Cool …
M But ⁸_____ (she / not pay) for it all! We ⁹_____ (pay) her back for the ingredients.
A So what ¹⁰_____ (I / do)?
M ¹¹_____ (you / clean) the house!
A Oh, fantastic … I get all the best jobs …

d Choose the most natural sentence to follow sentences a and b in each pair.
1. a ☐ I'm going to have a party.
   b ☐ I'm having a party.
   1 It's this Saturday. Do you want to come?
   2 I don't know how many people to invite. What do you think?

2. a ☐ They're going to arrive in the afternoon.
   b ☐ They're arriving in the afternoon.
   1 They're not sure what time yet.
   2 They've arranged for a taxi to meet them at the station.

3. a ☐ Are we going to play tennis on Saturday?
   b ☐ Are we playing tennis on Saturday?
   1 Yes, I've booked the court for two o'clock.
   2 Yes, what time do you want to play?

4. a ☐ She's going to study all day tomorrow.
   b ☐ She's studying all day tomorrow.
   1 She's got an exam next week, and she wants to pass.
   2 She's got classes from 9 am to 6 pm.

5. a ☐ I'm going to fly from Dublin to Berlin.
   b ☐ I'm flying from Dublin to Berlin.
   1 Which airline do you recommend?
   2 My plane leaves at 8 am.

e ≫ Now go back to p. 38.

4B *will / won't / shall*

a Look at the sentences. Is each sentence a promise (*P*), an offer (*O*), a decision (*D*), or a suggestion (*S*)?
1. ☐ Shall I get some milk from the shop?
2. ☐ Shall we go for a walk?
3. ☐ I'll drive you to the station if you like.
4. ☐ I think I'll have spaghetti.
5. ☐ Don't worry. I'll call you later.
6. ☐ Let's we go to the beach.
7. ☐ I won't be late for the meeting.
8. ☐ Shall we have chicken for dinner?

b Choose the correct word in *italics* to complete the sentence.
1. A I need to go to the station.
   B *I'll / I shall* call a taxi for you.
2. A This document is secret.
   B Don't worry – I *won't / shall not* show it to anyone.
3. A This box is really heavy!
   B *Shall / Will* I help you to carry it?
4. A Those shoes are in the sale. They're only £30.
   B Great! *I'll / I shall* take them.
5. A *Shall / Will* we go out tonight?
   B Good idea. Let's go to the cinema.
6. A I'm working late tonight. *Will / Shall* you cook dinner?
   B Of course.

c Complete the conversation with *will* or *shall* and the correct form of the verbs in brackets.

A ¹ _Shall we go_ (we / go) out to dinner tonight?
B Uh … well, I haven't got much money. ²_____ (I / cook) something for you at my flat?
A Don't worry. ³_____ (I / pay) for the meal.
B Really? Thank you! That sounds great. Where ⁴_____ (we / eat)?
A Let's go for Italian food. ⁵_____ (I / book) a table?
B No, it's OK. ⁶_____ (I / do) it. I know a good place near here. ⁷_____ (I / call) them now.
A OK. Can you call me after you make the booking? I'd like to know what time we're going to meet.
B Yes, ⁸_____ (I / call) you later. I promise. ⁹_____ (I / forget).
A Great. Talk to you later then. Bye.

d ≫ Now go back to p. 40.

151

5A must / have to / can

Necessary, a rule	Not allowed, a rule
Visitors **must** wash their hands. We **have to** wash our hands.	You **mustn't** eat in the classroom. We **can't** eat here.
Allowed	**Not necessary**
You **can** eat outside.	You **don't have to** wear a uniform.

Must and *have to* have very similar meanings.

Must is often used in written rules:
All employees **must wash** their hands.

People in authority use *must* when they are speaking, for example, teachers, doctors, etc.:
You **must turn off** your phone.

We use *have to* when we say what is necessary. It is very common in spoken English:
Doctors **have to work** very long hours.
I **have to leave** for work at 7:00 am

Mustn't and *don't have to* have very different meanings.

Mustn't means something is not allowed – it is important **not** to do something:
Students **mustn't talk** during exams.
You **mustn't eat** in here.

Don't have to means something is unnecessary:
Teachers **don't have to wear** a uniform.
He **doesn't have to work** because he's rich.

Can means something is allowed:
You **can take** a one-hour lunch break.
You **can borrow** up to five books from the library.

Can't is similar to *mustn't*.
It means not allowed / not possible:
You **can't eat** here.
Doctors **can't relax** for very long.

▶ 05.04 *have to* + infinitive

	I / You / We / They	He / She / It
+	We **have to work** hard.	She **has to leave** early today.
–	They **don't have to play**.	He **doesn't have to work**.
Y/N?	**Do** nurses **have to have** a degree? Yes, they **do**. / No, they **don't**.	**Does** he **have to wear** a uniform? Yes, he **does**. / No, he **doesn't**.

Can and *must* are modal auxiliary verbs. They are the same for all persons.

▶ 05.05 *must* + infinitive

	I / You / We / They / He / She / It
+	You **must arrive** on time.
–	Teachers **mustn't be** late.

Questions with *must* are rarely used in modern English.

💡 **Tip**
mustn't = must not

▶ 05.06 *can* + infinitive

	I / You / We / They / He / She / It
+	You **can leave** work early today.
–	The children **can't go** outside alone.
Y/N?	**Can** I **eat** here? Yes, you **can**. / No, you **can't**.

5B will and might for predictions

We use *will* and *might* to make predictions about what we expect to happen in the future.
Will shows that we are very sure:
I**'ll say** something silly. They **won't give** me the job.

Might shows we are less sure:
They **might ask** difficult questions. I **might not get** the job.

Will and *might* are modal auxiliary verbs. They are the same for all persons.

▶ 05.08

	I / You / We / They / He / She / It
+	You**'ll get** the job. You **might get** the job.
–	He **won't get** the job. He **might not get** the job.

Short forms: will = 'll, will not = won't

We usually use phrases like *I think …* , *I don't think …*, and *Do you think … ?* to introduce predictions when we speak.

▶ 05.09

	I / You / We / They / He / She / It
+	**I think** you**'ll get** the job. **I think** he **might get** the job
–	**I don't think** I**'ll get** the job.
Y/N?	**Do you think** we**'ll get** the job? **I think so**. / **I don't think so**. **Do you think** we **might get** the job? We **might**. / We **might not**.

We can also use *I'm sure …* before predictions with *will*:
I'm sure I'll say something silly.

Grammar Focus

5A must / have to / can

a Flavia works in a call centre. Read her office rules. Complete Flavia's description of her work with *have to*, *can* or *can't* and the words in brackets.

Office Rules
- Employees must wear a uniform at all times.
- Employees mustn't check emails during working hours.
- You mustn't talk to other employees during working hours.
- You must answer the phone within five seconds.
- Employees must always be polite to customers.

I'm telling you, Jo, it's a terrible place to work! The customers can't see you, but we still ¹ _have to_ wear a uniform all the time. You ² _____ (wear) your normal clothes.
I ³ _____ (check) my emails – it's not allowed – and I ⁴ _____ (speak) to my colleagues during the day! Fortunately, we ⁵ _____ (talk) to each other during our breaks!
When the phone rings, we ⁶ _____ (answer) it very quickly – within five seconds. And we always ⁷ _____ (be) polite to customers, but they're often incredibly rude to us! I really ⁸ _____ (find) a new job!

b Choose the correct option.
1 Visitors *mustn't* / *don't have to* eat in the building.
2 It's a relaxed office – you *mustn't* / *don't have to* wear a tie.
3 I start at 10 am, so I *mustn't* / *don't have to* get up early.
4 Employees *mustn't* / *don't have to* park in the customer car park. It is for customers only.
5 If there is a fire, you *mustn't* / *don't have to* use the lift. You must use the stairs.

c Complete the sentences with one of the expressions in the box. Use each expression once.

can   can't   doesn't have to   has to   must   mustn't

1 In my office, we _____ eat or drink at our desks. We have to go to the canteen.
2 My job's really nice. I _____ start work when I want and finish when I want.
3 She works from home, so she _____ drive to work.
4 Warning! Dangerous work area. Visitors _____ enter without permission.
5 Important! You _____ keep your visitor card with you at all times.
6 He _____ travel a lot for his job. Sometimes he goes to three or four countries in a month.

d ⟫ Now go back to p. 49.

5B will and might for predictions

a Duncan is planning to move to China for a year. Look at his predictions and complete his sentences with *will* / *won't* or *might* / *might not*.

	100% sure	50% sure ???
Good	learn about China meet new people try new things	learn to speak Chinese? travel around China? stay more than a year?
Bad	difficult language not much money no friends	tiring job? miss family? not like food?

1 I'm sure I __'ll__ learn a lot about China.
2 They have different food in China, and I _____ like it.
3 I'm sure Chinese _____ be really difficult, but I _____ learn to speak it a little.
4 I _____ have any friends at first, but I _____ meet new people.
5 My job _____ be tiring, and I _____ have much money!
6 I _____ try new things, and I _____ travel around the country.
7 I _____ want to stay more than a year, but I _____ miss my family.

b Correct the mistakes in the sentences below. Sometimes there is more than one possible answer.
1 She thinks she might to go to Spain for her holiday.
2 Which sights do you think you visit?
3 I sure the restaurant will be busy.
4 I'm sure it won't raining today – the sky's blue.
5 Do you think you might buying a new computer?
6 I'm sure I might change jobs next year.
7 He might not to arrive on time. The traffic's bad.
8 I won't think I pass my exam.

c Write questions using *will* and the words in brackets.
1 **A** Are you sure (you / enjoy) it?
   B Yes, I'm sure I will.
2 **A** Do you think (she / leave)?
   B She might.
3 **A** How much do you think (it / cost)?
   B About fifty pounds.
4 **A** When do you think (they / tell) us?
   B I don't know.
5 **A** Are you sure (we / finish) on time?
   B No. We might not.
6 **A** Do you think (I / get) an interview?
   B I think so!

d In which questions in **c** can you replace *will* with *might*?

e ⟫ Now go back to p. 50.

153

6A Imperative; *should*

We use the imperative and *should* to give advice – to tell other people what we think is the best or the right thing to do.

▶ 06.01 Imperative
The imperative is stronger than *should*. It tells somebody exactly what to do.

We can use it to give…
- advice:
  Try to get a good night's sleep.
  Don't stay up late.
- instructions:
  Don't turn right! **Turn** left!
  Come here!
- warnings:
  Be careful!

The imperative is the infinitive of the verb with no subject. For negative imperatives, use *don't* + infinitive:

Don't work so hard! You should take a break!

▶ 06.02 *should*
Should is less strong than the imperative. It shows that what we are saying is advice, not an instruction.

Should is a modal auxiliary verb. It is the same for all persons.

	I / You / We / They / He / She / It
+	You **should get up** early.
–	Children **shouldn't eat** a lot of sweets.
Y/N?	**Should** I **stop** eating sweets? Yes, you **should**. / No, you **shouldn't**.

We often use phrases like *I think …, I don't think …,* and *Do you think … ?* to introduce advice with *should*:
I think / **I don't think** you should go to bed.
A **Do you think** I should say I'm sorry?
B Yes, **I think so**. / No, **I don't think so**.

> 💡 **Tip**
> Adding *I think …* or *I don't think …* before *should* is more polite because it shows you are talking about opinion, not fact.

6B Uses of *to* + infinitive

The infinitive is the dictionary form of the verb (*go, swim, be, have,* etc.).

We use *to* + infinitive (*to go, to swim, to be,* etc.) in many different patterns.
The negative is *not* + *to* + infinitive (*not to go, not to swim, not to be,* etc.).

*Hello. I **want to go** to the Bahamas to swim with sharks. But I'm not sure **when to go**.*

*Er … isn't it **dangerous to swim** with sharks?*

▶ 06.10

1 Infinitive of purpose
Use *to* + infinitive to give a reason:
A Why did you go to Egypt?
B **To see** the sharks.
I looked in the mirror **to check** my hair.
Read a book **to relax**.

2 verb + *to* + infinitive
When two verbs go together in a sentence, certain verbs are followed by *to* + infinitive:
I **wanted to visit** Australia.
I **decided not to go** home.
Some of the verbs that follow this pattern are *choose, decide, want, would like, try, promise, expect, remember, forget, need, plan, learn* and *offer*.

3 adjective + *to* + infinitive
Many adjectives can be followed by *to* + infinitive:
I was **surprised to get** the job.
It's **important not to forget** people's names at work.

4 verb + question word + *to* + infinitive
Some verbs can be followed by a question word + *to* + infinitive:
I **forgot what to do**.
I don't **know who to ask**.
Can you **tell** me **where to go**?
I can't **decide what to wear**.

Some of the verbs that follow this pattern are *ask, decide, explain, forget, know, show, tell* and *understand*.

Grammar Focus

6A Imperative; should

Tony gets up late every morning and has to get ready for work very quickly. He doesn't have breakfast – he just drinks a cup of strong coffee. He drives to work – it's only about two kilometres, but the traffic is terrible. He checks his messages while he's waiting. At work, he drinks coffee all day and he doesn't stop for lunch – he eats pizza at his desk. When he gets home after work, he watches TV until about 1 am Then the next day, he does the same all over again.

a Read about Tony's normal daily routine. Write advice for him using *should / shouldn't* and the words in brackets.

1 (get up earlier)
   He should get up earlier.
2 (have breakfast)
   _____
3 (drink less coffee)
   _____
4 (drive to work)
   _____
5 (use his phone in the car)
   _____
6 (stop for lunch)
   _____
7 (eat at his desk)
   _____
8 (go to bed earlier)
   _____

b Tony's friend Andy is giving him advice. Complete Andy's advice with the imperative form of the verbs in the box. Be careful – two verbs need to be negative.

| drink | eat | get | go |
| set | spend | ~~start~~ | wake |

T I'm always tired these days. What should I do?
A That's easy. ¹ _Start_ the day with a good breakfast. ² _____ about half an hour on breakfast – it's really important.
T Half an hour? I don't have time in the morning.
A So ³ _____ up earlier. ⁴ _____ your alarm for six thirty. And then ⁵ _____ back to sleep – ⁶ _____ out of bed right away.
T Six thirty? Are you joking?
A No, I'm serious. Get up early, ⁷ _____ breakfast and ⁸ _____ so much coffee. It's bad for you.

c Correct one mistake in each sentence.

1 Everybody should to bring warm clothes.
2 How much money I should take?
3 Don't to be late for the party!
4 He shoulds be more careful.
5 Not spend so much money on the Internet.
6 You don't should check your email every five minutes.
7 What you think I should do to get fit?

d ⟫ Now go back to p. 58.

6B Uses of *to* + infinitive

a Match the sentence halves 1–7 with the endings a–g.

1 [e] It's dangerous
2 [ ] They went to the gym
3 [ ] He drove to the shops
4 [ ] It will be great
5 [ ] I'm going to bed
6 [ ] She was disappointed
7 [ ] She emailed the company

a to get some sleep.
b to buy some food.
c to visit Paris!
d to apply for the job.
e to text and drive.
f to do some exercise.
g not to pass her exam.

b Complete the sentences with the correct question word + *to* + infinitive.

| which to buy | what to watch | where to go |
| how to use | ~~what to do~~ | how to get | who to speak to |

1 I don't know _what to do_ about my problem.
2 Can you show me _____ this computer?
3 I can't decide _____ for my holiday.
4 Do you know _____ to the station?
5 I'm not sure _____ on TV tonight.
6 I like both these dresses. I can't decide _____.
7 Can you tell me _____ about getting a refund?

c Use the verbs in the box to complete the sentences with an positive or negative *to* + infinitive.

| ~~read~~ | eat | break | listen | wear | receive | go | arrive |

1 I bought this book _to read_ about sharks.
2 It's expensive _____ in restaurants every day.
3 I was annoyed _____ a reply to my email.
4 It's rude _____ when she's talking.
5 We promise _____ anything.
6 I don't know what _____ to the wedding.
7 You should leave now _____ on time.
8 I decided _____ to the party. I was too tired.

d ⟫ Now go back to p. 61.

155

7A Comparatives and superlatives

▶ 07.01

We use comparative adjectives and adverbs to compare two things or actions, usually with *than*:
John's **more interesting than** Michael.
He's **richer than** he was.
She drives **more carefully than** all my friends.

We use superlative adjectives and adverbs to talk about extremes, usually with *the*:
He's **the worst** guitar player in the world!
Who can run **the furthest**?
He played **the best** I've ever seen him play.

Less/least is the opposite of *more/most*. We can use them with all adjectives and adverbs:
I'm **less happy** than I was.
She drives **less slowly** than me.
It was **the least interesting** meeting ever!

We can use *as … as* to show that two things are equal:
He's **as tall as** me.
She drives **as carefully as** me.

We can use *not as … as* to mean *less than*:
He is**n't as clever as** me. (= He is less clever than me. I am cleverer than him.)
She doesn't drive **as carefully as** me. (= She drives less carefully than me. I drive more carefully than her.)

We often use comparatives or *as … as* to compare the past with the present:
He's much **better than he was**.
He's **not as bad as last time**.

We often use superlatives with *ever* and the present perfect:
This is **the best** meal **I've ever eaten**.
It was **the least interesting** book **I've ever read**.

Adjectives

One syllable	rich → rich**er**, **the** rich**est**
	big → big**ger**, **the** big**gest**
Ending in -y	easy → eas**ier**, the eas**iest**
	friendly → friendl**ier**, the friendl**iest**
Two or more syllables	careful → **more** careful, **the most** careful
	interesting → **more** interesting, **the most** interesting
Irregular adjectives	good → **better**, the best
	bad → **worse, the worst**
	far → **further, the furthest**
	quiet → quiet**er, the** quiet**est**
	bored / tired → **more** / **the most** bored / tired

Adverbs

One syllable	hard → hard**er**, **the** hard**est**
	late → lat**er**, the lat**est**
Two or more syllables	often → **more** often, **the most** often
	carefully → **more** carefully, **the most** carefully
Irregular adverbs	well → **better**, the best
	badly → **worse, the worst**
	far → **further, the furthest**
	early → **earlier, the earliest**

7B used to

We use *used to* + infinitive to talk about past situations and habits which have now changed. *Used to* tells us something was different in the past.
I **used to be** very thin. (= I was thin in the past, but I'm not thin now.)
He **didn't use to go** to the gym. (= He didn't go to the gym in the past, but now he goes to the gym.)
Used to has the same form for all persons.

▶ 07.09

	I / You / We / They / He / She / It
+	I **used to hate** tomatoes.
–	She **didn't use to wear** high heels.
Y/N?	**Did** you **use to be** good at sport? Yes, I **did**. / No, I **didn't**.

There is no present form of *used to*. Use the present simple.
I **play** tennis three times a week.
NOT ~~I use to play tennis three times a week.~~

> **Tip**
>
> **Used to and the past simple**
> We can usually use the past simple to talk about these situations/habits, if we make it clear that we are talking about a particular period of past time:
> He *was* in good shape **when he was younger**.
> **When I was a student**, I *went* running three times a week.
>
> It's natural to use a mixture of *used to* and the past simple when we write or speak about long-term past situations:
> In the 1950s, people **didn't use to drive** to work – most people **walked** or **cycled**.

Grammar Focus

7A Comparatives and superlatives

a Complete the sentences about three brothers: Alex, Eric, and Jack.

1 Alex is good at tennis, but …   Eric is _____better_____ than Alex.   Jack is _____the best_____ tennis player.
2 Alex is very fit, but …   Eric is _____ than Alex.   Jack is _____.
3 Alex has travelled very far, but …   Eric has travelled _____ Alex.   Jack has travelled _____.
4 Alex is very friendly, but …   Eric is _____ Alex.   Jack _____.
5 Alex drives carefully, but …   Eric _____.   Jack _____.
6 Alex works fast, but …   _____.   Jack _____.
7 Alex is fashionable, but …   _____.   Jack _____.

b Look at each group of sentences. Which sentence (a, b, or c) has a different meaning?

1   a I run faster than him.
    b He doesn't run as fast as me.
    c I run as fast as him.

2   a Her English is better than mine.
    b Her English isn't as good as mine.
    c She doesn't speak English as well as me.

3   a It's the most boring book I've ever read.
    b It's the least interesting book I've ever read.
    c I've never read a more interesting book.

c Correct the mistakes in the sentences.

1 He drives worse as me.
2 This is best film I've ever seen.
3 She isn't friendly as her sister.
4 I'm a good runner, but Tom's the faster in the school.
5 The weather is not as cold than it was.
6 The island was the more beautiful place I've ever visited.
7 This book is least interesting than the last one.
8 I don't speak French as well that she does.

d ⟫ Now go back to p. 68.

7B used to

a All of the sentences about the past are false. Change them so that they are true.

500 years ago …
1 People used to work in IT. *People didn't use to work in IT.*
2 People didn't use to work on farms.
3 People used to live as long as they do now.
4 Children's education used to be free.
5 Cities didn't use to be smaller than today.
6 People didn't use to travel by horse.
7 People used to use microwaves to cook food.

b Rewrite the sentences. Change the underlined verbs from the past simple to *used to*.

1 I <u>ate</u> a lot of chocolate when I was younger.
    I used to eat a lot of chocolate when I was younger.
2 People <u>wrote</u> a lot of letters in the days before email.
3 Where <u>did you live</u> when you were a child?
4 She <u>was</u> a manager before she stopped working.
5 <u>Did</u> your parents <u>read</u> you stories when you were young?
6 I <u>didn't like</u> vegetables when I was a child.
7 <u>Were</u> you a good student at school?
8 We <u>weren't</u> as fit as we are today.

c Look at the pictures of Mary and Jeff ten years ago and today. Write sentences about how they have changed. Use *used to / didn't use to* and the words in brackets.

1 _____ (Mary / have long hair)
2 _____ (Jeff / be thinner)
3 _____ (Jeff / wear suits)
4 _____ (They / look after the garden)
5 _____ (They / ride a motorbike)
6 _____ (They / own a car)

d ⟫ Now go back to p. 71.

157

8A The passive: present simple and past simple

Active:
Most verbs in English are active – the **doer** of the verb comes before the verb.

Francis Ford Coppola **made** The Godfather in 1972.
He also **made** … (We are talking about the person.)

Passive:
In the passive, the **object** comes before the verb.

The Godfather **was made** in 1972 by Francis Ford Coppola.
It **was filmed** in … (We are talking about the movie.)

We use passive verb forms when the main thing we are talking about is the **object** of the verb.

Some common uses of the passive are:
- when the doer isn't important:
  This house **was built** in the 1960s.
  (It doesn't matter who built it – the date is more interesting.)
  Thousands of copies of Gold: Greatest Hits **are sold** every year.
  (It doesn't matter who sells them.)
- when we don't know who did something:
  The picture **was stolen** last night. (We don't know who stole it.)
  This photo **was taken** in Barcelona. (I don't remember who took it.)

We form the passive with **be + past participle**, where **be** shows the tense of the verb, e.g., present simple.

▶ 08.02

	Present simple	Past simple
+	I **am chosen** for the school football team every year.	**Three** Godfather films **were made** altogether.
−	This car **isn't sold** in the USA or Canada.	The Harry Potter books **weren't written** for adults.
Y/N?	**Am** I **invited** to your party? Yes, you **are**. / No, you**'re not**.	**Was** The Hobbit **written** for children? Yes, it **was**. / No, it **wasn't**.

(See p. 168 for a list of irregular past participles.)

We use *by* to introduce the doer after the verb:
The Godfather was directed **by Francis Ford Coppola**.
This house was built **by my grandfather**.

8B Present perfect with *for* and *since*

We can use the present perfect with *for* and *since* to describe a situation that started in the past and continues now.

In positive statements, we use the present perfect with *for* and *since* with particular verbs which describe things that are often true for a long time: *live, work, know, have, be, like, love, hate, enjoy, own*, etc.

▶ 08.05

We use *since* to say when something started:
I've had this T-shirt since 2017.

have T-shirt
Past — 2017 — Now

We often use a verb in the past simple after *since*:
I've loved tennis since I was a child. (I was a child when I started liking tennis, and I still like it now.)

We use *for* to describe the length of time:
I've known him for a few days. (I met him a few days ago.)

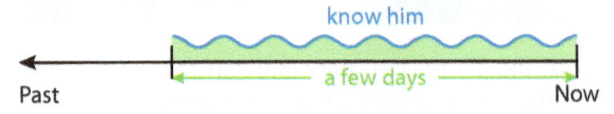

know him
Past — a few days — Now

We often use *How long …?* questions with the present perfect to ask about a period of time:
A *How long have you lived here?*
B *Since I was a child. / For about ten years.*

Remember, we form the present perfect with *have* + past participle.

> 💡 **Tip**
> We can also use *always* or *all my/your life*:
> *I've always hated cheese. / I've hated cheese all my life.*

> 💡 **Tip**
> - Don't use the present simple to talk about periods of time up to now. Use the present perfect instead:
>   *How long have you known each other?*
>   NOT *How long do you know each other?*
> - Don't use the present perfect for periods of time that are finished. Use the past simple (with *for, from … to*) instead:
>   *I lived there for two years / from 2016 to 2018.*
>   NOT *I've lived there from 2016 to 2018.*

He's been a member of the team since 1975.
He's faster than anyone!

Grammar Focus

8A The passive: present simple and past simple

a Rewrite these sentences in the passive using the highlighted words as the subject of the sentence. Don't include the doer.
1. Somebody wrote the story 200 years ago.
   The story was written 200 years ago.
2. A company made my car in Germany.
   _____
3. Bookshops don't sell that book in your country.
   _____
4. People eat sushi all over the world.
   _____
5. In the UK, DJs play the number 1 song on the radio every hour.
   _____
6. Somebody broke a window during the night.
   _____
7. The journalist didn't describe India very well in the article.
   _____

b Rewrite these sentences in the passive. Include the doer in the new sentence.
1. Frank Gehry designed The Guggenheim, Bilbao.
   The Guggenheim, Bilbao was designed by Frank Gehry.
2. Marilyn Monroe wore Chanel No. 5 perfume.
   _____
3. Every year, 3 million people visit the Taj Mahal.
   _____
4. A fire destroyed many parts of London in 1666.
   _____
5. Clyde Tombaugh discovered Pluto in 1930.
   _____

c Put the words in the correct order to make questions in the passive.
1. made / was / the / where / film
   Where was the film made?
2. was / the book / written / when
   _____
3. made / cheese / is / how
   _____
4. your bike / was / when / stolen
   _____
5. the statue / was / in France / made
   _____
6. who / her wedding dress / was / designed by
   _____

d ⟫ Now go back to p. 79.

8B Present perfect with *for* and *since*

a Write *for* or *since*.
1. _since_ last week
2. _____ a week
3. _____ a long time
4. _____ last weekend
5. _____ five minutes
6. _____ I was a child
7. _____ July
8. _____ 1,000 years
9. _____ yesterday
10. _____ months
11. _____ ten days
12. _____ I last saw you

b Rewrite the sentences with the present perfect and *for* or *since*.
1. I work here. _I've worked here since_ January.
2. I live here. _____ three months.
3. He holds the record. _____ the last Olympics.
4. She owns that car. _____ 2018.
5. They are married. _____ two days.
6. I don't listen to pop music. _____ a long time.
7. We are not friends. _____ we had a fight.
8. I don't have a TV in my home. _____ a few years.
9. He doesn't eat meat. _____ New Year's Day.

c Complete the questions in the present perfect.
1. How long _____ (you / study) English?
2. How long _____ (she / live) in this area?
3. How long _____ (Mr Bell / teach) at this school?
4. How long _____ (we / have) our passports?
5. How long _____ (he / be) a football fan?

d Complete the sentences. Use the past simple or the present perfect.
1. _____ (she / work) here for ten months.
2. _____ (she / start) work last July.
3. When _____ (you / buy) your car?
4. How long _____ (you / have) this car?
5. _____ (we / not see) him since last summer.
6. _____ (we / not see) him in October.
7. _____ (I / love) animals when I was a child.
8. _____ (I / love) animals all my life.

e ⟫ Now go back to p. 81.

159

9A First conditional

We use the first conditional to talk about a possible future situation and the result of that situation:

(possible future situation) **If** the weather **is** good this weekend, (result) we'**ll go** to the park.
(possible future situation) **If** I **pass** this exam, (result) I'**ll be** very happy.

There are two clauses in a conditional sentence: the *if* clause and the main clause.
The *if* clause can go before or after the main clause.

If I **pass** my exams,	I'**ll get** into university.	I'**ll get** into university	**if** I **pass** my exams,
if clause	main clause	main clause	*if* clause

To talk about a possible future situation, use the present simple in the *if* clause.

> **Tip** Never use *will / might* in an *if* clause.
> If **I go** to New York … NOT If I will go to New York …

To talk about the result of the situation, use a suitable future form, e.g., *will*, *might*, *be going to* or present continuous.

▶ 09.05

Statements
I'**ll get** a good degree **if** I **work** hard this year.
If he **works** hard, he **won't fail**.
If they **don't work** hard this year, they **won't get** a good degree.
Her teacher **might ask** her to repeat the year **if** she **doesn't work** hard.

Questions and short answers
What **will** you **do if** you **pass**?
If she **doesn't work** hard, what **will happen**?
If you **don't get** into university, **will** you **look** for a job? Yes, I **will**. / No, I **won't**.
Are his parents **going to** buy him a car **if he works** hard? Yes, they **are**. / No, they'**re not**.

> **Tip**
> - The word order in the *if* clause doesn't change in questions.
>   What will you do **if it rains**?
>   NOT What will you do if does it rain?
> - We can make short questions with *What if … ?*:
>   **What if** it rains?

If I pass the entrance exam, I'm going to study maths at the best university in the country.

9B Verb patterns

▶ 09.08

Some verbs are often followed by another verb. The two most common patterns are:
- verb + *to* + infinitive:
  I **hope to see** you soon.
- verb + verb + *-ing*:
  I **don't mind reading** about famous people.

verb + *to* + infinitive	verb + verb + *-ing*	Both
choose decide want would like promise expect need plan learn offer hope	describe discuss enjoy finish not mind stop keep think of	begin start continue prefer* like* love* hate*

Sometimes both forms are possible with no change in meaning:
He started **talking**. / He started **to talk**.
I prefer **talking** to my friends. / I prefer **to talk** to my friends.

To make a negative on the second verb in both verb patterns, *not* goes before the verb:
I decided **not to go** to the party.
I hate **not going** to work.

> **Tip**
> We can make negatives with either the first verb or the second verb. This sometimes changes the meaning:
> I **didn't choose** to go to the party.
> (I went to the party, but only because I had to.)
> I chose **not to go** to the party. (I didn't go to the party.)

> **Tip**
> *I **love going** to parties. ✓ I **love to go** to parties. ✓
> But remember, after *would like / love / hate / prefer*, you must always use *to* + infinitive:
> I **would love to come** to the party.
> NOT I would love coming to the party.

When a verb comes after a preposition (e.g., *on*, *by*, *from*, *about*), it is always in the *-ing* form:
You shouldn't **worry about talking** to strangers.
I'm **thinking of studying** history.

I enjoy reading about the lives of famous people.

Grammar Focus

9A First conditional

a Match the sentence halves.
1. [g] If you study hard, …
2. [ ] If you don't take a coat, …
3. [ ] You won't be late …
4. [ ] It'll be hard to get a good job …
5. [ ] If you drive too fast, …
6. [ ] If I get a place at medical school, …
7. [ ] He's going to travel around the world …
8. [ ] We might go to the beach tomorrow …

a if you don't go to university.
b if he has enough money.
c you'll get cold.
d I'm going to become a doctor.
e if you leave now.
f if the weather is nice.
g you'll get good marks.
h you might have an accident.

b Choose the correct options. All the sentences are about the future.
1. If you *pay / will pay* the bill, *I pay / I'll pay* you back next week.
2. If I *don't / won't* do some exercise, *I / I'll* put on weight.
3. She *isn't going to / doesn't* catch her plane if she *doesn't / isn't going to* leave soon.
4. What *do / will* you do if *there is / there'll be* a traffic jam?
5. If we *like / might like* the hotel, we *might stay / stay* a few more days.
6. They *won't / don't* enjoy the journey if they *won't / don't* get a seat.
7. *Are you going to / Do you* cook if I *get / might get* home late?

c Complete the conversations with the correct forms of the verbs in brackets. Use *will/'ll* or the present simple. All the sentences are about the future.

A I just bought an old car for £500.
B What [1]_____ (you / do) if [2]_____ (it / break) down?
A [3]_____ (I / ask) for my money back.

C If [4]_____ (it / be) sunny tomorrow, [5]_____ (I / take) the children to the park.
D That's nice. If [6]_____ (I / have) time, [7]_____ (I / make) a picnic for you.
C Great, thanks! But, if [8]_____ (you / not do), don't worry, [9]_____ (we / be) OK.

E [10]_____ (I / not finish) this essay tonight if [11]_____ (the cat / not get) off my laptop.
F Just push him off.
E If [12]_____ (I / push) him off, [13]_____ (he / jump) back up again.
F I'll put him outside.

d ⟩⟩⟩ Now go back to p. 89.

9B Verb patterns

a Choose the correct option.
1. They want *(to leave) / leaving*.
2. I enjoy *to play / playing* basketball.
3. Do you mind *to work / working* late?
4. We discussed *to start / starting* a business.
5. We hope *to visit / visiting* you soon.
6. Why did you choose *to live / living* in the city?
7. Please stop *to talk / talking* now and open your book.
8. They've offered *to help / helping* us.
9. We really need *to go / going* very soon.
10. You should plan *to save / saving* more money.

b Cross out the verb forms that are NOT possible in these sentences. Remember, after some verbs both verb forms are possible.
1. He began *to act / acting* when he was a child.
2. He chose *not to do / not doing* his homework.
3. He worries about *making / to make* mistakes.
4. I prefer *not to be / not being* late.
5. Do you mind *to start / starting* without me?
6. We're thinking of *to become / becoming* vegetarians.
7. The children continued *to be / being* noisy.
8. I like *to cook / cooking* for other people.
9. Would you like *to have / having* dinner with me?
10. We hate *to think / thinking* about money when we're on holiday.

c Complete the sentences with the correct forms of the verbs.
1. I don't expect _____ the exam. (pass)
2. She promised _____ late. (not be)
3. We don't mind _____ up early. (get)
4. I enjoy _____ on a uniform every morning. (not put)
5. They learned _____ English very quickly. (speak)
6. He couldn't concentrate on _____ his work. (do)
7. Which cities are you planning _____? (visit)
8. Did he choose _____ in the match? (not play)

d Complete the text with the verbs in the box.

~~hates~~   hated   started   discussed   didn't expect
thinks of   preferred   continued   needed

My friend says he [1]__hates__ speaking in public. He told me that when he [2]_____ getting up in front of a crowd, he feels terrified. I'm very surprised. I thought I knew everything about my friend, and I [3]_____ to hear this. He said that he [4]_____ feeling embarrassed around big groups of people when he was about 11 years old. He [5]_____ standing up in front of the class at school, and [6]_____ to feel this way as an adult when he [7]_____ to speak at meetings at work. We [8]_____ getting professional help for his problem, but he said he [9]_____ talking to friends about it.

e ⟩⟩⟩ Now go back to p. 91.

161

10A Second conditional

What **would** you **do if** you **saw** somebody fall down in the street?
I'd **stop** and **try** to help them.

We use the second conditional when we imagine a situation in the present or future. The situation is unreal, unlikely or impossible.

We describe the unreal situation in the *if* clause. We talk about the result of that situation in the main clause.
(unlikely future situation) ***If** I **stole** from work,* (result) *I'd feel bad.*
(result) *I'd take a holiday from work* (impossible present situation) ***if** I **had** more money.*

Use the past simple (and/or past continuous) in the *if* clause. We can use *would* + infinitive or *could* + infinitive to talk about the result.
***If** it **was raining** and I **saw** a hitchhiker, **I'd stop**.*
*I **could go** on more holidays **if** I **had** more money.* (*could* = it would be possible)

10.03

Statements
***If** she **crashed** my car, **I'd be** very angry.*
*He **wouldn't stop** to help **if** he **saw** an accident.*
***If** you **didn't have** a job, you **couldn't pay** the rent.*
*Hollywood **wouldn't stop** making films **if** people **didn't go** to the cinema.*
***I'd give** more money to charity **if** I **were** rich.*

Questions and short answers
*What **would** you **do if** you **lost** your job?*
***If** you **didn't know** the answers, **would** you **cheat**?*
*Yes, I **would**. / No, I **wouldn't**.*
***Would** you **buy** your child a motorbike?*
*Yes, I **would**. / No, I **wouldn't**.*

Tip

- When we talk about impossible present situations with *be*, we usually use *If I/he/she were*, not *If I/he/she was*:
  ***If I were** taller, I'd be better at basketball.*
- We can also use the second conditional to give advice with the phrase *If I were you* (NOT ~~*If I was you*~~):
  ***If I were you**, I wouldn't park there.* (I'm imagining the situation where I'm you.)

10B Quantifiers; *too / not enough*

Quantifiers

We use quantifiers before countable and uncountable nouns to describe the amount of something.

Countable nouns are things that we can count:
one book, five books.
Uncountable nouns are things that we don't usually count:
water NOT ~~*one water*~~, ~~*five waters*~~.

10.05

	Countable	Uncountable
Large quantity	*There are **a lot of** books.*	*There's **a lot of** water.*
No particular quantity	*There are **some** books.*	*There's **some** water.*
Small quantity	*There are **a few** books.* *There **aren't many** books.*	*There's **a bit of** water.* *There **isn't much** water.*
Zero quantity	*There are **no** books.* *There **aren't any** books.*	*There's **no** water.* *There **isn't any** water.*
Question	*Are there **any** books?* ***How many** books are there?*	*Is there **any** water?* ***How much** water is there?*

Tip

Be careful with the nouns *money*, *fruit*, and *furniture*. They're all uncountable in English. We can say *five euros*, *ten apples*, and *six chairs*, but NOT ~~*five moneys*~~, ~~*ten fruits*~~, and ~~*six furnitures*~~.

too / not enough

We use *too* to say something is more than the right amount:
*There are **too** many people. There's **too** much noise.*
We use *not enough* to say something is less than the right amount:
*There **isn't enough** food for everyone.*

10.06

		More than the right amount	Less than the right amount
Nouns	C	*There are **too many** people.*	*There **aren't enough** people.*
Nouns	U	*I eat **too much** cheese.*	*There **isn't enough** cheese.*
Verbs		*He **talks too much**.*	*He **doesn't talk enough**.*
Adjectives		*It's **too hot**.*	*It **isn't hot enough**.*
Adverbs		*She eats **too quickly**.*	*She **doesn't** eat **quickly enough**.*

very

We use *very* before adjectives and adverbs. There is an important difference between *very* and *too*:
*It's **too** small. / He's driving **too** slowly.*
(= I'm complaining about problems.)
*It's **very** small. / He's driving **very** slowly.*
(= I'm describing situations, not complaining.)
We use *very much* with verbs:
*I like it **very much**.* NOT ~~*I very like it.*~~

Grammar Focus

10A Second conditional

a Match the sentence halves.
1. [e] If you saw a celebrity in the street,
2. [ ] Would you help a stranger with their bags
3. [ ] If I didn't like my job,
4. [ ] If I saw an accident,
5. [ ] I could sell my motorbike
6. [ ] What would you do
7. [ ] I failed my exams,
8. [ ] Could she deal with the stress

a I'd look for a new one.
b if you were lost?
c my father would be disappointed.
d if she were a nurse?
e would you try to talk to them?
f if we needed some money.
g I'd try to help.
h if you were in a hurry?

b Choose the correct verb forms in each sentence.
1. If I *would be* / *were* rich, *I'd give* / *I gave* up work.
2. The film *would be* / *was* better if it *wasn't* / *wouldn't be* three hours long.
3. If *I'd have* / *I had* time, *I'd read* / *I read* more books.
4. What *would* / *did* you do if *you'd see* / *you saw* a snake in your room?
5. If you *wouldn't* / *didn't* buy coffee every day, *you'd save* / *you saved* a lot of money.
6. I *wouldn't* / *didn't* spend time with him if I *wouldn't* / *didn't* like him!
7. If you *would find* / *found* a lost phone, *would you* / *did you* keep it?

c Complete the conversation with the second conditional forms of the verbs in brackets.

A If [1]_____ (I / be) you, [2]_____ (I / not eat) those grapes.
B It's a supermarket. Nobody cares. If [3]_____ (I / not eat) them, [4]_____ (they / throw) them away.
A What [5]_____ (you / do) if [6]_____ (a shop assistant / see) you?
B [7]_____ (I / promise) to pay for them at the till.
A What if [8]_____ (they / not believe) you and [9]_____ (they / call) the police? [10]_____ (you / go) to prison for stealing grapes!
B You're being very silly! If [11]_____ (the police / come), [12]_____ (they / not send) me to prison. But [13]_____ (it / be) embarrassing.

d ▷▷▷ Now go back to p. 99.

10B Quantifiers; *too / not enough*

a Choose the best quantifier to complete each sentence.
1. Hurry up! We don't have _____ time!
   a some   b no   (c) much   d many
2. Just _____ chips, please. I'm not very hungry.
   a a few   b any   c a bit of   d much
3. Can I have _____ milk in my coffee, please? Not much.
   a a few   b no   c a lot of   d a bit of
4. You don't need to take _____ money with you. I'll pay for everything.
   a any   b no   c a few   d many
5. When I moved here, I had _____ friends. But now I have a lot.
   a a bit of   b much   c no   d any
6. I bought _____ books last week, but I haven't read them yet.
   a any   b no   c much   d some

b Tick (✓) the sentences that are correct.
1. There aren't much people here in the winter.
2. We saw a lot of lorries on the motorway.
3. Are there any empty seats in the cinema?
4. A bit of the vegetables were not enough soft.
5. I'd like a bit of bread with my soup.
6. I love too hot weather.
7. I don't earn enough money.
8. Was the test too much difficult?

c Correct the mistakes you found in the sentences in **b**.

d Write a sentence about each picture using the words in brackets and *too / not enough*.

1 (people / on the beach)
2 (soup / hot) 
3 (she / tall / to reach the shelf) 
4 (waiter / spoke / quickly) 
5 (service / here / slow) 
6 (Sorry, I / have / money) 

e ▷▷▷ Now go back to p. 100.

163

11A Defining relative clauses

We use defining relative clauses to define a noun. A relative clause explains what kind of thing, or which particular thing, we are talking about.
The film is about an android. ✗ (not specific enough – you don't know which film)
The film that is on TV tonight is about an android. ✓ (more specific – you know which film I'm talking about)
A vet is **a doctor**. ✗ (not enough information for a clear definition)
A vet is **a doctor that looks after animals**. ✓ (more specific – you know what kind of doctor)

To add a defining relative clause after a noun, we use a relative pronoun (e.g., *who, which, that*) or a relative adverb (e.g., *where*).

▶ 11.03

Use *who* or *that* when the noun is a person:
It's about a man **who/that** travels through time.
Use *which* or *that* when the noun is a thing:
There's an art gallery **which/that** stays open 24 hours a day.
Use *where* when the noun is a place:
The Matrix is about a world **where** computers control everything.

Who, which, where and *that* replace other words in the clause:
It's about a person ~~he~~ **who** travels through time.
There's an art gallery ~~it~~ **that** stays open 24 hours a day.
The Matrix is about a world **where** computers control everything ~~there~~.

11B Articles

		Things in general Ø = no article	Specific things	
			first mention	know which one
C	Singular		**a** man, **an** egg	**the** man, **the** egg
	Plural	**Ø** scientists	**some** scientists	**the** scientists
U		**Ø** chocolate	**some** chocolate	**the** chocolate

▶ 11.04

When we talk about plural or uncountable things in general, we usually use no article:
Ø Tourists sometimes have **Ø accidents** when they are climbing **Ø mountains**.

When we talk about specific things for the first time, we usually use *a/an* for singular nouns:
I met **a scientist**. She was wearing **a white coat**.
We found **an underground cave**.

We don't use an article for plural and uncountable nouns. We often use words like *some, any, much, many,* etc., or a number:
He put **some popcorn** in a bowl.
They found **8,000 soldiers**.
When we talk about specific things that we have already mentioned, we usually use *the*:
The popcorn popped.
The soldiers were all different.

We sometimes use *the* when we mention a specific thing for the first time:
- with a defining relative clause:
  The film that I saw last night was amazing.
- with a superlative adjective:
  Usain Bolt is **the fastest runner** in the world.
- when there is only one of something:
  He was **the only / the first** foreigner in the village.
  The sun was low in **the sky**.
- when we expect the reader/listener to know what we are talking about:
  Where's **the car**? (= my/your/our car)
  He got a taxi from **the airport** to **the hotel**. (= the airport that he arrived at, the hotel he was staying at)
  They saw a man in **the ice**. (= the ice on the mountain)

We don't use articles for the names of most places, including countries (e.g., *Vietnam, China, Austria*) or cities (e.g., *Vienna, X'ian, New Orleans*) and other places (e.g., *Mount Everest, Lake Winnipeg*).
But there are exceptions: *the USA, the UK, the Alps, the Nile, the Golden Gate Bridge.*

> **Tip**
> There are some phrases where you can't change the articles. You just have to learn the phrase:
> *by accident / by chance / on purpose;*
> *in bed / at home / at work;*
> *by car / by plane / on foot*

11A Defining relative clauses

a Write the correct word – *who, which, that,* or *where* – to complete the sentences.

1 A dictionary is a book _____ contains words and definitions.
2 An architect is someone _____ designs buildings.
3 That's the cinema _____ they show films at midnight.
4 She's the girl _____ lives next door.
5 What do you call a machine _____ cuts paper?
6 The restaurant _____ we met was very quiet.
7 The shop _____ sold nice cards has closed down.
8 The chef _____ works on Fridays isn't here today.

b Cross out the relative pronouns that are NOT possible.

1 The car *who / which / where / that* won the race was a Ferrari.
2 The area *who / which / where / that* he lives is very nice.
3 I have a friend *who / which / where / that* loves science fiction.
4 That's the office *who / which / where / that* I used to work.
5 I read about some scientists *who / which / where / that* are studying time travel.
6 The film's about a planet *who / which / where / that* it's dark all the time.
7 He made the discovery *who / which / where / that* won the Nobel Prize.

c Correct one mistake in each sentence.

1 The actor he played the doctor was very good.
2 Where are the shoes what were under the stairs?
3 Is there a shop which I can buy a sandwich near here?
4 A smoke alarm is a device tells you when there is a fire.
5 A man who fixed my dishwasher says he knows you.
6 Our wedding pictures were saved on the laptop it broke.

d ≫ Now go back to p. 109.

11B Articles

a For each noun, decide which article (*a, an, the* or *Ø*) is NOT possible. Cross out **one** wrong article.

1 *A / Ø / The* books are expensive.
2 We went to *a / Ø / the* shop.
3 They come from *Ø / the* India.
4 *A / Ø / The* tourists often used to come here.
5 *An / Ø / The* ice is dangerous – you can fall down easily.
6 We found it by *a / Ø* chance.
7 They made *a / Ø / the* clothes in that factory.
8 I need to go to *an / Ø / the* airport.
9 She's at *Ø / the* work right now.
10 *An / Ø / The* Indian food is delicious.

b Decide if the underlined words are the same thing or two different things. Write *S* or *D*.

1 He didn't find the book that he was looking for. But he found a really interesting book in the cupboard. _D_
2 He put some popcorn into a bowl and it popped. Then he put some chocolate into a bowl and it melted. ___
3 Two climbers were going up a mountain. Far ahead, they could see somebody on top of the mountain. ___
4 He took a photograph of his son and entered it in a competition. He was very surprised to see the picture on TV. ___
5 I saw a girl at the station. She looked like the girl who lives next door, but she has black hair. ___
6 **A** I sent you a message about school. Did you get it?
  B No, I don't think so. Maybe you sent the message to somebody else. ___

c Complete the story with the correct articles: *a, an, the* or *Ø*.

In 1738, some engineers near ¹_Ø_ Naples in ²___ Italy wanted to build ³___ palace for ⁴___ king of Naples, so they started digging ⁵___ hole.

They found ⁶___ wall under the ground. ⁷___ wall had ⁸___ beautiful paintings on it. After more digging, they found ⁹___ whole city.

¹⁰___ city was Pompeii, which was destroyed by ¹¹___ volcano nearly 2,000 years ago. The discovery showed ¹²___ world exactly how ¹³___ people lived 2,000 years ago.

d ≫ Now go back to p. 111.

12A Past perfect

*When I got home, my goldfish **had disappeared**.*

We use the past perfect to describe an event in a time period that leads up to another past event or time period. We use the past simple to describe the more recent event or time period:
*By 2016, I **had left** London and **had moved** to Cambridge.* (I did this before 2016.) *I **got** a job ...* (I did this in 2016.)

We form the past perfect with *had/hadn't* + past participle. The form is the same for all subjects.

▶ 12.02

	I / You / We / They / He / She / It
+	I **had** / I**'d left** before he arrived.
–	He **hadn't arrived** when I left.
Y/N?	**Had** you **seen** him? Yes, we **had**. / No, we **hadn't**.

(See p. 168 for a list of irregular past participles.)

The past perfect is often used with the past simple. The two clauses are often joined with *when, because, so* or *by the time*.

When + past simple, past perfect
When I **got** home, my goldfish **had disappeared**.

Past simple, because + past perfect
I **was** late **because** my car **had broken** down.

Past perfect, so + past simple
We**'d** never **been** to a concert before, **so** we **were** very excited.

By the time + past perfect, past simple
By the time the class **had finished**, we **were** all tired.
By the time + past simple, past perfect
By the time she **called**, her sister **had gone** home.

12B Reported speech

When we talk about what someone said in the past, we often use reported speech:
I don't know what happened. (direct speech)
→ *She **said** she **didn't know** what **had happened**.* (reported speech)

We usually use the verbs *say* and *tell* in the past simple. After *tell*, you must include the person who was spoken to:
*My sister **said** (that) ...*
*My sister **told me** (that) ...*
We can also include *that* before the reported words – however, it's not necessary.

We change the verb forms in the reported words by shifting them back one tense.

*My sister **told** me she **didn't know** what **had happened** to my best shoes. But I didn't believe her.*

▶ 12.07

Direct speech	→	Reported speech			→	
present simple	→	past simple	I **don't like** this book.	→	He said he **didn't like** the book.
can	→	could	You **can** start eating.	→	He said we **could** start eating.
will	→	would	She**'ll** be angry.	→	I told him she**'d** be angry.
present continuous	→	past continuous	I**'m watching** TV.	→	He said he **was watching** TV.
am/is/are going to	→	was/were going to	I**'m not going to** sleep.	→	He said he **wasn't going** to sleep.
past simple	→	past perfect	I **saw** you break it.	→	She said she**'d seen** me break it.
present perfect	→	past perfect	I**'ve** never **been** to London.	→	I told them I**'d** never **been** to London.

> **Tip**
> Don't forget to change the pronouns (e.g., *I, you, she*) and possessives (e.g., *my, her, your*) in reported speech, depending on who you are talking to.
> *'I like **your** shirt!' she said.* → *She said she liked **my** shirt.*

Grammar Focus

12A Past perfect

a Complete the text with the past perfect form of the verbs in brackets.

Staff at a supermarket were surprised to find a tiger in their shop on Monday morning. The tiger ¹ _had gone_ (go) into the supermarket because it was hungry. It ² _____ (break) the door to get in, but the alarm ³ _____ (not go) off because the shop manager ⁴ _____ (forget) to turn it on. The tiger ⁵ _____ (make) a terrible mess in the shop. It ⁶ _____ (find) the meat section, and it ⁷ _____ (eat) a lot of the meat from the fridges. The police gave the tiger some more meat with a drug in it. When the tiger ⁸ _____ (finish) eating the drugged meat, it fell asleep. Then the police took the tiger back to the zoo. The tiger ⁹ _____ (escape) from the zoo the previous night after a zoo worker ¹⁰ _____ (leave) a cage open.

b Match the sentence halves.

1. [f] When she turned on the TV, …
2. [ ] Yesterday, I found some old pictures …
3. [ ] When I checked my emails after my holiday, …
4. [ ] By the time I started my meal, …
5. [ ] The flat was dark when we got home …
6. [ ] They didn't know what to do …

a everybody else had already finished.
b I saw that I'd received over 200!
c because they hadn't listened to the instructions.
d because we'd forgotten to leave the light on.
e that I'd drawn when I was a child.
f the programme had already started.

c Complete the sentences with one past simple and one past perfect form of the verbs in brackets.

1. Nobody __came__ (come) to the meeting because Jed _had forgotten_ (forget) to send the invitations.
2. Sofía _____ (arrive) late because her bus _____ (break) down.
3. My parents _____ (not go) to Rome before, so they _____ (be) really excited.
4. Fred _____ (not do) his homework when the teacher _____ (ask) for it.
5. By the time I _____ (find) the website, they _____ (sell) all the tickets.
6. The kitchen _____ (be) very messy because I _____ (not have) time to clean up.
7. I _____ (never fly) before, so I _____ (feel) very nervous.
8. _____ (the match / finish) when you _____ (get) there?

d Now go back to p. 119.

12B Reported speech

a Choose the correct option in the reported speech on the right.

1. 'I can swim 12 km.' — He said he *could* / *would* swim 12 km.
2. 'He's not going to go to the party.' — She said he *wouldn't going* / *wasn't going* to go to the party.
3. 'We'll call you when we get there.' — They said they *were* / *would* call him when they *got* / *get* there.
4. 'We saw him steal the laptop.' — They said *they'd seen* / *they've seen* him steal the laptop.
5. 'I'll go and get the car from the garage.' — She said *she'll go* / *she'd go* and get the car from the garage.
6. 'We like flying.' — We *told them* / *said them* we *would like* / *liked* flying.
7. 'You can come to the party.' — They said we *will come* / *could come* to the party.
8. 'I have been to Melbourne a few times.' — I said I *went* / *had been* to Melbourne a few times.

b Complete the reported sentences with the correct pronouns and possessive adjectives.

1. 'I don't want to see you tonight.' — She told me __she__ didn't want to see __me__ tonight.
2. 'All of my friends are going to the cinema.' — He said all of _____ friends were going to the cinema.
3. 'You can't go out until you finish your homework.' — He told us _____ couldn't go out until _____ finished _____ homework.
4. 'I left my book on the train.' — She told me _____ had left _____ book on the train.
5. 'You'll catch colds if you don't wear your coats.' — I said they would catch colds if _____ didn't wear _____ coats.
6. 'You can't tell me what I can and can't do!' — I told my parents _____ couldn't tell _____ what _____ could and couldn't do.

c Now go back to p. 120.

Phonemic symbols

Vowel sounds

Short

/ə/	/æ/	/ʊ/	/ɒ/
teach**er**	m**a**n	p**u**t	g**o**t
/ɪ/	/i/	/e/	/ʌ/
ch**i**p	happ**y**	m**e**n	b**u**t

Long

/ɜː/	/ɑː/	/uː/	/ɔː/	/iː/
sh**ir**t	p**ar**t	wh**o**	w**a**lk	ch**ea**p

Diphthongs (two vowel sounds)

/eə/	/ɪə/	/ʊə/	/ɔɪ/	/aɪ/	/eɪ/	/əʊ/	/aʊ/
h**air**	n**ear**	t**our**	b**oy**	f**i**ne	l**a**te	c**oa**t	n**ow**

Consonants

/p/	/b/	/f/	/v/	/t/	/d/	/k/	/g/	/θ/	/ð/	/tʃ/	/dʒ/
picnic	**b**ook	**f**ace	**v**ery	**t**ime	**d**og	**c**old	**g**o	**th**ink	**th**e	**ch**air	**j**ob
/s/	/z/	/ʃ/	/ʒ/	/m/	/n/	/ŋ/	/h/	/l/	/r/	/w/	/j/
sea	**z**oo	**sh**oe	televi**si**on	**m**e	**n**ow	si**ng**	**h**ot	**l**ate	**r**ed	**w**ent	**y**es

Irregular verbs

Infinitive	Past simple	Past participle
be	was /wɒz/ / were /wɜː/	been
become	became	become
begin	began	begun
blow	blew /bluː/	blown /bləʊn/
break /breɪk/	broke /brəʊk/	broken /ˈbrəʊkən/
bring /brɪŋ/	brought /brɔːt/	brought /brɔːt/
build /bɪld/	built /bɪlt/	built /bɪlt/
buy /baɪ/	bought /bɔːt/	bought /bɔːt/
catch /kætʃ/	caught /kɔːt/	caught /kɔːt/
choose /tʃuːz/	chose /tʃəʊz/	chosen /ˈtʃəʊzən/
come	came	come
cost	cost	cost
cut	cut	cut
deal /dɪəl/	dealt /delt/	dealt /delt/
do	did	done /dʌn/
draw /drɔː/	drew /druː/	drawn /drɔːn/
drink	drank	drunk
drive /draɪv/	drove /drəʊv/	driven /ˈdrɪvən/
eat /iːt/	ate /et/	eaten /ˈiːtən/
fall	fell	fallen
feel	felt	felt
find /faɪnd/	found /faʊnd/	found /faʊnd/
fly /flaɪ/	flew /fluː/	flown /fləʊn/
forget	forgot	forgotten
get	got	got
give /gɪv/	gave /geɪv/	given /ˈgɪvən/
go	went	gone /gɒn/
grow /grəʊ/	grew /gruː/	grown /grəʊn/
have /hæv/	had /hæd/	had /hæd/
hear /hɪə/	heard /hɜːd/	heard /hɜːd/
hit	hit	hit
hold /həʊld/	held	held
keep	kept	kept
know /nəʊ/	knew /njuː/	known /nəʊn/
leave /liːv/	left	left

Infinitive	Past simple	Past participle
lend	lent	lent
let	let	let
lose /luːz/	lost	lost
make	made	made
meet	met	met
pay /peɪ/	paid /peɪd/	paid /peɪd/
put	put	put
read /riːd/	read /red/	read /red/
ride /raɪd/	rode /rəʊd/	ridden /ˈrɪdən/
ring	rang	rung
run	ran	run
sit	sat	sat
say /seɪ/	said /sed/	said /sed/
see	saw /sɔː/	seen
sell	sold /səʊld/	sold /səʊld/
send	sent	sent
set	set	set
sing	sang	sung
sleep	slept	slept
speak /spiːk/	spoke /spəʊk/	spoken /ˈspəʊkən/
spend	spent	spent
stand	stood /stʊd/	stood /stʊd/
steal /stiːl/	stole /stəʊl/	stolen /ˈstəʊlən/
swim /swɪm/	swam /swæm/	swum /swʌm/
take /teɪk/	took /tʊk/	taken /ˈteɪkən/
teach /tiːtʃ/	taught /tɔːt/	taught /tɔːt/
tell	told /təʊld/	told /təʊld/
think	thought /θɔːt/	thought /θɔːt/
throw /θrəʊ/	threw /θruː/	thrown /θrəʊn/
understand	understood /ˌʌndəˈstʊd/	understood /ˌʌndəˈstʊd/
wake /weɪk/	woke /wəʊk/	woken /ˈwəʊkən/
wear /weə/	wore /wɔː/	worn /wɔːn/
win	won	won
write /raɪt/	wrote /rəʊt/	written /ˈrɪtən/

Acknowledgements

The authors and publishers acknowledge the following sources of copyright material and are grateful for the permissions granted. While every effort has been made, it has not always been possible to identify the sources of all the material used, or to trace all copyright holders. If any omissions are brought to our notice, we will be happy to include the appropriate acknowledgements on reprinting and in the next update to the digital edition, as applicable.

Key
U = Unit, C = Communication, V = Vocabulary.

Text
U2: Book cover from *Yes Man* by Danny Wallace, published by Ebury Press. Reproduced by permission of The Random House Group Ltd. Copyright © 2003; Solo Syndication for text adapted from 'Passengers on broken-down National Express coach get out and push it to bus depot', *Mail Online*, 26/10/2007. Copyright © 2007 MailOnline. All rights reserved. Distributed by Solo Syndication; **U3:** Text adapted from 'Have you ever stopped to help a stranger or been helped by a stranger?' *(Webb, G)*, 24/10/2012. Reproduced with kind permission of Gretchen Webb; **U6:** Guardian News & Media Ltd for text adapted from 'Experience: Sharks saved my life' by Caroline Spence, *The Guardian*, 26/09/2009. Copyright © 2009 Guardian News & Media Ltd 2009; **U7:** Smithsonian Magazine for the text from 'Interview: Jane Goodall on the Future of Plants and Chimps' by Joseph Stromberg, *Smithsonian Magazine*, 21/02/2013. Copyright © 2013 Smithsonian Institution. Reprinted with permission from Smithsonian Enterprises. All rights reserved.; Text from 'Oprah Interview Nelson Mandela'. Reproduced with kind permission of the Nelson Mandela Foundation; **U8:** Book cover of *Cambridge English Readers Level 3: A Puzzle for Logan* (MacAndrew,R), © Cambridge University Press, reproduced with permission, photograph by Paul Gardiner, courtesy of Film Edinburgh (formerly Edinburgh Film Focus); Book cover of *Cambridge English Readers Level 3: Eye of the Storm* (Loader,M), © Cambridge University Press; Book cover of *Cambridge English Readers Level 3: How I Met Myself* (Hill, D.A.), © Cambridge University Press.

Photographs
The following photographs are sourced from Getty Images:
U1: Matthias Ritzmann/Corbis; Rowan Jordan/E+; Xavierarnau/iStock/Getty Images Plus; Joseph Visaggi/EyeEm; Panic_attack/iStock/Getty Images Plus; Eric Audras/ONOKY; Richard Drury/DigitalVision; Sirinarth Mekvorawuth/EyeEm; ©fitopardo.com/Moment; FatCamera/E+; Andresr/E+; PNC/DigitalVision; **U2:** Mike Kemp/In Pictures; Seb Oliver/Cultura; Nldazuu/RooM; lucamato/iStock Editorial/Getty Images Plus; Levi Bianco/Moment; Jeff Greenberg/Universal Images Group; DavorLovincic/iStock/Getty Images Plus; DaniloAndjus/E+; Massimo Borchi/Atlantide Phototravel/The Image Bank; Xavierarnau/E+; Julien Viry/iStock Editorial/Getty Images Plus; Rmbarricarte/iStock/Getty Images Plus; Christine Wehrmeier/Moment; Viktorcvetkovic/E+; **U3:** Prasit photo/Moment; NurPhoto; Maskot; Filadendron/E+; Jose Luis Pelaez Inc/DigitalVision; Jozef Polc/500px Plus; SDI Productions/E+; Hispanolistic/E+; Kali/9E+; Laflor/E+, Chasing Light - Photography by James Stone james-stone.com/Moment; Starcevic/E+; JayBoivin/iStock/Getty Images Plus; **U4:** Philippe Bourseiller/Photolibrary/Getty Images Plus; Simonlong/Moment; Stone; Joshua Hawley/iStock Editorial/Getty Images Plus; WPA Pool/Getty Images News; Vladimir zakharov/Moment; Yoshikazu tsuno/AFP; Simonlong/The Image Bank; Tomohiro Ohsumi/Getty Images Entertainment; Yongyuan Dai/E+; Manjik/iStock Editorial/Getty Images Plus; SensorSpot/E+; Bojan89/iStock/Getty Images Plus; Mni Raks Bud Da/EyeEm; Mykola Sosiukin/EyeEm; Kali9/E+; Westend61; SolStock/E+; Imtmphoto/iStock/Getty Images Plus; Thomas Barwick/DigitalVision; **U5:** B.S.P.I./The Image Bank; Poramesstock/iStock/Getty Images Plus; Christian Ender/The Image Bank/Getty Images Plus; Georgijevic/E+; Daniela Ebert/EyeEm; Thomas Barwick/DigitalVision; Xavierarnau/E+; Hill Street Studios/DigitalVision; LL28/E+; Mangostock/iStock/Getty Images Plus; Bambu Productions/The Image Bank/Getty Images Plus; Izusek/E+; Don Mason; Ngampol Thongsai/iStock/Getty Images Plus; Eva-Katalin/E+; Nick David/Stone; FatCamera/iStock/Getty Images Plus; **U6:** Muslian/iStock Editorial/Getty Images Plus; EmirMemedovski/E+; 10'000 Hours/DigitalVision; Peter Dazeley/The Image Bank; Bymuratdeniz/E+; JGI/Jamie Grill; Demaerre/iStock/Getty Images Plus; Ivosevicv/iStock/Getty Images Plus; Deagreez/iStock/Getty Images Plus; Inusuke/iStock/Getty Images Plus; Brent Durand/Moment; Thomas Kline/Design Pics; Bo Tornvig/Photographer's Choice/Getty Images Plus; Graiki/Moment Open; Emir Memedovski/E+; MangoStar_Studio/iStock/Getty Images Plus; Terry Vine/DigitalVision; Westend61; Drazen_/E+; **U7:** Steve Smith; Marla Aufmuth/Getty Images Entertainment; Steve Granitz/WireImage; Penelope Breese/Hulton Archive; Allen Berezovsky/Getty Images Entertainment; Samir Hussein/WireImage; Gary Miller/Getty Images Entertainment; VCG/Visual China Group; Amy Sussman/Staff/Getty Images Entertainment; H. Armstrong Roberts/Retrofile RF; Dennis P Hallinan/UNIC NA/Archive Photos; Lambert/Archive Photos; Tom Kelley Archive/Retrofile RF; AzmanJaka/E+; Portra/E+; Wavebreakmedia/iStock/Getty Images Plus; Jetta Productions Inc/DigitalVision; **U8:** Jim Dyson/Getty Images News; ERIC FEFERBERG/AFP; Bettmann/Bettmann; Gijsbert Hanekroot/Redferns; Carol Yepes/Moment; Gary Hershorn/Corbis News; Tim Graham/Getty Images News; Jan Kruger/Getty Images Sport; David Aliaga/MB Media/Getty Images Sport; Quality Sport Images/Getty Images Sport; Tottenham Hotspur FC/Tottenham Hotspur FC; Izf/iStock/Getty Images Plus; Nisa and Ulli Maier Photography/Moment; Bigjohn36/iStock/Getty Images Plus; Val Thoermer/EyeEm/EyeEm; PeopleImages/E+; Vm/E+; Lacheev/iStock/Getty Images Plus; Aldo Murillo/iStock/Getty Images Plus; Tim Robberts/DigitalVision; Jerome Tisne/The Image Bank; Portra/E+; **U9:** Tim Warner/Getty Images Sport; Vera Anderson/WireImage; Stephane Cardinale/Corbis Entertainment; Steve Granitz/WireImage; Frederick M. Brown/Stringer/Getty Images Entertainment; Mike Marsland/WireImage; Paul Archuleta/Stringer/FilmMagic; Caiaimage; Luis Alvarez/DigitalVision; DragonImages/iStock/Getty Images Plus; Monkeybusinessimages/iStock/Getty Images Plus; Ishii Koji/DigitalVision; Russell Monk/The Image Bank; **U10:** Andrew_Howe/E+; Maskot/Maskot; Jeffbergen/E+; Mapodile/E+; Mint Images/Mint Images RF; **U11:** Pierre Perrin/Sygma; Photo 12/Universal Images Group; The State/Tribune News Service; Stephane Cardinale/Corbis Entertainment; Grassetto/iStock/Getty Images Plus; Katya_Havok/iStock/Getty Images Plus; Picturegarden/The Image Bank/Getty Images Plus; AFP; Danny Lehman/The Image Bank; Bjdlzx/iStock/Getty Images Plus; Yarochkins/iStock/Getty Images Plus; YakobchukOlena/iStock/Getty Images Plus; **U12:** Antagain/iStock/Getty Images Plus; Dorling Kindersley; Okea/iStock/Getty Images Plus; PrinPrince/iStock/Getty Images Plus; Antagain/iStock/Getty Images Plus; Dieter Schaefer/Moment Open; Make_Video_Company/iStock/Getty Images Plus; Ibrahim Suha Derbent/The Image Bank/Getty Images Plus; M Swiet Productions/Moment; Caiaimage; FG Trade/E+; Warren Faidley/The Image Bank; Win McNamee/Getty Images News; The Washington Post; **C:** Photoevent/E+; Fcafotodigital/iStock/Getty Images Plus; Nv Dèn Buy Xariy Sirichay/EyeEm; Roberto Machado Noa/LightRocket; KempMartin/iStock/Getty Images Plus; Thomas Northcut/Photodisc; Ivosevicv/iStock/Getty Images Plus; Katya_Havok/iStock/Getty Images Plus; **V:** Anterovium/iStock/Getty Images Plus; Orchidpoet/E+; Pavel Skopich/EyeEm; Badahos/iStock/Getty Images Plus; Andrey Nikitin/iStock/Getty Images Plus; Istanbulimage/E+; Tatniz/iStock/Getty Images Plus; Popovaphoto/iStock/Getty Images Plus; ProArtWork/E+; Adisa/iStock/Getty Images Plus; Cjp/E+; Stevica Mrdja/EyeEm; Arthur S. Aubry/Photodisc; Watchara Piriyaputtanapun/Moment; AleksandarNakic/E+; Samotrebizan/iStock/Getty Images Plus; Heide Benser/The Image Bank; Baranozdemir/E+; GlobalStock/E+; Bambu Productions/The Image Bank/Getty Images Plus; Izusek/E+; Mangostock/iStock/Getty Images Plus; Ngampol Thongsai/iStock/Getty Images Plus; Dougal Waters/DigitalVision; David Buffington/Photodisc; Jupiterimages/PHOTOS.com/Getty Images Plus; Fuse/Corbis; Don Mason; DreamPictures; Hero Images; Scyther5/iStock/Getty Images Plus; Technotr/E+; Nisa and Ulli Maier Photography/Moment; NurPhoto; Val Thoermer/EyeEm; WebSubstance/iStock/Getty Images Plus; Slingshot/Stone; Lzf/iStock/Getty Images Plus; Puckons/iStock/Getty Images Plus; Vm/E+; PhotoTalk/E+; Aaron Black/The Image Bank; Skynesher/E+; Georgette Douwma/Stone; Bigjohn36/iStock/Getty Images Plus; Pgiam/iStock/Getty Images Plus.

The following photographs are sourced from other sources/libraries:
U2, C: Copyright © Albanpix. Reproduced with kind permission; **U4:** Geoffrey Robinson/Shutterstock; **U8:** RTRO/Alamy Stock Photo; Lebrecht Music & Arts; **U12:** Suzi Eszterhas/Minden Pictures/FLPA.

Cover photography by Creative Frame Studio/Moment/Getty Images.

Commissioned photography by Gareth Boden.

Commissioned video stills by Rob Maidment and Sharp Focus Productions: **U1–12**.

Illustrations
QBS Learning; Mark Bird; Mark Duffin; Sean KJA; Jo Goodberry; Dusan Lakicevic; Carrie May; Jerome Mireault; Roger Penwill; Gavin Reece; Gregory Roberts; Martin Sanders; Sean Sims; Marie-Eve Tremblay.

Audio production by Leon Chambers and by Creative Listening.

Typeset by QBS Learning.

Corpus
Development of this publication has made use of the Cambridge English Corpus (CEC). The CEC is a computer database of contemporary spoken and written English, which currently stands at over one billion words. It includes British English, American English, and other varieties of English. It also includes the Cambridge Learner Corpus, developed in collaboration with the University of Cambridge ESOL Examinations. Cambridge University Press has built up the CEC to provide evidence about language use that helps us to produce better language teaching materials.

English Profile
This product is informed by English Vocabulary Profile, built as part of English Profile, a collaborative program designed to enhance the learning, teaching, and assessment of English worldwide. Its main funding partners are Cambridge University Press and Cambridge Assessment English, and its aim is to create a 'profile' for English, linked to the Common European Framework of Reference for Languages (CEFR). English Profile outcomes, such as the English Vocabulary Profile, will provide detailed information about the language that learners can be expected to demonstrate at each CEFR level, offering a clear benchmark for learners' proficiency. For more information, please visit www.englishprofile.org.

CALD
The Cambridge Advanced Learner's Dictionary is the world's most widely used dictionary for learners of English. Including all the words and phrases that learners are likely to come across, it also has easy-to-understand definitions and example sentences to show how the word is used in context. The Cambridge Advanced Learner's Dictionary is available online at dictionary.cambridge.org.